Memories of Appalachia

HAROLD RALEY

TotalRecall Publications, Inc.
1103 Middlecreek
Friendswood, TX 77546
281-992-3131 TEL
www.totalrecallpress.com

All rights reserved. Except as permitted under the United States Copyright Act of 1976, No part of this publication may be reproduced, stored in a retrieval system, or transmitted in any form or by any means electronic or mechanical or by photocopying, recording, or otherwise without prior permission of the publisher. Exclusive worldwide content publication / distribution by TotalRecall Publications, Inc.

Copyright © 2020 by: Harold Raley

ISBN: 978-1-59095-649-6
UPC: 6-43977-26494-7

Printed in the United States of America with simultaneous printings in Australia, Canada, and United Kingdom.

FIRST EDITION
1 2 3 4 5 6 7 8 9 10

Judgments as to the suitability of the information herein is the purchaser's responsibility. TotalRecall Publications, Inc. extends no warranties, makes no representations, and assumes no responsibility as to the accuracy or suitability of such information for application to the purchaser's intended purposes or for consequences of its use except as described herein.

The scanning, uploading and distribution of this book via the Internet or via any other means without the permission of the publisher is illegal and punishable by law. Please purchase only authorized electronic editions and do not participate in or encourage electronic piracy of copyrighted materials. Your support of the author's rights is appreciated.

To My Parents

Authors Bio

Novelist and short story writer, linguist, philosopher, and professor, Harold C. Raley holds degrees (BA, MA, PhD) in English, Foreign Languages, Humanities, and Philosophy. Named Distinguished Professor, he has taught languages, literature, and philosophy in American and foreign universities. His publications include fourteen books of fiction, history, language, and philosophy, and approximately 150 articles and essays on wide-ranging topics in professional journals and newspapers.

Table of Contents

Authors Bio iv
Introduction vi
Chapter 1: "Jist Tolable" 1
Chapter 2: Early Times and Old Days 8
Chapter 3: Family and First Memories 15
Chapter 4: Wayward Relatives 29
Chapter 5: Hard Times and Country Cooking 36
Chapter 6: Ancestors and Other Relatives 39
Chapter 7: A Year on the Cook Place 49
Chapter 8: Life at Grandma Hooper's 58
Chapter 9: The Log Cabin Year 72
Chapter 10: The Red Hill 88
Chapter 11: A Year at Bethlehem 96
Chapter 12: The Walker Farm 106
Chapter 13: Pursued and Perplexed 117
Chapter 14: Other Aggravations 120
Chapter 15: School and Romance 126
Chapter 16: Free Enterprise 137
Chapter 17: Too Soon the Victory 140
Chapter 18: Disappointments 142
Chapter 19: Mr. Carl Walker 146
Chapter 20: War and Renaissance 149
Chapter 21: Labor, Lightning, and the Lord 154
Chapter 22: Driving and Peddling 161
Chapter 23: From Empire to Romance 168
Chapter 24: The Unraveling Years 175
Chapter 25: Arkansas Traveler 187
Chapter 26: Empty Pockets 198
Chapter 27: Geraldine, Darrell, Janice, Joyce 202
   A. Geraldine 203
   B. Darrell 206
   C. Janice 210
   D. Joyce 214
Chapter 28: Random Recollections 218
Chapter 29: Misadventures 226
Chapter 30: Roads Not Taken 229
Chapter 31: Michigan, Military, Misery 237
Chapter 32: One Bale for College 255
Afterthoughts 266

Introduction

A celebrated philosopher once said that in order to understand anything human we must tell a story. However, this human narrative is not about *what* we are. That kind of information is the business of science, which teaches us about our physical nature. But the real story of our life, the human portion, is *who* we are, and it begins where science and nature end. Biography, not biology, is the true human narrative.

No one can write our narrative for us, and no one should. For we are the novelists of ourselves, the composers of our personal melody of life. Daily we add pages to our story or notes to our song. Animals, our only flesh and blood companions in this world, are what they are by Nature's decree, but we humans are who we become primarily by our personal choices. This means that of all God's creatures, only we have the freedom—and therefore the responsibility—to choose how we live our life, and if necessary, to reconsider, to rectify, to repent and rewrite our story if it is sordid or change our tune if our music is discordant.

I take these distinctions to heart in this writing. It is the story of the things I did for the first twenty years of my life and what happened to me as I did them. In a general sense, this is the description of any life, great or small, and mine conforms to the pattern with nothing exceptional to recommend it. Mine is the unremarkable tale of an obscure life in an obscure place. Yet I cannot dismiss it as insignificant, for that would imply that I am judge and jury of life's meaning, which I am not, not even of my own life, most of all, my own life.

Within this general pattern, I admit that I write these events also out of curiosity. After I left the lower Appalachian country and its ways, I began a life so different in assumptions and obligations that it is hard to tie it to what followed. This writing is an attempt to make sense of it all, and for reasons that I do not fully understand. Much of life in those times, to quote the poet Wordsworth, seemed to be about "old, unhappy, far-off things, and battles long ago." But I would be the last to declare them meaningless now. The older I get, the more I believe that the tiniest flower that fades unseen, the loneliest sparrow that falls unnoticed, register their being on the Creator's grand scale. All things matter and link in secret ways we do not perceive. This is why wiser minds than mine tell us to walk by faith and not by sight.

Harold Raley

Chapter 1:
"Jist Tolable"

With a few short interruptions, I spent the first twenty years of my life (1934-1954) close to the Old Corn Road that runs for eighteen miles along the top of Brindley Mountain just south of the Morgan-Cullman County line in North Alabama. Geographically, the region is the southernmost extension of Appalachia wedged between the Tennessee Valley on the north and lower lands to the south. Working as hired hands and tenant farmers for half of those years and on our own sixty-four-acre farm for the rest, my family moved back and forth across the Old Corn Road but never far enough to escape hard times.

Illness was a common part of our troubles. Most of us, myself included, were hardy without being healthy, and though often sick, we had a habit of waiting to go to a doctor or a hospital until we were all but ready to die. And when we finally went, some of us never came back alive. I think that's why I have never really gotten over my childish fear that doctors and hospitals exist to kill people. My adult mind knows better, but my baby brain doesn't. And if we are honest with ourselves, we all know that our infantile mind still controls many, if not most, things in life. To this day I have a primitive fear of the "Whitecoats." My blood pressure rises so high in their presence that they go into panic mode, thinking I'm about to die in their office. Then I have to listen to their sermons about lowering it. Once out of their office, however, things return to normal and I forget their lectures and often ignore their prescriptions.

Anyway, what I was going to say is that by today's standards folks in our world lived and died early in the old days. Life in those times was slow in its pace but often short in its span. According to the older timetable—just beginning to change in my generation, men reached full manhood at twenty-one, middle age at thirty-five, old age at fifty, and for most, the graveyard not long thereafter. Women were often married as soon as they grew to be "husband high," were pregnant in their teens, well along into their physical decline by thirty-five, and spent and lusterless by forty-five or fifty. Even among people who survived beyond six or seven decades it was rare to find a man of sixty still able to put in a full day's work in the field or a woman up to the rigors of caring for a family or herself by that age.

But grievous though they were, we bore our ailments like badges of honor and described them with painful pride. It was almost bad manners not to have a respectable list of miseries to trot out at every gathering. Toothaches, earaches, colds, and bronchitis were common ailments, while pneumonia, tuberculosis, failing eyesight, rheumatism (arthritis we call it today) were ever present threats to health. Cancer (which many people thought was contagious) and heart disease were not so common then as today. Obesity, the scourge of modern America, was almost unknown in those times. Women had a different assortment of mysterious sufferings about which children, especially we boys, had only the vaguest notions. It gave a person a sort of backhanded prestige and local fame to have the most spectacular pains. But the maladies had be genuine; nothing lowered you quicker in eyes of neighbors than fake ailments to get out of work or to hide the embarrassment of good health.

The Good Lord, it seemed, seldom saw fit to be gentle with us "up on the Mountain" as we said in my family, but neither did He forsake us altogether. We had our good moments, too, and even in our darkest days and deepest sins we knew that God was on His throne and everything as it ought to be in Heaven, even if our life was often belly up.

Life was hard but simple, and it took little to entertain us, unlike today when entertainment is full-time work for a lot of people: round-the-clock movies and music, food, drink, drugs, tablets, telephones, YouTube, Facebook, shopping, Tweet, sports, TV, and noise. Never an idle moment, yet seldom a full one either. I have long argued that noise and speed are sin's closest relatives. In contrast, Jesus and the biblical saints never seemed to rush, yet they always got there on time. Time waited for them. It runs from us.

Far from saintliness, we had our own brand of disorderliness back in the old days. Life for us was mostly a daily round of unplanned deviations, sudden emergencies, frequent calamities, and few completions. Things had a way of never getting done, that is, if they ever got started in the first place. Things ran us, we didn't run them. Our days were too full of breakdowns, distractions, accidents, drunk and derelict people for us to plan our life and stay on a schedule. We claimed to admire people who live planned, orderly lives, but maybe we weren't being completely honest with ourselves. Orderliness seemed a little unnatural and stifling to us, and I think we unconsciously conspired to see that it didn't happen to us.

Consequently, we hardly ever got the things we wanted and mostly didn't want the things we got. But even if things had a way of ganging up on us, we saw nothing wrong with the way we lived. It took many years of hindsight and softer living for us to realize just how impoverished and chaotic life back then had been. By comparison, we were rich in later life before we were amazed at how poor we were in earlier times. But there was a pride along with the self-pity we felt for ourselves. Years later and far away from the Corn Road for many of us, we tried to outdo one another in describing how bad the old days were. Of course, all that was only in distant retrospect after time had softened our memories. At the moment, our poverty seemed as natural as the air we breathed. Sure, life was hard; it had always been hard, and we reckoned that it would always be so. We took Jesus at his word: "Sufficient unto the day is the evil thereof." Some people—my mother for example—had a vision of a better life, but daily calamities saw to it that it remained just that: a vision and never a reality.

As for the bigger picture of the world, we knew little and cared less about the causes that people squabble over today. Even though most Corn Road people had a mystical respect for the U.S. government in those times, they—and we—took it as a plain fact that all lower orders of politicians were self-serving and corrupt. Not that we considered ourselves responsible for their mess; nobody I knew voted. With few exceptions, we were democrats by inclination, but that was as far as we went in politics. We had better things to do with our money than pay poll tax and plenty of wiggle room to do it in. There were no red lights or stop signs to hinder us in Corn Road country, no papers to fill out or income taxes to pay, no clocks or deadlines to fret over, and no mandatory inoculations for children and dogs.

In general, we did not break the law so much as ignored it. There may have been laws about disposing of large carcasses like a dead cow or horse. If a mule or horse took a notion to die on us, we put a chain around its neck and let our surviving horses or mules drag it off to a convenient ditch for buzzards and varmints to devour. The slant of the sun regulated our work and rest. We had a withering contempt for people who valued a signed paper over a man's word and handshake, even though, as I recall, as many promises were broken as honored.

Though ever short of money, we had all the freedom we could stand: we could drive our unlicensed, uninsured, and uninspected wagons on either side of the road we pleased and like our squawking chickens, cross it anywhere and anytime we took a notion. It was true that police and highway patrolmen fined folks for driving a car without a tag or driver's license, but at least they did so when we were in their territory. But they went too far when they told us that we had to have a license to hunt and fish. What's the world coming to, we asked one another indignantly. No wonder we considered law officers to be our natural enemies, one more harassment we poor people had to put up with. We put their meddlesome requirements in the same idle category as truancy laws and hunting permits and ignored them all. Luckily or otherwise, city officials generally did not enforce these statutes out in the country where we lived.

As for education, we reckoned that it was a good decision for those able and patient enough to learn. But ignorance of ciphers and letters was no shame or drawback if a woman was virtuous and a good cook and seamstress, and a man, honest, hardworking, and not given to chasing skirts or obsessed with the bottle. People in general believed that an education was a passport to a good job and an easier life than farming, but it was too remote from our rural life for most to pursue beyond basic schooling—if indeed that far. There were still a good many illiterate folks around when I was a child. In fact, some of them would seek my mother's help when they needed documents explained or forms filled out.

Two dimensions of life from those early years are still fresh in my memory: one was the common toil of working the stingy, often stony mountain land, fighting the crab grass, and gathering the meager harvest of cotton and corn; the other for me personally, a rich overlay of bookish imagery and romanticism that for me rounded off the rough edges, soothed the worst hurts, and invested my world with ideal beauty and heroism that sensible realists would have searched hard—and in vain—to find. I learned early to keep my bookish fantasies mostly to myself. They had no place in common conversation. For the most part, we were too concerned with scrounging up our daily fare to bother with poetic fictions. And any extra psychic or mental energy we might have usually found expression in religious exaltation for the righteous or drunken escapades for the sinners.

The Corn Road wound its way through all these experiences, linking them like an eighteen-mile metaphor. It seems reason enough to weave my memoirs around it. Oddly enough, however, even though we came close, we never actually lived on the Corn Road itself.

The washboard-bumpy, deep-rutted Corn Road I knew is no more. True, its modern paved version follows the same roadway, but today it is a speedy convenience for our cars not an indelible stamp on our spirit. The horse and wagon were a fixture of rural life—and had been for untold ages past—but the upstart automobile has always been too swift and impatient to really be a part of country life. For this and other reasons, today the Corn Road traffic is heavier, but its humanity is less. Neither the mud nor the memories of the Old Corn Road stick to us as they did in those far-off days. No creaking, mule-drawn wagons etch their iron-rimmed tracks in its muddy ruts; no scuffling, rock-throwing boys strut its sandy curves; no Sunday-splendored, bright-ribboned girls giggle their flirtatious secrets along its way; no porch-sitting neighbors laze away the hours in smoke, snuff, spit, and gossip, waving to the passing world. Like everybody else, they have withdrawn to air-conditioned isolation and traded the real world and people for the bogus stars and virtual images of television.

All this reminiscing is a moment of nostalgia, not a complaint. My generation had its Corn Road years and they are gone, a little era that slipped away unnoticed, unmourned, and unmissed into yesteryear. After all, most of us were eager to serve our time there and rush off to what we hoped would be a better life elsewhere. Maybe we take a kindly view of old times we were impatient to outlive not because they were good but because we do not have to confront their hardships again. Their problems were resolved for better or worse, and things that have been resolved lose their drama—and often their pain—and sink back into an ideal and unthreatening sentimental landscape.

They say that what doesn't destroy us makes us stronger. Surely that is an exaggeration, for some experiences leave us forever maimed and diminished. What is more certain is that even the worst of times mellow with newer time. And a good thing, too, for otherwise life might be unbearable. In any case, younger generations have no call to walk where we walked. They have other roads to travel, other ruts to negotiate, other memories to build.

Maybe my Grandmother Mary Raley summed up in two words what I have been trying to say in several. When people would ask her how she was and how things were going, Grandma would answer, "jist tolable." That was Grandma on her good days and bad. Many years have passed, and I have walked a good piece down many other roads, some good, some not so good. But after it's all said and done, all the gains and losses tallied, and all the comparisons made, life on any road, fast or slow, new or old, may even out to be as Grandma described it: "jist tolable."

Chapter 2:
Early Times and Old Days

Centuries before white settlers reached our part of North Alabama, the ancestors of Chickasaws, Cherokees, Creeks, and other native American tribes traveled along well-established trails in the region. One called Black Warrior Path began at Melton's Bluff on the Tennessee River and ran southward through parts of present-day Lawrence, Morgan, Cullman, and Blount counties. Crossing Brindley mountain at a location that in time would be named Day's Gap and then renamed Battleground after the Civil War battle there, it intersected with the east-west High Town Path that was said to stretch for a thousand miles, spanning the entire southeastern United States. A modest eighteen-mile section of the ancient High Town Path became the Old Corn Road.[1]

Exactly how and when the Old Corn Road acquired its modern name remains something of a mystery. But the most reasonable explanation I have heard is that early-day Morgan County farmers, whose valley lands were fertile but whose creeks were too slow for milling, hauled their corn up to gristmills on the swifter streams of Brindley Mountain. Naturally they made use of the High Town Path, renaming it the Corn Road. The gristmills themselves are long gone, and officially so is the road itself. Like all the Cullman County roads, it has lost

---

[1] General Andrew Jackson and scout David Crockett reportedly made use of both paths on their punitive expedition against the Creek Indians in 1813. In some instances, the US government also used these trails as boundary lines to determine—perhaps arbitrarily—the claims and territories of Native American tribes.

its human name and been dehumanized to a number: County Road 25. (May the flowers wither and the grass die for whoever came up with such an ugly scheme.) Anyway, for us born in an earlier age the original names were grandfathered in. For us the County Road 25 will always be the Old Corn Road.

As I said, the road runs just south of the Cullman-Morgan County line, marking a watershed for much of its length.[2] From most of its northside ditches water flows to the Tennessee River; from its south side to creeks that empty into the Warrior River and eventually the Gulf of Mexico at Mobile. This fact, which my mother told me, impressed me mightily, and as a boy I used to run back and forth across the road thinking I was crossing from one part of the world to another. It surprised me that no one else among family and friends seemed to care which way the waters parted.

Cynical people told an equally commercial but more disreputable story about how the old Indian road got its name. According to them, it was called the "Corn Road" because whiskey makers from the forests of Winston and Lawrence County hauled their corn mash "white lightning" along the road to customers in neighboring counties. Which version is the truth? Probably the first lays the stronger claim, but it is also true that a lot of moonshine whiskey was hauled—and drunk—on the Old Corn Road as I was growing up.

Despite my certainty that we lived near a road that grandly divided the world, most people would consider our region to be one of the most out of the way places imaginable. Not only was it a splayed flank of Appalachia but a location remote from towns or sizeable settlements. To this day when people ask me to

---

[2] Before the formation of Cullman County in 1873 most of this area was in Morgan County. The rest was Blount County.

pinpoint my birthplace, I have trouble telling them. In recent decades I have called Hartselle my hometown because the Texas wing of my family knows it best, but in fact, I grew up "on the Mountain," as we called it, ten or twelve miles to the south. In fact, mention just about any place and we lived several miles from it. Our mail came from Vinemont in Cullman County, but I was nearly grown before I ever laid eyes on its post office. When we lived over in Morgan County, Decatur was our county seat, but it was normally beyond our reach on the Tennessee River at the far north end of Morgan County. Dr. Howell, who came out to check on my Mother and me after I was born at home, wrote "Falkville" on my birth certificate, but we lived nowhere near it. I went first to Ebenezer School, then to West Point, both several miles distant.

My first memory of church was lying on a quilt or blanket in Round Top Church in the Valley where our Raley ancestors lived for several generations. I was a few months short of my second birthday. (I had a fairly good memory at the time—sadly not so sharp today.) I remember that it was stifling hot, probably in July or August, and the women, towering big above me, were furiously fanning themselves. The church was loud with voices and music, and I was afraid some of the women might step on me. The church building burned down later that fall (1936). I remember a good many things from that early time, including a very unpleasant one when I was still wearing a diaper that an old man—so he seemed to me—kept annoying me by pulling it down. I think he was my Grandfather Hooper who died in 1936. We revered the church and respected its teachings in general but did not attend regularly because we lived too far away. I remember walking with Momma across two mountains to Fairview Holiness Church at the foot of Burney Mountain. I was probably close to four by then. We lived with my Grandmother

Hooper, now widowed, on the Burney Mt. Road. Fairview Church also burned down later and was rebuilt further north on the Lacon Road, and much later rebuilt again closer to Hartselle. (I deny having anything to do with burning either church.) Later, we walked or rode in a two-horse wagon westward along the Corn Road to East Battleground Missionary Baptist Church, which was established in 1940 after a preacher named May held a revival in the area. First Mr. Wiesner and later neighbor Harvey Cook were the two preachers I remember. Depending on which one could beat the other to church, Miss Tressie Cole or Mrs. Willie Heck Blackman supplied music for hymns on an old donated piano. Our neighbor Mrs. Helton, who worshipped in an upscale Church of Christ near Longview on Highway 31 and scorned Baptists, Methodists, Holy Rollers, and other denominations she considered to be religiously defective, sarcastically called our church "Dough ball" and the name stuck for many years.

None of these accusations of theological or geographical backwardness, however, bothered us in the least. For if some folks might think we lived far off the beaten track, we knew better. The Corn Road was home and for us the very nerve center of our world. Later I read a philosopher who argued convincingly that anywhere we are becomes the center of the universe for us. I have always liked the idea because it dignifies what other people dismiss as backward regions. To me all places were divinely created and share in the grace of the Creator. It is the reason why no matter where I find myself, I hardly ever fall into boredom—I started to say "the sin" of boredom, but I have no reason to be too critical of people who do not know what it is to "hold infinity in the palm of your hand and eternity in an hour."

On rare, wonderful Saturdays we and fifteen or twenty other

people would pay a quarter each to ride the back of Olin Brazile's truck east along the Corn Road and then south on Highway 31 to Cullman, the county seat. There we would spend the day, the women walking, talking, window shopping, and rummaging through the bargain merchandise at stores like Watson's, Stieflemeyer's, Ponder's, and Romine's, while the men hung out at the Court House and at mule barns and farm supply stores, checking out the animals, mulling over plow points, trace chains, horse collars, sweeps, scratcher teeth, plough lines, and harness; or smoking, whittling, spitting, watching, and catching up on news with friends and former neighbors. For young people there was the thrilling prospect of flirtations and romance in the teeming streets, and for the tougher big boys and pool sharks the dark, smoky confines of several pool rooms with the rack and crack of billiard balls, loud bragging and "cussin'" over made or missed shots, and the latest gossip about fights, shootings, knifings, bootleggers, and loose women, the Devil's own territory, according to religious folks. On the white steps of the 1912 Courthouse (now demolished and replaced by a newer structure a couple of blocks away) itinerant preachers harangued idle crowds about hell fire punishment for sins and argued biblical points verse for verse with fractious, self-taught country theologians. One Saturday a wandering preacher made an astonishing claim before a skeptical crowd. "I know the whole Bible by heart. Name any chapter and I can tell you every verse in it," he boasted. They laughed in disbelief until they tested him, and he passed. People shook their head in wonderment. (Later I published a story, "Miracle in Meridian," based in part on my impressions of his talent.)

Cullman was really two cities in those days. Downtown and especially West Cullman were the territory of late-arriving Protestants of one stripe or another, whereas East Cullman was dominated by the soaring spires of the Catholic Church,[3] Sacred Heart School for girls, Ave Maria Grotto, and St. Bernard College for men, legacies all of Cullman's German Catholic founders. For us these institutions seemed to belong to another universe, for we had little to do with them except to spread lurid gossip about what we believed were their heretical beliefs and strange rituals. As late as World War II some people hinted darkly that "them ole Germans up 'ere in Cullman has got shortwave radios and they're probly telling ole Hitler and Tojo ever'thang they know." In fact, similar suspicions about the earlier Cullmanites in World War I had encouraged the last of the German speakers to switch to English. But even as we ignorantly questioned their patriotism and disparaged their faith, we, and especially Momma, admired their hardworking thriftiness and excellent Catholic schools.

Before I was old enough for the pool halls, I sometimes listened a bit to the courthouse sermons and debates or, seated on the courthouse steps, read a favorite book or comic book. But the toy basement at the Western Auto store was also a great lure. Not that I could ever buy very much, but the variety of toys roused in me many a rich fancy. Too bad money was always too short to make dreams come truth. (Even then I knew that my childhood would soon be over, and the toys would lose their magic.) Lunch might be a fifteen-cent hamburger or ten-cent hotdog "with ever' thang on it" or a moon pie, and a nickel Grape, Orange, RC, or Coca Cola (a "Cocola") at places like Bud Sheats's restaurant. (Bud was from Battleground and one year

---

[3] Cullman was founded in 1873 by Colonel Kullmann and his followers who had first settled in Ohio, around Cincinnati, I think it was. Until then the Sand Mountain plateau was very sparsely settled and largely bypassed in the relentless westward surge of early settlers. The thrifty German farmers showed how versatile and productive the land could be and soon Anglo settlers followed them. Colonel Kullmann (d. 1895) is one of the unsung heroes of Alabama, having brought more settlers into the State than any other person.

we rented a farm from him.)

If I had an extra fifteen cents, I first hurried to see a matinee "show" at the Cullman Theater. (I looked young enough to get in on a half ticket—for those twelve and under—until I was fourteen.) Daddy had taken me to see my first western movie in 1941. It starred obscure western actor Bob Steele and the shootouts, saddle acrobatics, and fistfights were thrilling beyond description. But I was mystified by the stagecoach wheels that seemed to spin backwards and maybe a little scornful of the cowboys, especially the villains, because they fired so randomly and missed most of their targets. In our part of the world rifle and shotgun shells were hard to come by and we had to make every shot count. The serials were wildly exciting—and always ended with a train or other menace bearing down on the helpless heroine tied to the railroad tracks or a tree—but we didn't get to town often enough to see the final episodes. The 2 pm movie started too late for us to see it, for Olin left for home around three or three-thirty.

Gathering ourselves for the return trip was usually an exercise in comic futility almost worthy of my favorite idiots: The Three Stooges. First, we would notice that some of our folks were missing. "I seen 'em over yonder by the Courthouse," somebody would say. "I'll go git 'em." Then while they were gone, the missing persons would show up and others would be dispatched to find the searchers. Meanwhile, the searchers would return, and the process would start all over again until finally somebody got the bright idea to stay put by the truck and wait until they all came back. It worked, but by the next trip we forgot that wisdom and repeated the same crazy routine.

Chapter 3:
Family and First Memories

If you take the Burney Mountain Road north from the Corn Road and go a winding country mile past the Red Hill, across another ridge, and over the Morgan County line to a little beyond the South Powell Road Cutoff, you come to what was called the Hale farm on the left at the Bertha Road fork where around 8 p.m. on November 23, 1934 (a Friday), weighing in at 9 ½ lbs., I was born second by four years to my sister Geraldine in the family of William Barthel Raley and Vernie (Verna) Lou Hooper Raley.

Geraldine was born back on Burney Mountain, the first stop on the family's slow migration south from the Valley, the ancestral land of the older Raley generations, to the hills of lower Morgan and Cullman counties.

Redheaded, gospel-singing Jett Hale had lost the farm to the Evans family in the Depression, but his name lingered. Headed up by older brother Howard, the Evans family of Falkville foreclosed on so many mountain farms during the Depression years of the thirties that a story began to make the rounds. Do you mind if I tell it? I take your silence for consent.

It seems a sinful neighbor died and went to Hell.
Looking around, he noticed a big black wash pot
turned upside down. "What ye got under that
wash pot?" he asked the Devil. "Howard Evans,"
the Fiend whispered with a worried look. "And
don't you look under it. If ole Howard gets loose,
he'll have a mortgage on Hell quicker'n you can spit."

Now back to my story. Momma said she had in mind to name me "Maurice," or maybe "Morris," but decided against it because of a local scoundrel—and third cousin as I discovered many years later—by that name. I never knew where my parents got "Harold" and "Cecil," for to my knowledge these names had not appeared on either side of the family. Momma said I was born with a tooth, an oddity that caused her considerable discomfort since she breast-fed all her children. My Aunt Mary Woods was the midwife who helped deliver me and many other babies in our region. She was regarded as a professional because as everybody said in respectful tones, she had a "certificate."

Born March 30, 1908, Momma was twenty-six when she gave birth to me. Daddy was almost a year younger—February 4, 1909. In coloring, temperament, personality, and interests, they were as dissimilar a couple as you could imagine in that time and social setting, and one glance at their physical differences was enough to suggest that they were incompatible in nearly everything else. Momma was only a smidgeon, if that, taller than 5', redheaded, florid of complexion, round-faced, short-legged, and heavy later in life. (Daddy was 6'2" and slender until middle age.) In her early years Momma moved swiftly about her chores, but by the end of her life all her actions except walking seemed to be in slow motion. She had a tendency to scatter her efforts among her many tasks so that she completed few of them on schedule and to her satisfaction. By nature, however, she was thrifty, hardworking, and burdened with worries about our precarious circumstances. She confided to me in her later years that she worried not only about things that happened but also about things that might happen.

Her morbid mindset reflected the outlook many Corn Road women—none more so than her three Hooper sisters—had on life in those days. It was considered unseemly for women to appear lighthearted. Good women talked mostly about bad things. With solemn seriousness and gruesome details, they tried to outdo one another in describing wasting illnesses, incurable aches, inhuman abuses, and other calamities of life. The inherited stories passed down through many generations of hardscrabble life had deposited in their minds and souls the conviction that everything awful not only could happen, it already had and probably would again. Consequently, they did their best to impress us with the sufferings of life and to prepare us for the worst.

Momma's perennial but ever frustrated hope was to have a family free of outside distractions and united in the common cause of overcoming poverty and assuring our future. Momma suffered much when life—or Daddy, to be more precise—denied her this dream. She was often depressed, a condition that seemed to be an inherited trait in the Hooper family and occasionally a problem for me (and, I suspect, for my siblings). But she was not one to endure her lot in silence. She never failed to remind us how hard her life was or to describe her trials and tortures in greater detail than any of us cared to hear. The truth was that we no more listened to her complaining than we did to the wind blowing and were genuinely surprised and dismayed the few times she was obviously sick. She nagged Daddy constantly with good reason but poor psychology, for the more she complained the more he withdrew in manly silence and indulged his own whims.

"Don't never git in a argument with a woman," he would counsel me. "Jist walk off when they light in on you."

Unlike Daddy, who made friends easily with everybody, Momma had a less charming personality. Nowhere was their difference more obvious than with children, for whereas they loved Daddy, Momma had to work hard to win them over. She always viewed Daddy's easy popularity as one of life's unfair favoritisms. But his charismatic personality had serious drawbacks, too; all kinds of lowlife characters, drunks and drifters, were attracted to him and took advantage of his generous spirit. Momma complained bitterly but to no avail. Daddy was a friend to all, but it was usually a one-sided relationship: his so-called friends were nowhere to be found when he was sick or in need.

In keeping with an ancient custom, when our parents married in 1929 relatives donated enough old furniture to the new couple to set up housekeeping. They used it the rest of their married life; if I recall correctly, adding only a couple of straight back chairs. In 1944 a neighbor, I think it was Bill Mckenzie, gave us an old couch, armchair, and organ. As best I remember, Momma never had any more furniture of her own until she was widowed in 1968. She passed on in 1997, a few months short of ninety. From her mother she inherited a bookish bent and a love of learning, and even though the endless drudgery of life left her little time for books, she remembered nearly everything she read, and, unfortunately, believed everything in print. She lived in an age of much greater innocence than our time. This caused her to believe that the government would not let people publish things that were untrue. (Ah me! Dear innocent Momma! If only you had known how much misinformation and rank stupidity find their way into print!) A consummate seamstress and quilter, Momma also had a marked artistic talent, which with rare exceptions she was unable to express until her widowhood many years later. She wrote a beautiful hand, and even though her spoken English was only slightly better grammatically than the unpolished country speech of our region, her letters were impeccable in grammar and spelling. I always double checked both when I wrote to her. It would not do for her PhD son to make a mistake that would have shattered Momma's naïve illusion that I knew practically everything. For she also made the mistake of equating education with intellect.

Speaking of education, among the several disappointments of her life perhaps none pained her more and longer than the circumstances that shortened her formal studies. She loved everything about school, and when she talked about her school days at Battleground her eyes would light up and she would relive some of the happiest years of her childhood. Not only was she the best speller hands down in the school but maybe the fastest runner as well on the playground. She claimed she could beat the boys in a footrace. I had my doubts until I saw my sister Geraldine try to outrun her one day to escape a switching. My sister ran as fast as normal young legs could carry her, but Momma's short legs were awesomely faster, a blur of motion, and Geraldine was soon in tow for her punishment. Of course, I stood by smugly and watched, relieved that I had escaped—for the moment—little Momma's redheaded wrath and stinging hickory withe.

After seventh grade and a stellar performance at Battleground School, Momma had her heart set on high school. In those days that meant boarding away from home. Her parents agreed to the expense and Momma had her bags packed for departure the next day. But by morning for reasons she never understood and in truth never got over, her parents had changed their mind and so ended Momma's formal studies. I can only guess at the depth of her disappointment. Later she delighted in my academic progress, and even though I cannot remember ever being consciously aware of it, I think one reason I went on to and through high school, college, and graduate school was so Momma could vicariously live out her old dreams. These accumulated disappointments probably had a corrosive effect on Momma's youthful exuberance and spontaneous affections. I remember when I was very small, she would clasp me to her bosom and hug me with a joyous love that bonded us forever. But as time went on, her demonstrations of maternal love became rare and then ceased entirely as she withdrew more into her own sadness. Her withdrawal bewildered me. I missed her embrace and wondered—without ever putting it into words—what had happened, just as I wonder today whether it might have caused some of my childhood health problems.

Thinking about her long life shortly before she died, I realized with a degree of astonishment that I had never known Momma to tell a lie, not even a little white one. I asked her about it, and she answered simply, "My parents taught me to tell the truth." When she passed away in September of 1997, I mentioned her truthfulness to my siblings—Geraldine, Darrell, Janice, and Joyce. They agreed with me that indeed Momma never lied.

Daddy was as different from Momma as daylight is from dark. In love with forest and stream, he seemed to be a man born out of his time. The old American frontier, not the farm, would have been his natural setting. Like a latter-day Daniel Boone, he farmed sporadically and haphazardly only when not busied with his primary pursuits of hunting, fishing, roaming, and visiting. They told how as a near-feral boy he would escape for days at a time into the forested slopes of Burney Mountain, returning home eventually with ruined shoes and torn clothing. Daddy knew every creek, bluff, cave, and trail for miles around. His contact with animals and nature had at least one dire consequence: at a very young age he contracted a severe case of what he described as "rabbit fever" (Lyme Disease?) and was bedridden for several weeks. Recovered at last, he had to learn how to walk all over again. Repeating something Grandma Raley had told her, Momma said he was never the same afterwards, which was her way of saying that his emotional and intellectual maturity was stunted by the illness. Momma was born old when it came to responsibilities; Daddy, though wise in many ways, to some degree always remained an adolescent. It was both his charisma and his shortcoming. He finished sixth grade at Round Top School in the Valley but read little. But he had a lively imagination and sometimes would tell stories when we were picking cotton. He also loved flowers. Somewhere in that big man there was a poetic spirit.

Daddy was acquainted with all the forest herbs and their medicinal qualities. Much to my later sorrow, I scorned most of this woodland knowledge, convinced that it was superstitious ignorance that could not stand up to my bookish learning. The only part of his lore that interested me at the time was his revelation that ginseng sold for twenty-five or thirty dollars a pound. I immediately set out to find some along streams and creeks, but all I ever located was bitterroot, a plant that superficially resembles ginseng. I think by the time I discovered its monetary virtues we lived south of its range.

Daddy wandered the woods as stealthily and silently as an Indian, often standing motionless to watch animals or men unaware of his presence. (And he saw some strange things.) He was a master hunter and for many years trapped animals and tanned hides in the frontier way. At the same time, he was respectful of wildlife and often would rescue and doctor birds with broken wings or animals with mangled paws. He scorned men who hunted or fished only for pleasure and did not consume what they had killed or caught, and he had a withering contempt for people who posted their land with "No Trespassing" signs, which he usually ignored. He had acquired considerable veterinary skills, and people would come from miles around to get his help if a cow was having trouble calving or if it was time to castrate hogs. He may have picked up some of his knowledge from some books his father had, but mostly he learned from experience and an instinctive understanding of animals.

He always kept hunting dogs, mostly "tree dogs" for squirrel and 'possum—they could also double as rabbit dogs—and running hounds for foxhunting. Only occasionally did Daddy hunt quail (we called them "partridges"), and I cannot remember our having bird dogs, though I may have forgotten one or two. Because of a Bible passage—"Thou shalt not accept the price of a dog"—Daddy would not sell or buy canines, but he occasionally traded them. Regardless of the breed, they were always hungry and a leaping, snapping menace whenever I tried to run out the backdoor holding a "biscuit and butter" as high as I could. "A fat dog won't hunt," he explained. He fed them just enough to keep them in ravenous hunting form.

As much as he loved his dogs, however, Daddy had a rule that they were never to come into the house. "Bein' in the house rurns their nose and they can't foller a scent," he told us. I adopted his prohibition when I married, and, happily, a dog-free house contributed in no small way to our domestic peace. I love dogs outside but only tolerate them inside. Luckily, they always seem to like me.

Usually Daddy had two or three guns, maybe two 12-gauge shotguns, or sometimes a 16-gauge, and a .22 squirrel rifle, leaning in the corner next to his bed. He kept the shells in a head-high cabinet near the fireplace. He warned us sternly never to play with the guns, never to load them indoors, and never to point them at anyone. After hunting, Daddy would open the breech to make doubly sure they were unloaded. The guns were never a temptation to us, and we grew up accepting them as a natural part of our world.

"No work on Sunday" was an inviolable rule in our house, and Daddy looked with scorn on neighboring farmers indifferent to the biblical injunction regarding a sabbath day of rest. But while I respected his vehemence and was delighted to agree with him for my own lazy reasons, I always suspected the prohibition also suited Daddy's own leisurely preferences as well. Daddy and I had very different personalities, but usually we got along fine. From an early age, he treated me as a full-fledged person and respected my opinions, something that helped me deal with all kinds of people.

Because Jesus said—if I recall the passage correctly—that "No man having put his hand to the plow and looketh back is fit for the Kingdom of Heaven," Daddy took it literally and would not look back at furrows he had plowed. The rows were often crooked and messy, for even at his best he was unconcerned with the aesthetics of his farming. This was especially true in the early spring when he laid off Momma's garden, that is, plowed the furrows for planting. Meticulous Momma, orderly by nature, would protest the meandering rows, while indifferent Daddy would take his team and go away to the field, leaving Momma to take her trusty hoe and straighten them out as best she could while complaining aloud to anybody or nobody why "Barthel just won't do anything right I ask him to do." They both had their ways of sabotaging each other.

In retrospect, it is obvious that both were deeply unhappy and disappointed in their marriage. Daddy was admired, liked, and respected by nearly everybody within a twenty-mile radius, but at home all he heard was Momma's everlasting complaints about his failures. She never understood that what a mature man needs and wants more than anything else is the respect and support of his wife and those close to him.

As for Momma, she was embittered by a husband who was indifferent to her dreads and demands. He was never physically abusive, but he could not, or would not, respond to a wife whose disapproval of him was unrelenting. From my standpoint, both were right and both wrong. The result was a family that was outwardly respectable but inwardly dysfunctional. We were monetarily poor, but at a deeper, unspoken level, we were, or at least I was, emotionally off center. Momma once confided to me that if there had been other livelihood options open to her she would consider taking us children and leaving him. I would not have blamed her, for I understood her grievances, but at the same time I faulted her for her divisive criticism that resolved nothing and ruined much. As I said, Daddy's response to her carping was silence and withdrawal, never physical violence.

But if Momma and Daddy were as different as fire and water, at least they had one strong bond: they agreed on matters of common morality. For all his roaming and drinking in his youthful years, Daddy was, by all accounts, not one to stray from his marriage vows. Taking his cue from Grandma Raley no doubt, he detested sexual immorality with a vehemence that surprised those accustomed to his easy-going manner in other matters. There was talk that his own father was not so puritanically disposed, and I suspect that Daddy saw and resented the suffering the fact or suspicion caused his mother. The day before Daddy was buried in June of 1968 a certain uncle, whose name I will not mention here, told me that when they were young, he once tried to persuade Daddy to stop at a house of ill-repute in Cullman.

"Ye can stop if ye want to, but I aint," he told his wayward brother.

My uncle added that Daddy would never have anything to do with easy women except to respect them. Other men told me the same thing. Once he learned that a married man was harassing a local divorced but respectable woman whom Daddy had befriended—with Momma's encouragement, I should add, for in such matters she trusted him implicitly. Daddy was furious with the man and threatened to "whup" him if he didn't cease his unwanted advances. His philosophy was simple: he respected all women and tried to instill by example that principle in me.

"Ye always have to respect a woman, even if she don't respect herself," he once told me.

I think it was the only time he verbalized to me his version of chivalry. I never forgot it, even if I did not always live up to his teaching. Daddy was an honest, truthful man, but unlike Momma who always told the truth in a direct, unvarnished way, he was prone to tell things in a pleasant way that soothed feelings and kept peace, skirting or omitting harsher topics that might upset others. Nevertheless, his patience and goodwill had limits. He was a proud, independent man prone to towering rage if he thought a man was belittling him or trying to make him do something against his will. Daddy could be easily led but never pushed. He would do anybody a favor, but he could not be forced or coerced to violate his principles. And it was dangerous to try. In his prime he was uncommonly strong. My Uncle Elton said he saw him lift the front end of a Model T car, and Daddy himself told me of once knocking a balky mule off its feet with his bare fists.

If Momma was unselfishly accommodating in her own right, Daddy was generous to an alarming degree to any and all in need. People were aware of this and, as I said earlier, many took advantage of his largesse. Money, tools, time, and labor he would offer without question or hesitation, and I think his father was the same way. The old saying that the shoemaker's children go barefoot often applied to us. For Daddy helped everybody, but his own family often seemed to be last in line. But I have to say that I remember him handing me his last half dollar once when I wanted to go to a movie in Cullman. Needless to say, many of the borrowed items were never returned, and often we lacked a certain plow or tool because some friend or neighbor had borrowed it—forever. When he died, someone "borrowed" his .22 rifle and, of course, never returned it to Momma.

On a broader scale, retrieving borrowed money in a community that had so little was usually a lost cause. It was enough to satisfy every man's honor for the borrower to remember and acknowledge the debt—"I'm gonna pay you back just as soon as I get the money"—and after such an avowal it was bad form to insist on actual repayment. In this way debts could be carried for years without offense or breach of friendship.

My family lived only a year or two at the Hale place and I have but one hazy yet angry memory of those first years. I alluded to it earlier. I recall standing up in an automobile wearing only a diaper and being pestered by an old man. It must have been in the fall of 1935. He kept pulling down my diaper and talking foolishly to me. The man may have been my Grandfather William A. Hooper, who died in December of 1936. (I think I said this earlier.) I have always regretted not having a positive memory of Grandpa Hooper who by all accounts was a decent, hardworking, and intelligent man. By trade a bricklayer, he worked on the Wilson Dam and other major projects in North Alabama. Many years later when my mother passed away, I inherited his Bible, and what he wrote in it moved me and gave me a truer moment of insight to the Christian gentleman he really was. He may have had the same problem with children that I saw later in my mother: a tendency to say or do the wrong thing at the wrong time—try to kiss them ("steal some sugar"), for example, or threaten to take them home with her. Mother meant well but unlike Daddy, she was tense and usually did poorly with children at first acquaintance. It was a trait I noticed in several of her relatives. The few times my gruff, snuff-dipping Aunt Itra Hooper Parish, Grandpa's Hooper's sister, ordered me to come to her for a snuff-tainted kiss, my first impulse was to run for my life.

There was another event that I seem to recall—but it may be my recollection of a story I was told—of how I chewed up and swallowed a handful of cigarette butts that Daddy or my uncles had thrown in the fireplace. I turned green and was deathly sick, but the effect of my misery was permanent and positive: I never had the urge to smoke, even though nearly every boy I ran with took naturally to tobacco as the manly thing to do. But I was strong ("stout" as we used to say) with a pretty good set of fists and believed I could defend myself without cigarettes, snuff, or chewing tobacco.

About that same time, or maybe a year or so earlier, my Uncle Bertis Raley "saved" my older sister Geraldine at another fireplace. It may have been before I was born when they lived on Burney Mountain. It seems she got too close and ran or fell headlong into the fire. Uncle Bertis pulled her out before any real damage was done. But we always repeated the story with the conviction that Geraldine might have perished if Uncle Bertis had not acted so quickly. Ever afterwards he was a "hero" in my eyes, and although later he moved several miles away to Jones Chapel and my contacts with him were few, he remained one of my favorite relatives.

Geraldine was less lucky playing with our first Cousin Ralph James, our Aunt Burlie's older son. When she was about three, they were cutting wood as they had seen the men do. Geraldine was holding the limb and Ralph was chopping with a hatchet. Unfortunately, he missed and cut off two of Geraldine's fingers at the first joint. Daddy said they buried the fingers, but Geraldine was crying with pain. So they dug up the fingers, which the ants were devouring, put them in a little snuff can and reburied them. The pain subsided and Geraldine soon recovered, adjusting so well that hardly anyone ever notices that her ring and little fingers are shorter on her right hand.

In those days, many mothers dressed girls and boys alike in loose-fitting, robe-like garments. I became so attached to my "dress" that I cried angrily, so Momma said, when it came time to change my garb to boy's clothes. It was probably a good thing we had never heard of modern psychology. In some mysterious way people seem to "catch"—or induce—conditions they read about.

I had better luck keeping my little aluminum plate with the ABCs in a continuous circle around its border. I cannot remember not knowing the alphabet because of that early exposure, and I ate from the plate—probably my version of a security blanket—until I was ten or so and it wore out. To this day I visualize the alphabet as a circle, like one of those mythological looped serpents with their tail in their mouth. Armed with my circular alphabet, by about age four or five I started figuring out words by picture association in the Sears Roebuck and Montgomery Ward catalogs. By matching four familiar letters with the picture of a hunting decoy, for instance, I learned "duck," the very first word I learned to read. I worked out my own unorthodox vowel sounds and was intrigued and mystified by the phonetic relationships of words. By my first day of class at Ebenezer School in September of 1941 I had taught myself to spell and recognize random words. Then that very morning it suddenly all came into focus in Mrs. Butler's class and I could easily read whole sentences. That afternoon when I got home to the log cabin where we were living my mother asked me what I had learned my first day at school.

"Momma, I learned how to read!" I responded proudly.

Chapter 4:
Wayward Relatives

There are many collateral narratives to tell about these Appalachian years. One of them begins with Aunt Mary Woods, the midwife for whom I always had much affection. She was the large, kind, and unflappable wife of my alcoholic great uncle Ambrus Wood, or Woods, as the surname had become. He was "Uncle Am" to us and brother to my grandmother Mary Woods Raley. Aunt Mary was the matriarch of a clan expertly versed in most of the vices any of us knew anything about. In no particular order, these included drinking, lying, larceny, profanity, promiscuity, laziness, and general worthlessness. Aunt Mary took it in stride and somehow kept her wayward family from total disintegration.

Uncle Am certainly contributed to her woes, but unlike most of his children, he also retained enough moral fiber and sense of responsibility to keep a job and save the family from total ruin. In earlier times he had been a hard scrabble farmer like his father but left the farm during World War II to work for the L&N railroad. When Friday and payday came, he started drinking and usually didn't stop until Sunday. Then began the melodrama of getting Uncle Am sobered up and fit for work on Monday. Somehow with Aunt Mary's calm, expert help he always made it. Years later, however, a boxcar load of telephone poles fell on him and crushed his body. Although he survived the accident, doctors said he would never walk again. Consequently, the railroad settled a considerable compensation on him. As I remember the account, with his new wealth Uncle Am bought a fine automobile, found a driver, stocked up on liquor, got himself a young woman to ride around with him, and went on the longest binge of his life. As I heard the story, in a moment of drunken generosity he handed over a considerable portion of his cash to Aunt Mary, whereupon she bought them a house and squirreled away the remainder. Eventually, having squandered the rest of his fortune, Uncle Am reportedly begged Aunt Mary to return the money he had given her. She refused, and for the rest of their days they had a nice home and adequate provision. Aunt Mary was, as I said, calm in the midst of her incredibly chaotic circumstances. Against all odds, by the way, Uncle Am made an unexpected recovery from his injuries and—thanks mainly to Aunt Mary—lived to a respectable old age.

Some of their children were not so tough or fortunate. Daddy's first cousin Leo "Bode" Woods, who looked startlingly like my father when they were young, went little or never to school but needed no education anyway to teach him what he did most and best: lie, steal, drink, and fornicate. He once robbed the bank in Falkville—a small Valley town—of a few hundred dollars. Law officers caught him a few miles south in Lacon. He then served eighteen months or so in Alabama's Kilby Prison. He had many brushes with police and sheriffs and lived with a thief's natural dread of the law. But for all his shortcomings, he was a likable man and one of the most engaging liars I ever knew. He had a square, manly face, honest, pleading blue eyes, and enough good will and generosity in him to win the confidence of people. Unfortunately, he also had a habit of stealing anything not nailed down once he gained their trust. He farmed some now and then and worked a little here and there, but his enthusiasm soon diminished as his thirst grew and before you knew it, he had abandoned home and plow—and wife if he happened to have one at the moment—and was off to find his next drink or commit his next theft. He ended his life as senselessly as he lived it. Drinking as usual, so I was told, he jumped or was thrown from his Cousin Howard Woods' car. Seemingly out of danger from a concussion and released from the hospital, he died unexpectedly the next day.

His brother Leon Woods was handsome with a sunny disposition, and while he shared many of Bode's vices he also had a greater endowment of virtues. He was not the liar and thief his brother was, nor did he need to be. His smile, good humor, and charm were more effective. Behind his back, my mother stoutly claimed to detest him for his drinking, immoralities, and infringements on my father's time. Yet the minute he showed up flashing his broad smile and teasing Momma in his handsome, good-natured way, she forgot her anger and soon would be laughing at his stories and antics. Illiterate like Bode, Cousin Leon had natural good manners and people could not help liking him. He thought it was a waste of a young man's life if he did not spend all his waking hours chasing and bedding every available female. He had a perverse version of the biblical injunction, "Ask and ye shall receive." As Leon inversely summarized his philosophy, "if ye don't ask fer it, ye don't git none." We all understood his meaning. Leon practiced as well as he preached and was broadly ecumenical in his conquests. No woman was too high and haughty and none too low and ugly for his taste. His name was often associated with unfaithful wives, cuckolded husbands, and deflowered daughters. Childhood poliomyelitis caused him to limp noticeably on his left foot, but it only seemed to make him more attractive to women. Unlike cowardly old Bode who ran away as readily as he lied, Leon would stand and fight if he had to, but there was not a bitter bone in his body, only a man-child who frolicked his way through life and grew old without growing up. It was a wonder to us that somebody hadn't shot him years earlier or that he didn't die from bad whiskey, knife fights, drunken brawls, or numerous car wrecks. But he always came away laughing and unscathed. We shook our heads and reckoned that he was a scoundrel who happened to be born under a lucky star. Unlike us, he hardly ever worked but somehow always had smoking tobacco and a little money in his pocket and his clothes were always clean.

Only once that I can recall did his fabled luck almost run out, and it involved the most sensational murder case our area had ever known. A Mrs. Haney was returning home through a lonely wooded stretch of Powell Road when a neighbor named Lang assaulted her. He raped and killed her in a pine thicket, then brutally mutilated her body. Her bag of groceries purchased at Bibb's store on the Corn Road fell by the wayside. A little later old Leon came whistling and limping along and always with a keen eye for anything requiring no work, happily appropriated the provisions and took them home. The case created a sensation at the time (late 1940s) and in the course of the investigation Leon was picked up for questioning. Eventually he was cleared when Lang was arrested, but not before he had received the fright of his life. He went to church, accepted Jesus, and promised to change his ways. The experience affected him so deeply that he kept his promise for, oh, maybe two or three whole weeks, about as long as his Christian walk lasted before backsliding into his old life after he was saved and baptized at a Dough Ball revival.

An earlier incident was resolved less traumatically. In 1943, I think it was, a training plane, probably a B-17, crashed on the mountain a few miles west of our house. By this stage of World War II, the sky was often full of training planes and we were used to them. That day I was playing outside, idly aware of the drone of its engine, and had even turned to watch it once or twice as it circled. There was lightning in that direction and a bolt may have struck the plane. For all at once the droning turned into a screaming whine which suddenly ceased. Within hours the news was out that a plane had gone down killing the crew. Curious people started going down the Davis Gap Road to the crash site. Who but Leon would be one of the first to arrive on the scene, and who but he would find the billfold of one of the doomed crew members? The money it contained was tempting, but to his credit Leon turned it over to military investigators when they showed up and questioned him. (Rumor circulated, however, that at least one other man kept money and personal effects he found.) Not long afterwards my parents and I, along with family members and other curious people, walked down the mountain side to witness the devastation for ourselves. The plane had struck the side of the mountain with such force that its twin engines and fuselage gouged out ten-foot craters. We found aluminum shards embedded in surrounding trees and learned that twisted metal, human flesh, and other remains were scattered over a wide area.

Leon married a beautiful, blonde neighbor girl, eighteen-year old Marie Cook, with whom I—at age three or four—also declared myself to be in love. To be truthful, it was a tossup whether I like her or her cookies more. At my solemn request, she promised to wait for me until I grew up, but soon afterwards she married Leon. I was crushed; it was my first romantic disappointment. Many years later when, finally, she had enough of Leon's drinking and womanizing and divorced him, I reminded her of her failed promise.

"Harold," answered the still pretty Marie, "I probably would've been better off if I'd waited for you!"

I never saw Marie again, but her words were a gratifying little vindication of my childish dream. She and Leon had five handsome children, one of whom—Billy—was severely handicapped with spina bifida and lived only to age thirteen or fourteen.

Hubert Woods, brother to Bode and Leon, did his part to uphold the ill-repute of the siblings and there were stories about his early hell-raising escapades as well. But to me his personality was less impressive and when I came to know him he was not as creative and vigorous as his brothers in their fulltime pursuit of vice. What I have said of Bode and Leon will more than cover the familiar misdeeds of their less energetic sibling. Hubert, a navy veteran of World War II, was married for a short turbulent time to Rosie Milligan, one of Henry Milligan's daughters, as celebrated for their sexual laxity as Henry was for his religious fervor. Years later Hubert married another Rosie, but I have little recollection of her.

If Leon was determined to get all the sexual favors he could, some of his sisters were said to be just as dedicated to spreading theirs around to all the men who asked. To this neighborly generosity some of the girls added the customary family traits of drinking, lying, and general wantonness. My Grandmother Raley railed mightily against her wayward nieces, though I cannot remember her saying anything critical about Uncle Am and Aunt Mary. I am not sure Grandma even knew about the men their daughters were said to entertain, but she was convinced that no good could come of women with hemlines above their knees and cigarettes in their mouth. Decent women didn't smoke, and good women covered their legs, she said. Everybody agreed with Grandma, of course, probably including men who helped the girls light their cigarettes and lift their skirts.

Yet for all their faults, the Woods girls were loyal to family and relatives when the test came. And come it did. When I was about seven James Edwards, my Uncle Aaron's ("Bufus") second son, was harassing us at the bus stop on the Corn Road beside Aunt Bea's little house. Recently James had turned so mean the bus driver had to order him off the bus. He retaliated by throwing rocks through the school bus window and threatening to beat us up. He was a beefy boy of thirteen or fourteen, but my cousin Lena ("Lenar") Woods was a rangy, exceptionally strong girl of seventeen or so. When she heard what James was threatening, she marched out and challenged him in our defense. Old James charged her like a baby bull. Whereupon, as I recall, she picked him up and threw him over her back as we little ones cheered. James fled in disgrace, and Lena was forevermore our champion, her courage and strength more than making up for her alleged moral deficiencies.

Because the Raleys generally adhered to a higher moral plane than Uncle Am's clan, his family furnished us a steady supply of entertaining gossip about things forbidden to us. But even though we routinely condemned their conduct, as Grandma Raley, Momma, and others had taught us, I think my cousins and I secretly admired some of our notorious kinfolks, especially our cousin Lonzo Johnson, son to Geneva Woods Johnson (later Milligan) and grandson to Uncle Am and Aunt Mary. Unlike us, Lonzo enjoyed complete freedom of speech, for he had mastered at an early age a rich, eloquent profanity which he launched without the slightest inhibition or punishment at any person or circumstance that displeased him. On the other hand, we rehearsed our anemic little cussing vocabulary only when we were sure no adult was around.

But even more we envied Lonzo his trained dog that he would hitch to a little red and yellow wagon and ride up and down the dirt road, manfully cursing the toiling canine the same way neighboring plowmen blasphemed against their wayward, balky mules. Grandma Raley and the women of our family were duly scandalized, of course, but in comparison to Lonzo our list of amusements seemed pale indeed at the time.

Chapter 5:
Hard Times and Country Cooking

The 1930s were Depression years, or so they said, but we Corn Road people and I suppose others in Greater Appalachia could hardly tell the difference between good times and bad. We were poor before the Depression and only slightly poorer after it started. They used to say jokingly you could tell when hard times were easing when a rabbit ran across the road and only one man was chasing it.

We grew and canned much of our own food and when they were in season, picked blackberries and gathered wild poke ("poke salad"). Around 1939 or 1940 the first pressure cookers came out and farm families were allowed to buy them from the government for $10 with payment deferrable until harvest. Most families took shelled corn to Russell's grist mill—or later to Floyd Bibb's mill, both a mile apart on the Corn Road. The miller would dip out a portion for his profit and the rest of the milled grain we hauled home to make cornbread. Flour, coffee, sugar, Cayenne black pepper, Bruton snuff, County Gentleman smoking tobacco or Brown Mule chewing tobacco, and a few other commodities we had to buy when we could. The women made and mended many of our clothes. #50 or 60 grade thread was always high on the list of indispensable goods, and often Momma sent me to fetch it from McCravy's or Bibb's store. Wives and mothers who were poor seamstresses were pitied, and for good reason. Unfortunately, Grandma Raley was one of them, and my Grandma Hooper, herself an exquisite seamstress, could not conceal her horror over Grandma Raley's crude stitching.

Every now and then Daddy or my younger uncles would supplement our diet with squirrels, rabbits, or fish. And for several winters there was molasses from Grandpa Raley's syrup mill. I was as squeamish about food as a poor country boy could afford to be, but with effort I could stomach just about everything except possum. For after I got a look at one's grinning face and reptilian looking tail I was convinced that God never meant such creatures for the human diet. Once when my Aunt Christine Johnson, I think it was, served it on my plate and then asked me how I liked it.

"I'm eatin' it, but it just won't go down," I answered with considerable distress. We were easily amused, and family members laughed at my remark for days.

Our chickens roamed everywhere they pleased around barns and fields and supplied us with eggs if we could find their nests before the egg-sucking hounds or wild animals got to them. Some people, including Uncle Bemis, had hardy, semi-wild guinea hens that laid more eggs but were better than chickens at hiding their nests.

My favorite everyday food was a soggy combination of "sweet milk" and cornbread, though later I learned to enjoy a buttermilk mix almost as much. Nevertheless, I must have had a touch of what nowadays they call lactose intolerance, for I regularly suffered from colic and stomach aches as a toddler and had a chronic iron-deficiency anemia until I was almost in my teens. I loved bologna and pinto beans, but these were town luxuries that I seldom sampled.

Most families had milk cows and raised hogs. Hog-killing around the time of first frost was a grand event that gave us children firsthand experiences with squealing animal slaughter, singeing odors of hair and skin, bubbling cauldrons of fat, and expert slicing of the hanging carcass. For days afterward, we gorged ourselves on pork, especially bacon, liver, and souse meat. Our food contained huge amounts of animal fat and starch, but we walked, worked, or played off most of what they call "calories" today. It was rare to see a fat person. It was essentially the same food our ancestors had eaten for centuries. Indeed, in most ways not much had changed for people like us in hundreds of years. Unbeknownst to us changes were just over the horizon, but for a few more years the old ways would continue.

My favorite fall activity, however, centered on Grandpa Raley's syrup mill. My uncles would cut and haul the cane, and we would feed it into the press to be crushed by the huge revolving wheels powered by a droopy, circulating mule. The juice flowed down a sluice into a huge copper pan or vat under which Grandpa stoked a fire. He kept the juice from congealing prematurely with a long iron instrument fitted to slide between the raised dividers. Meanwhile, having tired of feeding the press, we children would jump and slide down the cane pummings, or crushed stalks, and chew on the ultra-sweet cane sections.

I was not as enthralled with Grandpa's blacksmith shop, because my job there was to work the bellows until my arms hurt. Nevertheless, it was fascinating to watch the iron turn red hot and the water sizzle when they dipped the fiery metal—horseshoes or turning plow points and sweeps—in it. Though not as versatile as Grandpa Raley, Daddy also did some blacksmithing and several times I watched him trim horse and mule hooves to fit them to the iron shoes. One trick was to get the horse or mule to stand still for the fitting, for sometimes they would kick or sag down on the smith's back. The square horseshoe nails had to be inserted at just the right angle so they would come out of the hoof ready to be bent and clipped off. I always watched with some apprehension, afraid he would drive the nail into the quick and injure the horse. He never did.

Chapter 6:
Ancestors and Other Relatives

More than a century earlier—around 1818—my great-great-great Grandfather Charles Raley came to Morgan County from Kershaw County, or District, South Carolina. A Revolutionary Veteran, he was eligible for land, so I understand, when Alabama was opened to white settlement. His Grandfather, also Charles Raley, was born in 1705, perhaps in Antrim County, Ireland, but it could have been England, Virginia, or upper North Carolina. The name is English in origin, but some of the English settled in Ireland in the 1600s.[4] The original American Charles Raley seems to have settled first in Onslow County, North Carolina. His son, also named Charles and also a Revolutionary War veteran, was born in 1740 either in Onslow or perhaps in Ireland. The third Charles Raley was born in 1764 in Onslow, North Carolina, but shortly thereafter the family removed to Kershaw District, South Carolina. Sixteen-year-old Charles joined the Revolutionary forces in 1780, fought in several battles, and finished the war under the command of General Marion. He married Sarah Owen (born October 17, 1774) Nov. 5, 1789 (his 25th birthday) and they were the parents of several children, including Owen Raley (born 1801), who was to be our direct ancestor.

I am not sure just where Charles Raley first settled in Morgan County[5] but the Raleys were among the founders of Cedar Plains

---

[4] I talk about the Raley lineage in my history of the family.

[5] This information is found in my history of the Alabama Raleys.

Church, one of the oldest in Alabama. In any case, in the latter years of his life Charles Raley lived close to Round Top Church, probably on the old Raley place a mile or so across the fields at the foot of Burney Mountain. Pensioned as a Revolutionary War veteran in 1832, he died in 1839 and may have been the first person buried in Round Top cemetery. In a special ceremony at the 2003 Raley reunion held at Round Top Church the Sons of the American Revolution unveiled a Revolutionary War marker for his grave. At long last Great-Great-Great-Grandfather Raley had a fitting tombstone.

My Great-Grandfather William Marlin Raley (1831-1900), grandson of Charles and son of Owen, was a Union soldier in the Civil War—1st Alabama Calvary, USA. He was said to be a gentle, soft-spoken man of deep convictions. At his death, he left the valley farm to his youngest son nineteen-year-old William Thomas Raley who was to become my grandfather. Tom Raley, as he was known, whose forename, so I was told, was Gordon until he changed it to Thomas, was a tall, rawboned, slightly ferocious looking young man with oiled down, center-parted hair in old pictures. Later in life he became quite heavy. In 1903 he married Mary Elizabeth Wood, or Woods, daughter of William (Uncle Bill) Woods.

Great Grandfather Woods was a hard-fighting, hard-drinking Irishman with a handlebar mustache, lively blue eyes, and an irreverent disposition. I knew him when he was old and his mustache white, but he had been a powerfully built man, especially in his arms and shoulders. In his prime, his strength, agility, and fighting skills were the stuff of local legend. They told how he once swam the Tennessee River and claimed that he was never "whupped" in a fight, of which he supposedly had many. My Uncle Bemis believed he was the strongest man in Morgan County. I once heard that on Election Day—like many other occasions an excuse for drinking—he would draw a circle on the ground and being of Republican sentiments, would dare any democrat to step inside with him. And he made short, dirt-eating work of any man brave—or foolish—enough to accept his challenge. Even in his eighties he was still a vigorous hunter and fisherman and his spirit was as lively as ever. As a young man he fell in love with and married petite, pretty Sarah Hardin and remained faithful and devoted to her until her death in 1933. But lonely and still vigorous in his eighties after her death, he ran off with a young woman of dubious reputation. Eventually his scandalized family caught up with the pair and persuaded him to give up his folly. He once boasted that he drank a pint of his homebrewed moonshine whiskey every day for forty years. Unfortunately, he passed on this alcoholic taste to some of his descendants, especially son Ambrus, whose story I summarized earlier. Indeed, each succeeding generation seemed to increase his vices and diminish his virtues.

As his years increased, Grandpa Woods must have given some thought to his eternal destiny. They tell how Hobert Junkins and his brother, evangelists who were running a revival—it may have been at a Baptist Church near Eva—went to Grandpa Woods' house to invite him to the meeting.

"Humph, might think about it," he answered gruffly and said nothing more.

That night there was a commotion in the overflow crowd that spilled out into the yard. A loud voice, backed by strong elbows told everybody to "stand aside!" It was Grandpa Woods pushing people out of his way to get to the altar. And so at long last, the old man made his peace with God. In other revivals Reverend Junkins held him up as an example. If God could pardon such a notorious reprobate as Bill Woods, he explained, He will pardon anybody's sins.

Born in 1860, Great Grandfather Woods died in 1954 at ninety-four. I remember the day my sister Geraldine called me at Athens College to tell me the sad news. I recall in particular a conversation I had with him when I was thirteen or fourteen and concerned that I was not growing as fast or as tall as some of my friends.

"Them that grows fast fade first," he responded, scanning my compact body approvingly with his twinkling blue eyes. "And them that grows slow and study'll stay stout the longest."

Since I couldn't do anything about my growth, his words gave me some comfort.

Grandpa Woods almost died many years earlier. He and a neighbor, Anderson by name, I think it was, were plowing down in the Valley when lightning struck them and their mule team. The mules were killed instantly but remained standing upright, propped against each other. Mr. Anderson was also dead, and Grandpa Woods was unconscious for an undetermined time before making a full recovery.

His daughter, my garrulous Grandmother Raley who preceded her father in death (1883-1948), was short and redheaded while Grandfather Raley (1881-1950) was tall with raven black hair (perhaps from Cherokee ancestors in his Tennessee grandmother's bloodline). Their offspring were an interesting combination of both gene pools. Uncle Bemis, their firstborn, had brown hair and a heavy beard with, as I recall, some red mixed in. Burlie, the second child and one of two girls in the family, was auburn haired with reddish tints. Barthel, my father, had darker hair but very blue eyes. My redheaded mother used to say with some envy that in the sun he "turned brown without blistering," a trait that certainly neither she nor I shared. Uncle Bertis had sandy to reddish hair and blue eyes. On the other hand, Uncle Tolbert had black, wavy hair and unless my memory has failed me, brown eyes. Uncle Athel was of nearly the same coloring of hair, eyes, and skin as Bertis. The last two sons, fraternal twins Felton and Elton, both had dark hair, but whereas Felton had dark eyes, Elton's were blue. (Elton was my last paternal uncle to pass on. Felton died in the summer of 2006, Elton in 2008.) Azalee, the baby and only other girl, had auburn hair that darkened some with age, but she had the freckled, delicate white skin of a redhead.

At about six-three, my Uncle Felton was the tallest of the Raley boys, while my father was next at six-two. In his prime, Daddy was acknowledged as the strongest of these big men who in their youth prided themselves on their strength, lifting ability, and fighting skills. Unfortunately, my father also ruined his back eventually with these juvenile displays of strength. Uncle Bemis might have been as tall as my father if he had straightened up, but he had a pronounced hump. Unlike his beefier brothers, he was lean and hard ("tough as a pine knot," they used to say) and in endurance and stamina probably he could match up with any of them. He chewed tobacco all his life after Grandpa Raley used it to worm him as a boy. In his later years his teeth were worn nearly to the gum. For her part, Burlie (or Burley—not sure of the spelling) had a quarrelsome nature and was prone to say things in a blunt way that ruffled feelings and caused disputes. She had married Charlie James to spite her father, so I was told, for his having broken up her romance with another man, a former sailor, I believe. Charlie was a hardworking, successful farmer who always spoke kindly to me. Nevertheless, Burlie often scorned him and by all accounts their marriage was an unhappy union that produced five first cousins, Ralph, Imogene, twins Mildred and Marie, and Owen.

Unlile Burlie, Azalee, second daughter and last child, was the soul of gentle goodness. She was not much older than some of her nieces and nephews and was so protective of us that we used to say with utter conviction that if any of us were certain to make it to Heaven, it had to be Azalee. I never had a reason to change my mind about her.

She married Joe Frick and had an only child, Brenda. Their marriage was a sturdy one and as a couple they were very close. But their economic circumstances were always precarious. As a young man Joe was the victim of a malicious prank that limited his working ability. A fellow worker, perhaps a cousin, ran up behind and tickled him while he was carrying a sack of cement. Joe dropped the sack and fell backwards on the concrete. His back was ruined for life.

When I was about eight Daddy brought one of the younger Frick boys to the house and asked me to play with him for an hour or two. I tried, drawing a circle on the ground so we could play marbles, but Billy, I think his name was, seemed dazed and unable to understand what I was saying. Daddy explained that the boy had had a hard life. Today we would say that he was probably the victim of a dysfunctional family. I never saw him again but often wondered what became of him.

Bertis was the practical joker of the Raley clan and many stories were told of his pranks. Once he and some boys got a cowbell and while the other boys rang it across on the mountain slope, Bertis went up to a neighbor's house to announce in somber tones that his cow had slipped through the pasture fence and was running loose. The neighbor ran out to retrieve her, only to fall headlong over a wire that Bertis had strung across the pathway. Another time when Uncle Bemis was courting Aunt Viola, whom he later married, Bertis hid under their buggy and rode all the way to the Valley (three or four miles distant). (He had also briefly courted Viola.) Later he related every word they said. An easy task, he said laughingly, since they only spoke once or twice about topics like the weather. Nothing was safe from his wit and sarcasm. If he suspected someone was lying, he was as adept as a skilled lawyer in the way he would nonchalantly repeat the same questions from different angles until the liar tripped himself. Then Uncle Bertis would pounce and ridicule his victim. It was better to tell him the truth from the very first.

Of all my Raley uncles, Bemis was the one with whom I had the most contact. His birthday came one day after mine, and we used to joke that I was a day older. Although he may not have talked much as a courting man, in later years he liked nothing better than to chat for hours. I never saw him in a hurry or concerned about time, but his daughter Mary laughingly tells of one exception to his lifelong unhurried pace.

As her story goes, Uncle Bemis and his son-in-law L. E. Shaneyfelt were working on Bemis's barn. Aunt Viola called them to dinner (lunch). "In a little bit!" they answered and kept on with what they were doing. Mary called them again. Same response. This went on for a while. Then all of a sudden, here came L.E. and Bemis running as fast as they could, chased by an angry black racer snake they had disturbed. With his usual terror of snakes, Bemis threw his hammer at the serpent, but it fell in an abandoned storm pit and he was never able to find it again.

Bemis had what we would call today a pathological fear of snakes, living or dead, which incidentally I shared. On the other hand, my father, who loved animals, would pick them up and handle them. He may have been bitten once or twice. He told of one other time Bemis got in a rush. My daddy was up to his usual tricks with snakes and in a perverse moment tossed a dead snake at his older brother. Daddy said Bemis came at him eyes blazing with anger and ready to fight. I don't think Daddy ever played that trick on Bemis again.

"Beem," he said with respect, "will fight you over a snake."

What I remember fondly about Uncle Bemis was the way he

would spend hours talking to me as if I were a grown man. Even so, once he shot me. It was an accident, of course. He was hunting down below his house and just as I walked into the woods, he fired at a squirrel, I think it was. The shotgun pellets, their trajectory spent, started sprinkling all around and a couple of them struck me harmlessly. So, no damage was done, but we had a lively topic to talk about for a while.

Uncle Bemis had a memory that bordered on total recall, a trait he passed on to his children. It seemed to me that he remembered in detail everyone he had ever known. He could have reconstructed whole chronicles of our world if we had asked him. I regret that we did not record his recollections before he passed on in 1977. Almost more than about people, he loved to tell stories about horses and mules, for he lived close to these animals and respected them as much as he loathed snakes. He could recall not only the names, ages, and colors of horses and mules from days long gone but would describe in impressive detail their character and quirks.

Uncle Bemis had one oddity about him that I never understood fully—probably because I never asked him to explain it. He was, of course, a Christian, yet he did not think it was necessary for him to join a church. He often attended "Dough Ball" and other churches with us but on his own independent terms that everybody respected.

In my boyhood I was especially fond of Felton (born 1920) who gave me basic lessons in auto mechanics. He patiently explained the firing sequence, timing, and the principles of the gasoline engine. On a few occasions I watched to see how he repaired motors, for he had the reputation of being a good mechanic. While snaking logs when he was fourteen or so and in the midst of a growth spurt a log rolled down and broke his leg. The broken leg ended up several inches shorter than the other so that it was hard for him to walk, especially behind a plow. He tried different jobs, including several years in Cullman working for a combination junkyard-garage. For a while around 1941-42 he ran a small store across the road from Bethlehem Baptist Church. He and his wife Aunt Thelma once invited me to spend the night with them. That evening he gave me a stack of comic books, and for several years to come they remained a passion with me. Some of those comics—originals or very early issues of Superman and Batman—would be priceless today, but alas my mother tossed them out when I left for college.

A decade later, work for Felton petered out in Alabama and he announced that he was moving to Michigan where he had already worked for short periods. Other members of the family also went north in the post-World War II years: Tolbert, Daddy, my Cousin Armon Raley, and I, too, in due time. But none of us except Felton was really serious about living in the North. Out of options in Alabama and unable to farm because of his leg, Felton was determined to make a decent living for his family. He left Alabama early in 1953 and unlike the others, never returned except for short visits. We all missed him, Aunt Thelma, and son Rabon, for Felton had always been a sensible, strong, and caring man and many were the times the family could have used his wise, balanced counsel. Late in December of 1952 Felton sold Daddy and me a car heater for $6.00—at our request and on credit. A couple of weeks later he left for Michigan. The debt remained unpaid until I handed Felton $6.00 in July of 2001 at the Raley reunion. Felton had forgotten about the debt and Daddy had died, but for nearly half a century I remembered.

My Aunt Viola, Momma's younger sister, was less talkative than Uncle Bemis—and very slow about it when she did speak. But like Mother, she read a lot and had strong opinions about religion and moral conduct. Like many women in the pre-television era, she read romance magazines by the dozen. <u>True Confessions</u>, which contained some very lurid and erotic stories, was a favorite. (I read a few too.) Gruesome detective stories were almost as popular, but we were shocked and disillusioned when the Haney murder was written up and bore only a distant resemblance to the facts of the case. For the first time, I think, our naïve trust in journalism and the printed word was shaken.

Chapter 7:
A Year on the Cook Place

Around 1937 we moved a mile or so south of the Corn Road to the Cook place where I met Mrs. Cook, Marie, and Edith. Our house, located about a quarter of a mile past the Cook home, was at the end of the road, unless you counted the rough wagon road that continued on by the barn, around the woods, and down into the Cook Cove. Geraldine was going to school by this time and there were no other children around for me to play with. But intensely absorbed in my games, I never thought about being alone, much less about feeling lonely. Company and solitude were, and have remained, equally appealing to me.

I cannot say the same for my mother who, I am sure, often suffered from loneliness. My father worked at various jobs in his younger years—cutting dyewood, WPA, hiring out to do manual labor—and spent a lot of time away from home. Even in the best of times he invented ways to be away from home: hunting, fishing, or roaming around the countryside talking with people. To my mother's horror, he sometimes drank and came home late. The occasional drunkenness that seemed to her comical in my bachelor uncles she found repugnant in Daddy. To make matters worse, she never missed an opportunity to berate him for his shortcomings. As I said earlier, it was an unhappy pattern that was to cause them much sadness throughout their marriage.

There were several memorable episodes—at least for me—during the year we lived on the Cook farm. I remember Chancey Cook, for instance, trotting past our house on his way to lunch (dinner) and then running back to his plowing in the back fields or down in the Cove. Chancey, who never failed to have a friendly word for me, was reputed to be one of the hardest working men in the community. People said of him respectfully that he had been gassed in World War I and never got over the effects. Chancey was a bachelor and when World War II came, he either joined or was drafted again. He served only a few weeks, though, before the army released him. The hardest working man we ever saw was, so they said, not up to the rigors of military life.

Chancey also performed dental work in the community. When I was twelve or so and had a painful, abscessed molar, Daddy took me to his house one night. Chancey looked at the tooth, took out his evil-looking, stainless steel pullers and, after telling me to be tough, got a grip and proceeded to pull, twist, and grind on the tooth until it popped out. Then he and Daddy talked about crops and hunting as I rested a few minutes until my body stopped trembling. Daddy offered to pay him, but in good Southern country style Chancey graciously declined. We both told him several times we were "much obliged" and walked back home through the woods. The gum healed nicely and by the time I needed dental service again, I went to a town dentist.

Chancey died ten or fifteen years later about the same time as Cousin Bode, I think, but in a totally different yet equally senseless way. As I heard the story (for by then I was no longer living on the Corn Road), Chancey teamed up with Brasher Sheats. It must have been the destiny of these good men to meet up in a working duel. For if there was any man in that country who worked as hard as Chancey, it had to be Brasher. He lived next to a right-angle curve of the Corn Road in Battleground where he cared for his impoverished family. But Brasher and his wife met their poverty head on by working like people possessed.

People said of Mrs. Sheats that she would "drop a young'un in the mornin' and be back out workin' in the field that evenin'." True? Maybe not, but it was a myth that grew out of a truth about her grit and tolerance for pain.

Chancey and Brasher began sawing logs with a crosscut saw. Now a crosscut saw is one of those ultimate tests of stamina and manhood. Your partner—and opponent—crouches face to face, eyeball to eyeball, with you across the log. You pull and he pushes; you push, and he pulls, as if you were trying to wrest the saw out of each other's hand. The saw, doused now and then in kerosene to keep it free of clogging gum and sap, sings its way through the wood. The sawdust piles up, the section drops, and you move to the next cutting. And so it goes, until your arms are dead with exhaustion and your lungs heave from exertion. For most men a moment comes when one of them gives in and with a twinge of embarrassment and to the knowing nod of the other, will offer a little rest to his partner.

But Brasher and Chancey were not your ordinary run of men who sensibly rest when fatigued. Instead they sawed on and on and on, for much stronger than their bodies, was their fanatical will to labor. And so still they sawed until they had sapped their last reserves of strength. I do not know the details, but after that duel neither man ever recovered and both sickened and died not long thereafter.

Mrs. Cook was the soul of sweetness. Her skin was smooth and creamy white, for like many women of her generation she never ventured out bareheaded in the sun. Geraldine and I felt welcome in her home and given the incentive of the wonderful cookies she and her daughters Marie and Edith made and the way they pampered me, I soon began begging Momma to let me go up to Mrs. Cook's house.

There was, however, a terrifying enemy on the way. In order

to get to the Cook house, I had to pass by their barnyard where a huge tom turkey gobbler ruled over his females. He took a disliking to me and would come running towards me the moment he saw me. I have been called a turkey more than once, but that was the first time I had ever been mistaken for one. I always tried to sneak by, but he would spot me and with a horrifying gobble and shaking of his ugly red wattle he was after me and the chase was on. But the sugar cookies, pretty Marie, kindly Edith, and gentle Mrs. Cook made the ordeal worthwhile. The Cook ladies always laughed and told me not to mind the gobbler, but at three and a half or four I lacked the size and speed of foot to be nonchalant about an enemy taller and tougher than I was.

Once past the gobbler I enjoyed many pleasant visits to the Cook home. One day sitting with them on the porch I saw a team of oxen snaking logs out of a stand of timber beyond their pasture. Little did I know that I had just witnessed the tag end of an era, for that was the first and last ox team I ever saw. Long after I had moved away from the Corn Road, I heard to my sorrow that during the last years of her life Mrs. Cook suffered from acute dementia and peppered her speech with profanity. It was the last thing I would have suspected of the gentle lady I knew.

Her married sons Harvey and Othell ("Shorty") Cook lived nearby. Shorty was a successful farmer out on the Corn Road, and Harvey moved into the Bibb home and followed Preacher Weisner as our pastor at Dough Ball.

For some of those years we had no team or wagon and usually walked everywhere. I remember standing with my feet in the back pockets of Daddy's overalls and holding on to his shoulders. It was late one summer day as the four of us took a shortcut across the pasture on our way home. The reddish sunlight reflected off the enameled surface of something half buried in the silt of the small stream that gathered in the pasture and flowed behind our house into the forest. I asked what it was and was amazed to learn that someone had thrown away a stove. A stove! What an unthinkably wasteful thing to do! We were too poor to discard anything.

One day Daddy accidentally drove a cotton stalk into his foot and could not work for many days.[6] Uncle Elton came over to plow his cotton for him. Earlier when Daddy was cutting dyewood the axe slipped and slashed several tendons across the top of his foot. Luckily the doctor managed to reattach the tendons and soon Daddy was as good as new.

When bad thunderstorms came, country people liked to take refuge in "storm pits," or cellars, that is, underground shelters that were reinforced with wooden beams and equipped with crude benches. Some had shelving for canned goods. Toads, spiders, snakes, and other creatures loved the moist, musty interior. Once during a storm when we had taken shelter in the pit near our house, lightning struck a tree and ran down the trunk and out through its roots cut flush with the dirt wall where I was leaning my head. I received a terrific, bell-ringing pop that left no lingering effects I know of. Momma was holding me in her lap and got a good jolt also.

Some people took the fear of storms far too seriously. Daddy used to laugh and tell how on his way home late one clear, calm night he saw some simpleminded neighbors—their surname may have been Chapman—huddled in their storm pit by the side

---

[6] What I actually remembered was Daddy cutting his foot while trimming a tree down in the pasture, but my Uncle Elton assured me that the wood chopping accident happened years earlier. He remembered the cotton stalk episode because he had to come over and plow for Daddy. I trust his memory more than mine in this case.

of Burney Mountain Road.

"What you'uns doin' in there?" he asked.

"Don't ye see that bad lightnin' over yonder?" they answered. Daddy said they had seen a searchlight sweeping the skies many miles away over Decatur.

Geraldine caught the measles at school that year and gave them to me. Luckily, I had a mild case and if memory serves barely curtailed my daily playing. The chicken pox she brought home the next year was even milder and I hardly knew I had it.

Uncle Tolbert had lived with us for a few months some years earlier, but I do not recall his stay. He remembered, though, and always had a special fondness for Geraldine and me as a result. Uncle Athel stayed with us some that year at the Cook place, and I remember one incident fairly well. He went off one day and got a little drunk—well maybe more than a little—and being the good soul that he was, on the way home he bought a sack of flour to help out the family. The sack had a hole in it and by the time he got home, carrying the flour over his shoulder, he was ghostly white from head to foot. Momma took one look at him and burst out laughing, much to his embarrassment. He tried to explain but his tongue was too thick with alcohol to make much sense.

"Vernie, I thank I'm jist about drunk," was all he could say.

Speaking of drinking, once or twice Shorty Cook and some other men had to help Daddy home. In Daddy's case, that could be dangerous, for he liked to fight when he had too much to drink. And he could do real damage with his strength and oversized fists.

Cousin Leon found out the hard way. One day when Daddy was drinking, Leon and two or three of his buddies—probably drinking moonshine too—met him walking alone down the Burney Mountain Road. Leon allowed as how it would be "a good time to give ole Barthel a whuppin'." Now Leon had nothing against Daddy that I know of. In fact, he was probably his favorite cousin. But cousin or not, a little manly fighting would stir the blood and give them something to brag about. So, they challenged Daddy and told him they were going to "whup his ass," in Leon's words.

"You'uns can try whenever ye feel like it," Daddy replied casually, patting his butt.

They did but despite their best licks, as Leon laughingly told it later, Daddy knocked them around and down as if they had been little boys. As I said earlier, Leon was not one to hold grudges and losing the fist fight only served to increase his admiration for Daddy.

Later that year after Athel had gone home, our Aunt Mary Foust, my Grandmother Hooper's sister, came to stay with us. Years later I learned that Aunt Mary left her daughter Alma's house because of a spat with her son-in-law Lecil Griffin, but at the time her visit was simply a pleasant interlude in my life. Aunt Mary would hold me in her lap, talk to me, and read me stories. I came to love her deeply and missed her when she went back home.

Nevertheless, my life had its unhappy moments. One day after Aunt Mary left, as I recall, it seemed to me that everybody in the house was conspiring to make me feel wretched. I was indignant and decided to run away from home. I walked down the wagon road toward the Cook Cove and hid behind a fallen tree trunk. Hours passed and it grew dark, but still I stayed in my hiding place. I could see the lamplight in the window back at the house and the thought of Momma's food was becoming enticing. Though still smarting over their slights, after a time I made a silent truce with my family and walked back home. As I opened the door, they all started laughing. It seems that the tree trunk was charred, and black soot covered my face and hands. I think Geraldine called me "Little Black Sambo" and Momma laughed as heartily about my black face as she had about Uncle Athel's white one. At first, I didn't think it was very funny at all, but after I had washed and eaten supper, the world looked much better to me. It seems remarkable now that they were not really worried about a three-and-a-half year-old boy hiding in the woods at night. But of course, the world has greatly changed since those days long ago.

That fall my parents started picking the cotton. I was too young to work but not too little to pester the pickers. Not knowing what else to do with me, my parents put me in a little cotton storage house on the wagon road just across from the infamous tree where I had blackened my face. I soon tired of the place and even though they had bolted it from the outside, with some effort I managed to loosen a plank and get out. Finding them over at the back side of the cotton field, I promised to behave, and my parents promised not to put me back in the cotton house. At least they kept their promise.

My chronic anemia or avitaminosis had several effects. I was plagued by carbuncles, my skin cracked painfully, and at times I had dull pains in my legs. Once as Momma and I were walking up the hill to the Corn Road I felt for a moment that I could go no further. Momma asked me what was wrong, and I answered, "This ole hill is just to-o-o heavy." She laughed at my odd misuse of adjectives and repeated my words to the family, but the aches and pains were real.

For a few years I also suffered from occasional seizures, "spasms," Momma called them. Daddy compared them to the howling "fits" the dogs had. Often these were accompanied, or maybe caused, by terrifying nightmares. In one particularly memorable dream in 1941 a loathsome green animal was chasing me with vicious intentions and my aching legs would not carry me fast enough to get away. Momma came to my bed and asked me what was wrong. I described the pursuing monster as "a green possum" not because it was but because that was as loathsome a description as I could come up with. As I said, I never liked possum. Luckily for me that was the last real spell I had, though I confess that I faked one or two more to get Momma's attention.

Chapter 8:
Life at Grandma Hooper's

One December day in 1938 we walked over to Grandma Hooper's house located on the Burney Mountain Road just beyond my birthplace, the Hale place where, as I recall, Charlie and Burlie James were now living. It started snowing and we spent that night and several more at Grandma's. The next morning, we awoke to a frozen, snow-white world that kept us inside for days huddled beside the roaring fireplace. I was thrilled at the sight and persuaded Momma and Grandma to let me play for a little while at a time in the snow. The temperature probably dipped into the teens.

Not long afterward we moved into Grandma Hooper's house. It was a three-story frame structure filled with the accumulated books, papers, letters, trunks, and clothes of several generations. My sister Geraldine and my cousin Mary would take me up to the third story, dress me in some of the ancient garments and shoes, and put me on display for the amused family. I liked to rummage through the old letters, books, and a page of cartoon drawings in The Progressive Farmer magazine.

Even though I loved my Grandmother Hooper dearly, I cannot now remember anything she ever said to me. There was a profound and peaceful silence about her and when she spoke her words had the quality of a whisper. Her face was smooth and unlined, for like Mrs. Cook she did not expose her skin to the sun. There was an indefinable world-weary sadness in her eyes. No doubt she missed my Grandfather Hooper very much, for Momma told me they were very close. She read incessantly, and

Momma told me that she had taught school. I trusted her implicitly, for I knew with a child's certainty that she was an infinitely kind person completely without guile or malice. The strongest recollection I have of her is of a thin, erect lady always dressed in a long-sleeved, floor-sweeping black dress buttoned to the chin. At night, lamp in hand, she would glide silently about the dark, high-ceiling house checking to see that everything was in order. Compared to the garrulous, roughhouse Raleys, she seemed to come from another world.

And in a manner of speaking she had. If my memory is correct, on the Hooper side of the family they remembered their English origins in Dartmouth, England, and unlike the always rural Raleys, in her immediate family Momma had the urban experience of living in Alabama City (now absorbed by surrounding cities) near Gadsden where Uncle Hays Hooper later settled. Even though it was before Child Labor Laws and Momma worked in a textile mill, she always looked back on those years as some of the happiest of her childhood. Then they moved to the Battleground community and bought the oak-shaded Laney house by the Corn Road. For a time, they sold eggs and other commodities and were conveniently close to a store and school. There the family was also happy. But then, Momma said with regret, because her parents did not approve of some of the rude "Georgia" people that had recently settled in Battleground, they sold their home on the well-traveled Corn Road and bought the remote, lonely farm down on the Burney Mountain Road. What were they thinking? Surely not about the welfare of their children. From then on until Momma finished seventh grade and her parents discontinued her education, she and her sisters and brother had to walk three or four miles to the Battleground school. By then Grandpa Hooper worked away from home and the family saw him only on weekends. I have wondered many times about their decision, but probably it must forever remain a mystery.

The Hays side of Grandma Hooper's family had produced, among other educated people, a banker, mayor (Cullman), and a pharmacist. There may have been a journalist in the mix also, but I never met any of them. Her mother Lettie (Leticia, I think it was), was the daughter of a Georgia planter and slaveholder in whose house two female servants, Hannah and Rebecca, catered to her needs and whims in the Antebellum South. They said of her that she never adjusted to life in the harsher post-Civil War conditions and that she made her daughters do for her what her slaves had once done. Grandma had not lost her mother's appreciation for high standards and retained an unpretentious trace of her family's vanished glory. If plain in its offerings, her table was always set in proper order and her dishes were finer than any I had seen. She kept an immaculate house, and with the help of her spinster daughter Irene and old maid sister Aunt Phoebe the yard was always swept clean and the shrubbery and flowers trimmed. For according to the standards of the time, she considered it slothful and disgraceful to allow grass to grow inside her hedgerows. Grandma Raley would not have disagreed more with her proper neighbor. "Lor-r-dy mercy," I can hear her saying, "who has time fer grass in the yard when ye have to cook and do day and night fer this bunch?" Every spring Grandma Hooper cleaned her house thoroughly and treated her mattresses for chinches. Although she never said so to me, I suspect Grandma Raley thought the Hoopers were a bit "quare" (queer), her favorite adjective for people that were just a little strange. (She would have had no inkling of the word's later homosexual connotations).

My health improved the year we lived with Grandma Hooper, maybe because the food was better and Aunt Phoebe

Waid could always be counted on for an extra biscuit and a thick slice of sugared butter. Not that she was gracious about it, for she was the very antithesis of her sister. She was illiterate and loud, whereas Grandma was eloquently polite, gentle, and well read. Although Aunt Phoebe nearly always had a harsh word to say, I soon saw through her tough talk and learned to manipulate her into doing what I wanted. Her favorite description of me was an exasperated prophecy, "Thunderation! You're more trouble than ye'll ever be profit!" When I was a little older and could lift her and whirl her around, she said of me that I was "stronger than Samson." She was wrong on the Sampson part, but she may have been right about the trouble and profit ledger of my life. Aunt Phoebe had helped raise several generations of children. In her last years she often called me "Hays" after Momma's brother and I never bothered to correct her. She had a collection of antique sayings and odd phrases. Once she dropped a plate, and even though it did not break Aunt Phoebe was annoyed anyway with the wayward dish. "I oughta stomp you into the very ground," she said to the plate.

As a living encyclopedia of superstitions, probably the most damage Aunt Phoebe did was to instill in me an unnatural fear of snakes. She told me how snakes would crawl into a sleeping person's mouth and coil up in their stomach, or how the fabled "hoop snake" would form a loop and roll down a hill to bite you, or again how some snakes got as big as a man's leg and could "swallow you whole." A year or two later these fearful lessons took effect. I spotted a brown snake, perhaps a rattlesnake, between our house and Uncle Bemis's and ran screaming in utter panic all the way home. A year or so later, my Cousin Armon Raley and I saw a big rattlesnake not far from Grandpa Raley's house and ran excitedly to tell my uncles the news. They killed the snake and complimented us for telling them. That made me feel better; nevertheless, my serpentine phobia was nearly as bad as Uncle Bemis's.

Unlike Grandma Hooper, simpleminded Aunt Phoebe never learned to read or write, as I said earlier. Nevertheless, she had strong opinions that her father, my Great-Grandfather Stokes Beason Waid, had instilled in her. She considered men to be an indecent waste of a woman's time and evidently had no idea at all of love and the tender sensibilities of life. It was said that she chased away the only suitor ever to come snooping around her house. Black people, she said matter-of-factly, had only half a soul. She informed me that her family was "Black Dutch," an assertion that puzzles me still, for the Black Dutch, like the Black Irish, have a dozen different stories about where they came from. Stokes Beason Waid was reputedly a hardworking man with a tendency to drink away his money as soon as fall crops were gathered and sold. Nevertheless, Aunt Phoebe revered his memory and took everything he ever said as gospel truth. Her mother, she informed us, had a "tutor," a distinction that in Phoebe's eyes raised her above the ordinary cut of mortals. My mother once tried to explain to her that a tutor was just a teacher that came to one's house, but Aunt Phoebe gave her a withering look and dismissed her words as unappreciative ignorance. I have a primitive photograph of Aunt Phoebe as a young woman. Except she doesn't look like a woman. Her hair is cut like a man's, and her features and expression have a masculine hardness about them.

Uncle Bud Waid, brother to Grandma and Aunt Phoebe, settled over in Winston County and I saw him only once or twice. He walked with a slight limp said to be the result of a fall he took while carrying a keg of the fine aged whiskey he made. In old age he drank only the whey of buttermilk which he extolled for its life-extending virtues. True, he lived into his nineties, but then so did some of his sisters who drank normal liquids. Aunt Phoebe herself made it to ninety (1863-1953) with an unpleasant disposition, an addiction to nicotine, and, according to Dr. Howell, a bad heart. He once advised her not to climb stairs or work outside, indeed, not to exert herself at all, advice she completely ignored. Aunt Phoebe took personal responsibility for running the world and was probably convinced that it would stop if ever she did.

Stories lingered in the family about the most terrifying sister of all, Aunt Jane Waid Allbritton, I believe her name was. It was said of her that so domineering was her character that she reduced her husband to servant status and so fierce was her hatred of Yankees in the Reconstruction Era that she would not allow anything blue in her house. She moved her family to Texas well before the end of the nineteenth century, settling, I think, in Nash, Texas near Texarkana. My mother had letters from one of her cousins there, redheaded like Momma. They corresponded for a time but never met. I read some of her letters and was captivated by her lively, noble spirit and wit. How often we see children overcome family negativity and form a noble contrast to their spiritually stunted parents!

That summer a "brush arbor" revival was held near the Corn Road. We may have attended a service, but my recollection is unclear. What I do remember was Daddy's sarcasm about the meeting. He laughed at the preacher's description of a sign from God: a white form moving in the night.

"All he seen was that ole white horse grazin' around out in the pasture," he laughed.

Despite a tendency toward sarcasm, a trait common to nearly all the Raleys, usually Daddy respected preachers and often befriended them. In later years he would invite wandering ministers to come home with him to rest and eat. Momma was unimpressed and looked on most of them as little more than bums and vagrants. But Daddy could be critical if he perceived a preacher was inadequate or an outright fraud. He told how one man he knew was standing in his field one day when he saw the letters G P written in the clouds and took it as a sign to "go preach."

"I imagine it meant 'go plow'," Daddy said with a disparaging laugh.

Before East Battleground Missionary Church was organized in 1940, we had no home church but instead attended services sporadically at several. I can remember going to Friendship Methodist (where Momma's people are buried), Bell Springs Baptist, Ebenezer Baptist (where the later Raley generations are buried), and over in the Valley, Fairview Church of God (home church of our Hardin relatives) and Roundtop Church (where the pioneer Raley generations are buried). One Sunday much to my parents' surprise, I told them I didn't want to go to church that day. They asked me why not.

"Because all that preacher ever preaches about is Jonah and the whale, Jonah and the whale."

They made me go anyway and guess what. Again the sermon was the story of Jonah and the whale. My parents were surprised that I had listened, for they had not remembered the previous sermons. I have always loved great preaching, especially by eloquent preachers who have a touch of poetry in their spirit. Even before I could say it, I have always believed that The Greatest Story ever told ought to be preached with all the majesty of language and devotion of spirit we can summon.

Two of the most beautiful and cherished traditions of our region were Decoration Day and "All Day Singing and Dinner on the Ground." The first, still observed in many regions of the rural South, was a designated Sunday of loving remembrance of deceased relatives and decoration of their graves with flowers; and the second, now all but abandoned as far as I know, were joyous, daylong gospel songfests with plenty of food spread on tables on the church grounds. Both traditions brought people together from miles around, and for young singles it was a splendid opportunity to meet members of the opposite sex decked out in their Sunday finery. Because several churches would select the same Sunday what today could be called "Decoration Day hopping" was popular with young men with automobiles—or swift saddle horses in earlier times. In the course of a Sunday they could visit several area churches to check out the scene and the girls. Many couples took their first steps toward love and marriage at these happy events.

Speaking of love, the year we lived at Grandma Hooper's I became infatuated with automobiles and spent considerable time drawing pictures of Model-A Fords. But there was almost no traffic on the Burney Mountain Road and the passing of a car once or twice a month was an event that brought us all running to look at them from doors and windows. I confess that once I scattered nails in the sandy ruts in hopes I could cause a flat tire and have a chance to get a better look at one of those fabulous contraptions. (My double-first Cousin Mary Raley Shaneyfelt had a similar desire and once scandalized several adults by announcing that she hoped Mr. John Bibb would have a wreck so she could get a better look at his car. She and I were kindred spirits, but hers was—and is—in nearly all respects much nobler than mine. She has always been a woman without guile, and I love her like a sister.) One day, two men in suits and ties in a shiny black car stopped briefly at our house. Grandma Hooper explained later that they were driving the "star route." I hoped they would return, and Momma told us they said something about a monthly run. But as far as I know, that was their first and last trip along the Burney Mountain Road. In any case, our mail delivery did not change. We still had to walk over a mile to the Corn Road to pick up our Vinemont Route 3 mail in a row of tin mailboxes in front of Mr. John Bibb's house. Actually, my family did not have a box. If we ever received any mail, and I do not remember any, it would come to Grandma Hooper's box marked "W. A. Hooper" and located next to my Grandpa Raley's box, "W. T. Raley".

Luckily for the rare automobile drivers on the Burney Mountain Road, my efforts to puncture their tires proved futile, just like Mary's destructive wish for Mr. John Bibb. But on rare occasions my Uncle Hays Hooper, wife Marzelie, and our cousins Alan and Aaron would drive over from Gadsden to visit Grandma Hooper. For us these visits were a festive and seductive glimpse into another world. Marzelie was a pretty woman with the finest clothes I had ever seen. Alan and Aaron were several years older than I and wise in the ways of the city. They used new words I didn't know and talked of unknown wonders like movies, bicycles, electric lights, and refrigerators. And unlike normal country people, they measured distances and locations not in miles, trees, roads, and landmarks but in odd reference points called blocks and streets. They seemed to dwell in a brighter, finer world, and our admiration for them was virtually limitless.

My curiosity about Uncle Hays's car—a late model Chevrolet—was overwhelming. In character much like his mother, Hays was a quiet, bookish, sad-eyed man who never raised his voice or objected to us playing in his car, changing gears, turning the steering wheel, and revving our imaginary engines over make-believe highways. From that time on, the automobile was for me a rolling symbol of freedom, the tangible means of transporting me from my small circumstances to the limitless world beyond my horizons. The romance with cars has lasted all my life.

In the beginning, however, my infatuation was a miniaturized affair. Somewhere I had seen, or perhaps imagined, that there were small motorized cars for children. The concept was perfect: a toy car that could take me to the faraway places I wanted to see. Not that my dreams were the stuff of mere idealism. I connected my desires to economics and began to pester my poor father for "a thousand dollars" to make my wish come true. At first, he and the other adults around me thought my outlandish request was humorous, but I was so unrelenting that everybody grew tired of it. At last one day as I kept interrupting his conversation with a visiting neighbor, my father said with an exasperated finality, "I done told ye fer the last time, I ain't got a thousand dollars!" The look on his face—anger and a growing suspicion that his son was seriously short of brains—plus a big hand about to do me major damage were warning enough for me to drop the topic. I still wanted the money and the car but for the time being had to add them to the long list of things I would do when I grew up and got free of people who thwarted my best plans.

But if obstinate adults blocked my dreams of a car, before long I was convinced that I was indeed rich. Unable or unwilling to come up with my demand for a thousand dollars, the adults chipped in and gave me stacks of pennies and nickels. Meanwhile, I had memorized a list of Mother Goose nursery rhymes and in the one about the "four and twenty blackbirds baked in pie" the verses declared:

"The King was in his counting-house counting out his money,
The Queen was the parlour eating bread and honey."

I dismissed the Queen as a silly woman who didn't know that according to Grandma Hooper, people didn't eat in parlors—whatever they were—but at the dining room table. But the King was another matter. An accompanying illustration showed the bearded monarch with stacks of coins almost exactly the size of mine. I made the logical leap to a happy conclusion: I was as rich as the King! Again, everybody laughed at me. I was beginning to think I was living in a household of idiots.

One day my irritation overflowed, and I decided—again—to run away from home. But unlike my first escape at the Cook place when I was three and a half, this time being much older and wiser at four and a half or five, I packed a few clothes in a sack similar to the tramp bag old Thad Morgan carried on a stick slung over his shoulder and set out towards Grandma's Hooper pasture. I got as far as the gate before it occurred to me to detour through the orchard for some juicy apples. But on the way, I heard a cowbell and saw that one of the cows had slipped through the fence. I ran as fast as I could back to the house to tell the family, forgetting my plans to run away.

Despite my occasional frustrations, the year at Grandma Hooper's was a happy time for me. I could not wait for the day to begin so I could play with my bottles, spools, and sticks—duly converted in my imagination into cars and trucks—in Grandma's yard or in the gullied ditches along the Burney Mountain Road, but not inside her hedgerows. In the summer the open windows in Grandma's house let in the breeze and let out music and news over her dry cell battery radio. (We had no electricity.) One day in 1939 as I was searching along the roadside for a new spot to play, the radio announcer broke in with the news that Germany had invaded Poland. I knew that something serious had happened, but the names and places sounded impossibly strange and much too remote to matter to us. I had heard about germs and knew something about poles and fence posts, and it seemed absurd to me that whole countries could be filled with such dirty and dull things. Good thing they were on the other side of the world.

Although Grandma Hooper's cat "Old Tom" refused to play with me, he did consent to let me hold him. His purring, arching stretches intrigued me, and his soft fur was soothing and warm. Tom was a consummate hunter and to impress us—as I supposed—with his skills he used to bring home mangled rats, lizards, and even small rabbits and deposit them under the beds. Sometimes the doomed creatures were not dead, and Tom would amuse himself by prodding them into tortured movement before pouncing on them again. Aunt Phoebe and Irene were duly scandalized by the gore, and Tom got many a broom poke as they tried to chase him out of the house. Years later when Grandma's house burned down and the family moved away, Tom reverted to a feral state and lived in the woods. I saw him once or twice, but he would no longer let people come near him. Apparently, the fire had traumatized him.

Only a few clouds darkened my sunny world that year. One was Thad Morgan the old tramp I mentioned earlier. He lived somewhere in the forested recesses between Grandma Hooper's house and the Valley, and mothers invoked his name to scare their misbehaving children. "He'll put you in his sack and carry you off if you're mean," we were warned. At first, I was not exactly sure what a "tramp" was, but I knew it must be something like the hobos Daddy talked about. Now and then old Thad would come up Burney Mountain Road on one of his mysterious journeys and we children would watch him in cowering fear as he trudged by silently and slowly, never giving us a glance.

The nearby woods held my other main dreads. Stories

persisted, probably from frontier times, of panthers ("painters") and wildcats, and a few of latter were apparently still around. Aunt Mary Woods, who used to live on one of the lower slopes of Burney Mountain Road, swore that one night she heard a "painter" screaming. "It sounded just like a tortured woman," she said. And there was the mystery of the foot path that emerged from the woods just in front of Grandma's house. Now and then I would get up enough courage to follow it to where—or to what—it might lead. The answer was nowhere, for after a few dozen yards it mysteriously ended without a trace. A long time passed before I realized that the woods must have served as a supplement to the outhouse where family members, particularly the men, went "outdoors," our euphemistic term for relieving themselves.

In those days the woods were crisscrossed by many trails, some of which had surely been there since Indian times, for like our predecessors, we walked everywhere and took as many shortcuts as we could. Today those trails are abandoned and grown over and the woods are much denser with undergrowth than in the old days when people walked, gathered roots and berries, and hunted in them.

Random arrow heads and old stories reminded us that these mountains and forests once belonged to earlier peoples, and just beyond the pasture on the other side of Grandma's house was a boulder etched with Indian art. One Sunday we all walked over to see it, and I still remember the stylized human forms, animals, and mysterious markings left by our Native American predecessors. Soon afterward, James Edwards, the bad boy from the school bus and Lena Woods incident described earlier, for no other reason than gratuitous wickedness, took it upon himself to deface the boulder, a wanton, destructive act that still angers me.

That year I got to know my Aunt Irene much better, and she

seemed to take a special liking to me that lasted the rest of her life. She called me "Snigglefritz" and though dour by nature, she would brighten in my presence and laugh at my antics. She shared a terror of snakes with me, but when somebody gave me a foot-long toy snake that seemed to twist in my hand I overcame my aversion enough to chase her around the house, fully enjoying the power it gave me. The oldest of the Hooper daughters and to all appearances a confirmed spinster, Aunt Irene surprised us that fall with a beau.

Her suitor, my future Uncle Aaron "Bufus" Edwards was the divorced father of three—or four—if you include a boy he refused to claim as his. I suspect there was some dissension in the family over the idea of a divorced man coming to call, but Irene's age and looks did not offer her other alternatives, and Bufus was permitted to pursue his courtship. I was a bit baffled by his abrupt and persistent presence, for until then I had monopolized Irene's time. Consequently, I made a pest of myself by intruding on their sessions. Neither seemed to mind; Irene would break into laughter as I entered, and Bufus, sensing perhaps that I was a fulcrum with which to leverage her affections, went out of his way to play with me. There was, however, a touch of sadism in his games. I was ticklish and he exacerbated the condition with a game he called "antsies," which consisted in pinching and tickling me until I was out of breath and begging for mercy. Nevertheless, I took a liking to Bufus that lasted the rest of his life.

Chapter 9:
The Log Cabin Year

When Bufus and Irene married not long afterwards and he became the man of the house, we moved into a two-room log house that Uncle Bemis had built on the west side of Grandma Hooper's property near my Grandpa Raley's place. In the meantime, Bemis and Viola had moved up the Burney Mountain Road to the Parker place on the Red Hill close to the Corn Road.

With its notched corner logs and the mud-chinked cracks between them, the log cabin duplicated the primitive frontier structures of a century earlier. Only the chimney had a finer profile than most of its ancestors. And Grandpa Raley was responsible for that feature. A stone mason of considerable talent, he built a handsome sandstone chimney that may still stand. And until a few years ago, so did the cabin, but invisibly so; for later Bufus enclosed the log core within an expanded and modernized exterior and added two more rooms and a small back porch to the original structure.

The cabin had no water well, so we were obliged to dip and carry our water from a cool, clear spring that flowed out of the rocks a couple of hundred yards below the house. Geraldine and I disputed whose turn it was to "tote Momma another bucket of water." One thing was certain: Momma seemed to use more water than any mortal woman had reasonable need of. But, my, how quenching and pure a dipperful of that water tasted on a hot day!

A quarter of a mile past the log cabin at the end of the road,

Grandpa Raley owned eighty acres of mountain land he had purchased a few years earlier from the railroad. He and my uncles cleared some of the hillsides, built a barn and a big smokehouse, and over a period of several months completed the four-room dwelling house. I can just barely remember going with Momma (in 1936) to see them while they were living in unbelievably cramped conditions in the smokehouse. I also remember the smoke of burning tree trunks, stumps, and limbs as they cleared the fields for cultivation.

The big fires kindled an incendiary fascination in me and not long after we moved into the log cabin, I went down to Grandma Raley's and told her Momma needed to borrow some matches. She fetched me a handful and I practiced trying to strike them with my thumb the way I had seen smokers do. Finally, I succeeded. The only problem was that the match was still in the pocket of my overalls and the flame set off others. By the time I emptied my pockets there was an angry, painful burn on my leg.

A day or so later, Geraldine and I were on our way to Grandma Hooper's.

"Looka here, Geraldine," I said proudly, "watch me start a fire!"

"You better not!" she warned.

I dropped a lighted match in a clump of dry sedge grass and the flames quickly leaped up and started spreading. I grabbed a brush and tried to beat out the fire. I finally succeeded but at the cost of getting my eyebrows singed. Tattletale that she was—just like me—Geraldine told Momma that "Buddy's got matches and liked to set the woods afire!" Having faced the flames, I now had to face the music about the matches. Grandma Raley allowed as to how "quare" she thought it was for me to borrow the matches in the first place, but she laughed heartily over the incident, as did nearly everybody except Momma. I was mortified until they all forgot about it.

Christmas was far from lavish in those days, and as the family economy began to disintegrate even more in my teenage years, we almost stopped celebrating it altogether. For her own peculiar religious reasons Momma herself did not believe in celebrating Christmas, but she did not express these ideas openly until after Daddy's death. In earlier years we would cut a small cedar, nail a couple of boards to the base of the trunk, and set up a minimal Christmas tree. On Christmas morning we might discover that Santa Claus had brought us children a simple toy, a little candy, and perhaps an apple and an orange, fruits which I long associated with Christmas time. The adults were past Christmas age and received nothing. Even though we honored the biblical account of the holy birth and talked about it at church, I do not remember any special service to commemorate it. At school we drew names and exchanged gifts in that manner (usually with a twenty-five-cent limit). A few of the kids forgot or ignored the obligation so that some ended up with nothing.

I learned very early—at three or four—that Santa Claus was a pious myth. That Christmas my parents gave Geraldine a doll. Later Aunt Burlie and Daddy were talking in my presence, and she asked him how much he paid for it. I put two and two together and came up with the astonishing truth that Daddy was Santa Claus, a deduction that my parents made no attempt to deny.

To my delight and astonishment, however, either that year or the next Daddy gave me a little red wagon for Christmas. It was not nearly as fancy as Cousin Gene Johnson's wagon or Lonzo Johnson's dog-drawn version with its removable sideboards and tailgate, but I enjoyed my wagon immensely and kept it for years. It was the best Christmas of my childhood.

We barely acknowledged birthdays and never with gifts. At

most Momma might bake a cake if she had time and the ingredients. (But not candles.) Other holidays and anniversaries such as Fathers' and Mothers' Day were not a part of our life, although at school we sometimes exchanged valentine cards, but only with sweethearts. Not until I was married did I realize that other people were concerned about such special events and holidays and expected gifts to mark the occasion. It took some doing to get used to the idea.

Shortly before we moved out of Grandma Hooper's house, Earl Sandlin moved his family into one of the Evans houses at the Powell road cutoff. (The Sandlins and Raleys had been friends for generations, ever since both families lived in the Valley near Round Top). There I got better acquainted with Tommy and Audrey Sandlin who were to become my good friends. We had visited the Sandlins at least once before when we lived on the Cook place, but I barely remembered Audrey and Tommy. Tommy was a little older than I and a bright, inventive playmate. Audrey was my age. We played back and forth between the two houses as often as we could, but our time together was limited. We all had chores to do, and Tommy was prone to sudden, acute headaches, perhaps due to a diabetic condition that seemed to worsen as he grew up. One day as I was walking past Grandma's pea patch muttering to myself about the interferences in my life, I yelled angrily, "And I aint seen Tommy in sixty-five years!" Aunt Irene, who was picking peas nearby, heard my vehement exaggeration and told everybody. Again, everybody laughed at my peculiar way of talking to myself.

That summer either Audrey or Attley Sandlin, Tommy and Audrey's younger brother, caught diphtheria. The Health Department quarantined the Sandlins and gave us shots so no one else caught it. I think the Sandlins lost part of their crop that year because of the quarantine.

Not long afterwards we had our second medical emergency. Geraldine got head lice at school and soon I was infected as well. Momma scrubbed and treated with us with several preparations, including a vile-smelling sulfur cure that did the trick. Having lice was considered to be not only a health hazard but a social stigma as well, and Momma was determined to rid her family of them as soon as possible.

Unlike Daddy who was indifferent about bathing and sloppy about his clothing, Momma harangued Geraldine and me about cleanliness, repeating the old adage that it "was next to godliness." I remember to this day the vigorous, almost vicious scrubbing she used to give my face, ears, and hands when I was little. With Daddy, however, she was less successful. She waged a constant battle to keep him reasonably clean and in fit clothes with his shirttail tucked in. He had a perverse genius for tearing his overalls and shirts while crossing barbed wire fences, climbing trees, or clambering over boulders.

Besides my occasional odd phrasing, for a few years I had a startlingly deep voice. During one of my bronchial illnesses Momma or somebody in the family had applied a concoction of home remedies that temporarily damaged my vocal cords and discolored the skin around my throat. My crying was unnerving to neighbors who said it sounded like a man's voice and carried for long distances. In time I outgrew the effects and my voice and skin returned to normal. In the meantime, I could sing very low notes. Mary and other playmates would ask me to me to sing "God Put a Rainbow in the Sky" so I could do the bass. It was my favorite song, but I also liked "The Wabash Cannonball" and "You are my Sunshine."

I was afflicted with bed-wetting for many years and not until I was thirteen or so, did I finally outgrow it. The embarrassment it caused me is indescribable.

After we moved to the log cabin, I got to know my Raley relatives better. Grandma Raley and Aunt Azalee worked and cooked incessantly for the family of five big men still living at home. But both women were happy as long as they had company. Both she and Azalee were prone to nosebleeds that continued for days on end. Most likely both suffered from high blood pressure and dietary deficiencies. Hypertension was common to both the Hoopers and Raleys alike and the probable cause of many early deaths in both families. Whenever the bleeding started, Grandma Raley and Azalee would take to their bed until finally it stopped, usually after two days.

Grandma Raley's education was minimal and as far as I know she read very little, if at all. What scanty information she had about the outside world came from Grandpa and her sons. Grandpa did not vote—nobody in our family did—but I think he had Republican leanings no doubt inherited from his Unionist father. Among other outlandish things, Grandpa reportedly told Grandma that President Roosevelt and Adolf Hitler were first cousins. I think she believed it to her dying day. Over at Grandma Hooper's house, on the other hand, Franklin D. Roosevelt was esteemed only slightly less than the very Christ. "He's for the poor man," they would say. Nearly everybody in the Hooper home took it for granted that President Hoover singlehandedly caused the Great Depression. If I was ever aware of the dichotomy of beliefs in the two households, I cannot remember it. Politics and the dissensions it caused were simply not a part of our lives.

One of the things I admired most about Grandpa Raley was his flyswatter. Huge of girth and stature and given to grave, manly speech that permitted no rebuttal or contradiction from his listeners, patriarch Raley would often punctuate the finality of his pronouncements with a lightning-quick zapping of pesky flies. I resolved then and there that I would get me a flyswatter as soon as possible. Occasionally I tried his when he laid it aside, but I could not match his speed or number of kills.

Informed of my interest and ability with words, Grandpa solemnly announced to the family, "This boy'll be a preacher."

"No, Grandpa," I dared to correct him, "I'm gonna be a teacher." I have no idea why I said it, for that profession had never crossed my mind before and I had all of two or three weeks of schooling.

Grandpa Raley's grandmother Ann, wife of Owen Raley, was a Hackworth whose family was related, so he claimed, to "Johnny Appleseed" of frontier fame and a fixture in American history textbooks. Less famous and purposeful than Johnny Appleseed but almost as much a wanderer was Uncle Johnny Wedgeworth, the other tramp in our lives. Johnny had no fixed abode but walked the earth incessantly accepting handouts and taking convenient advantage of hospitality. Grandma Hooper always offered him a meal when he came to her door for which he politely thanked her. He usually spent a few days at Grandpa Raley's. I barely remember him, but I do recall his long white beard and something of the stories he told. We children feared him for reasons that I cannot recall. Probably his strange looks. He was Grandpa Woods' uncle and thus related to Grandma Raley, but Grandpa Woods was ashamed of his vagabond uncle and could barely tolerate his presence. It was said of Uncle Johnny that he walked his two wives to death. He carried a metal cup around his neck and begged when family hospitality was not available.

Even though I enjoyed my visits to Grandpa Raley's house, at first, I still did not feel as comfortable there as I did at Grandma Hooper's. One day while we were visiting Grandma Raley I whispered to Momma that I wanted a "biscuit and butter."

Grandma Raley overheard me and declared with some hurt in her voice, "Lordy mercy, child, ye don't have to be bashful around here. Ye jist tell me if ye git hungry!"

Whereupon she brought me the biggest piece of cornbread and butter I had ever seen and the first time I tried that combination. It was better than my customary biscuit and butter and gave me the energy to play the rest of the afternoon.

Daddy and my uncles extolled physical strength over all other qualities except honesty, and to win their approval I tried to conform to their expectations. One day I came up with another of my celebrated sayings. Felton, I think it was, felt my biceps and asked me if I was a "stout" boy.

"I'm made out of iron," I replied to their laughter and hearty approval.

(In our dialectical English the way I really said it was, "I'm made av orn.") Later when I met Superman in the comic books I moved up to steel in my metallic claims and added flying to my list of ambitions.

Somebody told us that long ago an old Indian had buried his treasure on the spring side of the log cabin. Images of golden wealth fired our imagination and for a time Geraldine, Mary, Armon, and I, along with other cousins, speculated on its location and excitedly dug with hoe and shovel at likely spots. We created our own version of Erskine Caldwell's _God's Little Acre_ but found nothing but dirt and common sandstone.

Near our spring a giant overhanging bluff jutted out of the mountain and below it, boulders were strewn in cataclysmic chaos. We used to spend hours climbing and hiding in the crevices and fissures. Expanded, recombinant images of those rocks often loom in my imagination when I read stories with descriptions of boulders and mountainous terrain in them.

That fall—1941—I started to school. Because of my November

birthday I was nearly seven and only mildly apprehensive at the prospect. Momma dutifully prepared me a lunch of biscuits and sausage and I set off with Geraldine and Azalee to meet the school bus on the Corn Road. At the Hale Place we were joined by James and Bertha Edwards and at the Red Hill by Mary and Armon Raley. In all it was approximately a mile and a quarter to the bus stop.

We got to Ebenezer School about a half hour before classes started and no sooner had we arrived than Armon led me to the sedge grass meadow where the boys played at recess. The idea was to twist off the golden colored sedge ("sagegrass" in our language) and build a straw shelter to hide in. The minute we arrived we saw two boys mistreating a smaller one. Immediately Armon and I rushed to the rescue. He jumped one of the bullies and I took on the other. We put them to flight, but someone tattled to Mrs. South, one of the teachers, and Armon and I were summoned to her office. Learning that it was my first day at school, she rolled her eyes and wondered aloud how much trouble I was going to be.

"School hasn't even started and you're already in a fight. Why were you fighting, Harold?" she wanted to know.

"'Cause they was two of them big boys against that little boy," I answered.

"Now, you listen to me, Harold," she responded angrily. "We don't allow fighting here at Ebenezer. You have to obey the rules. Now will you promise me you won't get into any more fights?" she asked hopefully.

"Long's they aint two uv them big'uns against a little'un," I answered. "'Cause that aint fair."

She scolded me some more and let me go to my first class, cautioning Mrs. Butler about me. When I got home, I told Momma about learning to read, as I said earlier, but later I described to Daddy how I won my first-day fight. I think they were both pleased.

Our speech differed significantly from the language I was discovering in my readings. But I soon learned to slip easily from one linguistic mode to the other, reserving "proper" English for school and written assignments and reverting to our Corn Road vernacular elsewhere. In no way did I want to be laughed at for "talkin' proper" out of school the way we made fun of Bertha Edwards the times she tried it.

Speaking of Bertha, things were not going well for her in Aunt Irene's new family. Irene's hostility toward her stepchildren was unrelenting, and they more than repaid "Miss Irene," as they called her, with similar seething resentment. Bufus took Irene's side in the disputes and missed no opportunity to inflict savage punishment on his woeful offspring. I recall one Sunday when the Sandlins came to visit and James became so obnoxious that Mrs. Sandlin demanded he be punished. ("Laure," as Laura Sandlin was commonly called, was a loud, outspoken woman who did not shy away from conflicts.) Bufus obliged at once with a terrific beating far in excess of what James deserved. Whereupon Mrs. Sandlin turned her wrath on Bufus for beating his son worse than farmers whipped their mules. Gentle Grandma Hooper must have wondered what kind of barbarians had taken over her once peaceful home.

Leamon Edwards was about sixteen or seventeen at the time and within weeks he ran away from home and joined one of the armed services. I never saw him again that I remember, but we all read about him after World War II when he made national headlines by selling his children.

James stayed around a few more months before also hitting the road. But his path was to cross mine several more times over the years. Now it was two down and one to go for Aunt Irene.

But since Bertha was younger than her brothers, she stayed around several more years to bedevil her father and stepmother and to be abused by them in turn.

Probably it would take a team of psychologists to unravel the twisted lives of the Edwards children, considering the damage their parents and stepmother had done to them. People said that Bufus's former wife was a "bad woman" so openly notorious in her immoralities that the courts gave Bufus custody of all the children when he divorced her. All that is except son Gene whom Bufus refused to recognize. Folks said he was the nicest of the children and kind to his purported father, but once Bufus developed an opinion or a grudge he clung to it with pit bull tenacity.

Nor were we Raley children of any help in the matter. We resented James and Bertha as intruders in our life and had never experienced the degree of viciousness they displayed. Without warning Bertha would push Mary or the other girls off bridges and into roadside ditches. One afternoon gentle Azalee retaliated against James by pulling a strip from the picket fence along the front of the house where the Sandlins had lived and beating him over the head for his meanness.

"You better leave them alone, you nasty thing!" she screamed as she flailed away at the cowering James.

That same day on the way home from school Bertha attacked Geraldine, and even though Geraldine was older the unprovoked assault hurt her, and she started crying in pain and anger. I came to her rescue with a big rock which I hurled flush in Bertha's face. She was seriously hurt and ran home screaming to her father. That evening Bufus came over to the log cabin and for the first time he and Daddy had words.

A couple of weeks later in Grandma Hooper's orchard Bertha taunted us while standing under a tree with a concealed hornet nest. I took aim and jarred the nest with a sizable rock. The hornets swarmed out and covered the screaming Bertha whose face swelled to hideous size. I think Bufus had to take her to the doctor. Again. he and Daddy had words and—I learned later—almost came to blows.

Now, fighting Bufus would have been no laughing matter, not even for a man as strong as Daddy. Bufus was built like Neanderthal man, five eight or nine, hunched over, no neck to speak of, spindly legs and shuffling walk but with powerful arms, torso, and shoulders. His toughness and courage were beyond question. They said of Bufus that an opponent once broke his jaw with a pair of brass knuckles, but Bufus kept coming and others had to pull him away. As a young man he had wrestled some in Arkansas, and when the phony television version—which Bufus believed was real—became popular in the fifties, he regretted having left the sport. Luckily Bufus and Daddy settled their differences and spent the rest of their lives as good friends. My parents warned me about the rocks and out of respect for my throwing arm Bertha moderated her behavior, at least in our presence.

In fact, not many months passed before she switched behaviors entirely and began to get on intimate sexual terms with the big boys at school. Cousin Armon told me that she would crawl under the schoolhouse at recess and let the boys come to her one by one. Armon said there was a line of waiting boys but swore he never stood in it.

I owed Armon a lot and loved him like a brother. In fact, as double first cousins to him and Mary and constant playmates in our early years Geraldine and I almost were brother and sister to them. The close bond has lasted a lifetime.

Constant practice helped Armon and me develop dangerous precision in rock throwing. By the time I was ten or twelve both of us could bring down a sitting bird—and occasionally one on the wing. Any dog foolish enough to charge us was sure to be hit between the eyes and sent howling for cover. Provided I had a pocketful of rocks (as I always did) as I passed by houses, I had absolutely no fear of lurking dogs, an assurance that I have kept all my life. If only I had had such skill and confidence earlier when Mrs. Cook's old gobbler chased me!

A few years later some of the boys from the Panama community showed up to challenge Armon and me. It was a rare day when both my parents were gone, so there was no adult around to supervise us. All the Panama boys were friends of mine, but that Sunday for some reason they were in a hostile mood. The two Rainwater boys, Donald Cheatham, and Tommy Sandlin wanted to have a "cob fight" to settle our differences. Armon and I agreed, and the contest began. The only problem was that we soon ran out of corn cobs and substituted rocks instead. The inevitable happened. Armon or I—can't remember which—popped Charles Rainwater on the forehead. He went to his knees and an ugly knot came up on his head but luckily, he did not lose consciousness. Tempers flared, but as dangerous as Armon and I were and armed with more rocks, the Panama bunch threatened us from a prudent distance and beat a retreat southward toward home.

Early in the fall of 1941 after the Sandlins moved away, Johnny Jones and I were playing around the abandoned house. After we tired of running through the empty rooms, Johnny suggested that we break out all the windowpanes. Johnny was older and I thought I should do whatever he said, so I went along. Besides, it sounded like fun and involved rock throwing. Before long we had done all the damage we could and moved on to a drilled well over in the pasture. We dumped it full of rocks and tired from all our exertions, went our separate ways.

A day or two later, Daddy announced that the Evans brothers, owners of the property, were looking for the culprits who damaged the house and ruined the well. "Ye know anythang about that?" he asked. I told him the truth, and he said I might have to be put in reform school. I was ashen with fear and my legs trembled. School was one thing, reform school, altogether another. I made all kinds of promises never to do anything like that again. For days I waited fearfully for the Evans brothers to show up. They never did. My delinquencies ceased—for the moment.

As for Johnny, one night his father Marlo Jones loaded their things on their wagon and by morning had mysteriously disappeared. I never saw or heard of any of them again.

Mrs. Butler's initial apprehensions about me were unfounded, for I had no more fights I can remember my first year in school. On the other hand, learning was pure joy to me, and I could hardly wait for the school bus in the morning. In those days Ebenezer had a "primer" grade, something akin to the kindergartens of today. I spent only a few weeks in that category before Mrs. Butler put Jacqueline Hicks, Billette Edmondson, and me in advanced first grade and not long afterwards moved us up to second grade. I recall being a bit miffed when Jacqueline was promoted a few days before me. But cute, sweet, blonde, and well dressed, she was a teacher favorite, while I was rougher of speech and behavior and my clothing and grooming were decidedly inferior. Unlike West Point, Ebenezer had an early promotion policy that, had I stayed there, would have allowed me to graduate a year earlier. Several seasons later when Billette and my first-grade classmates from Ebenezer came to West Point after sixth grade to complete their high school, she was a year ahead of me. I lost track of Jacqueline.

Only one problem darkened my school bus journey to

scholastic happiness. On the way to Ebenezer the bus picked up high school senior Travis Russell who would roughly yank me out of my seat and smugly settle himself in my place for the longer ride to West Point. I protested to no avail and thoroughly detested and feared him. The very next year Travis was drafted and later died in Europe. I had mixed feelings when I heard the news: remorse for thinking so harshly of him, but also a timid notion that perhaps wickedness receives its due punishment after all.

We were lonelier in the log cabin than at Grandma Hooper's House. Daddy was spending much of his time working away from home, and if I remember correctly, drinking more. I recall one terrifying night when Momma, Geraldine, and I lay awake during a violent thunderstorm. The force of the wind rattled and shook the log cabin and for an hour the lightning flashes came so close together that it was almost as bright as day. We had no storm pit and we knew Momma was worried for our safety.

"I wish ye daddy was here," I remember her saying two or three times as we all huddled together in bed.

One afternoon Daddy came home weaving a bit, and as we gathered in curiosity around him, he scooped up a hot coal with the fireplace shovel, lit a cigarette, and then looked over at me.

"Do ye like me, boy?" he asked in an aggressive tone I was not used to.

"No," I answered tartly, "'cause you're drunk."

This displeased him and he thrust the hot shovel against my leg. I was unhurt but scared and cried out in fear. Instantly, with the fury of a mother bear, Momma rushed to my defense. Daddy realized, I think, what he had done and backed away from his enraged five-foot wife, making only a sheepish response to her screaming. To Daddy's mortification the story grew with Momma's repeated telling and helped persuade him to stop drinking.

It took another episode, however, to make his decision final. One Saturday night not long after the shovel incident, Daddy did not come home at all. I think the police had locked him up overnight in Cullman for drinking and fighting, but I am not sure of the dates and may have confused it with another time. At any rate, the next morning, Geraldine, Azalee, and I, all scrubbed and dressed in our best clothes, set off bright and early for Sunday school at Dough Ball Church. Just past the Hale place we met a shambling, disheveled man. It was Daddy but so dirty, unshaven, and ruffled that I, at least, did not recognize him at first. We all burst out laughing at the sight of him, and even though many decades have gone by as I write this, I can still remember the look of pain and shame on his face. He turned his head away and passed us on the far side of the road. That very day, or soon thereafter, Daddy resolved never to drink again. He proved to be a man of his word and I respected and admired him for keeping his promise. Not that he lost his desire for liquor. He confided to me many years later that he loved the taste and smell of whiskey. Luckily for me, I did not inherit the liking, and even though as a young man I drank at times for the alcoholic euphoria or social reasons, I have never liked the taste itself.

Chapter 10:
The Red Hill

Late in the fall of 1941 we moved into the old two-room frame house on the Red Hill across the Burney Mountain road from Uncle Bemis and Aunt Viola. The iron oxide that gave the hill its reddish tint also rendered the water almost undrinkable at first. But for me this odd singularity was beneficial, for I think it supplied me with the iron I had been missing and temporarily relieved some of my peculiar ailments.

Daddy rented the Helton farm and after several seasons of hiring out, returned to farming. It was a happy decision and now that he had stopped drinking, we were more united as a family. Furthermore, we made a bumper crop and Daddy was visibly proud of his enhanced status in the farming community. We "swapped" some work with Uncle Bemis. He and his family helped us with our planting and harvesting and we helped him with his.

The "we" must be understood advisedly, for my contributions naturally were meager. Daddy let me drive the team sometimes as he was turning the land in preparation for planting, but I was anxious to get behind the handles and plow like a man. Finally, one day as we were planting Uncle Bemis's cotton, they let me try my hand with the cotton planter. Everything went fine until I came to the end of a long row and yelled "Whoa!" to my mule. By that time my voice had faded back to normal childish insignificance and the mule paid not the slightest heed to my command. Instead she leisurely dragged me, the planter, and my pride into the bushes. Daddy and Bemis came over to rescue me, laughing at my wounded ego. It would be a year or two before I was ready to test my plowing skills again.

That year we grew closer than ever to Armon and Mary. He and I continued our rock-throwing contests, to which we now added expertise with rubber slingshots. We called them "flips" and carried them in our back pockets. Now we were a double threat to man and beast alike. Armon was in fact a bit older than Geraldine but emotionally he and I were closer in age and never quarreled.

I remember one painful exception to this happy rule. Once our cousin Owen James came to play with us and before long, he persuaded Armon to take sides against me. Angered by the conniving Owen, I wrestled him to the ground. Armon came to his rescue and rocks started flying, Owen was hit, and the adults summoned us all to the house. Uncle Bemis and Daddy switched Armon and me with hickory "withes," as they called them, while grinning cousin Owen looked on unpunished. It was, I believe, the first and last quarrel Armon and I ever had. I never fully trusted Owen again.

Mary was even sunnier of disposition than Armon and, like Uncle Bemis, an entertaining storyteller to boot. We all used to play for hours on end, at tag and hide-and-seek ("hide-n-seat" we called it), running from one house to the other, playing "ante over" the house with an old rubber ball, jumping ditches, or improvising games, riddles, and stories as we roamed up and down the wooded hillsides behind their house. Sometimes we would ride Uncle Bemis's old mule. The animal had remarkable patience and would allow two or three of us to ride at the same time. Eventually, however, she would tire of our antics and head for the low branch of a tree where we would all be gently dragged off. Mary had several favorite stories, among them Dickens's <u>A Christmas Carol</u>, which I read a couple of times at her house. She has always been one of my favorite relatives, as close to me as a sister. Our relationship has several more chapters that I will tell if ever I get around to writing about my life after the Corn Road years.

Speaking of deep affections, it's odd that I cannot remember when "Ole Ted" came into my life. He was a "feist" dog, according to Daddy's definition, which we understood generally to mean a small, nervous mixed breed unsuitable for hunting. Plain Ole Ted was as totally devoted to me as majestic Ole Tom, Grandma Hooper's cat, had been grandly indifferent. Whenever Bufus would start his "antsies" game with me Ted would growl, bare his fangs, and defend me with all his small ferocity. He shared all my games and I loved him as only a seven-year boy can love his dog. I was playing with him December 7, 1941, a Sunday, when Momma came out, her face drawn with worry, to tell me the Japanese had attacked Pearl Harbor. I wasn't sure which "Pearl" she meant but I knew it was a serious matter. And indeed, it was; the distant rumors of Germany I had first heard in 1939 would soon become a real war for people on the Corn Road.

Momma was fiercely patriotic. Sometime later the government called for a blackout of homes, lest the lights give the enemy clues and directions. Probably the message applied to urban centers and not to our area which had nothing of military significance. Besides our puny little kerosene lamp probably could not have been spotted a mile away, much less from an airplane. But loyal little Momma hung quilts over the windows anyway to do her part.

Summer came and with it a fervent revival at Dough Ball. I remember one impassioned sermon about the end of the world.

"Any minute could be the last fer this ole world," preacher May warned. "Jesus is a-comin' back when ye least expect it, maybe while you're asleep. And if he comes unawares and finds you unrepentant in your sins, ye'll go to Hell and burn forever."

I was thoroughly convicted and convinced of my doom, knowing all the bad things I had done. During the service we sang the hymn, "There's an All-Seeing Eye Watching You." That night I woke up in the wee hours of the morning, fearfully listening to the ticking clock, feeling the pounding of my heart, imagining God's great celestial eye peering down at me, and pondering the awful fragility of time and the certainty of my perdition if eternity should overtake me. The next day, or soon thereafter, as I was walking across Uncle Bemis's pasture thoroughly perplexed by these weighty theological fears and resentful that God might cut short my sunny, play-filled days, I uttered hateful words against Him, half expecting a bolt from the blue to strike me dead. I was sorry and regret to this day having said them.

On an earthly level Momma was concerned that we all have a decent burial when our time came. The insurance man, a Mr. Beck, brother of Aunt Thelma as I recall, came by once a month to collect the small premium. One day we saw him speeding up the Burney Mountain Road toward the house, raising a giant cloud of red dust behind his black Ford.

"Why was you drivin' so fast?" Momma asked him when he arrived.

"Well, Mrs. Raley," he responded, wiping his face with a red handkerchief, "the gas was gittin' low and I was tryin' to make it before it run out." Momma laughed heartily at the logical absurdity of his words, but Mr. Beck, not known for mental swiftness, looked at her in puzzlement.

Plans had been made for us to move into the Helton renter house up on the Corn Road. I was delighted by the prospect for I had always wanted to live on the big road itself with its automobile traffic and human activity. Several times I visited the empty house to savor its four rooms, electric lights, and ample playing area. Alas, the move never happened. The Heltons decided to reserve the house for their son Edgar Will who had just been drafted.

In the succeeding months he was joined by many other single young men, among them my Uncles Tolbert and Elton Raley who were drafted into the Army. Felton was 4-f because of his disability and Athel was turned down because of high blood pressure. Men like Daddy and Bertis were deferred because of family. There was an emotional moment when Tolbert and Elton left for their wartime assignments. It was the fall of 1942 and we were picking cotton when they came across the field to say goodbye.

"You be a good boy," Elton told me with tears in his eyes.

"I will," I promised as he gave me a hug.

Tolbert was several years older than Elton and more reserved than his twenty-one-year old brother. But his eyes were also teary.

Elton now looked like a different man from the skinny boy of prewar years. He had gained fifteen or twenty pounds in basic training and was as hard as a rock. We all wondered in awe about the mysterious transformation. Tolbert was already a mature muscular man when drafted and military training had not changed him very much. Not long thereafter Elton was sent to the South Pacific and we did not see him again until late 1945 or early 1946.

Tolbert, however, surprised us a few months earlier with an unexpected visit. He had gone AWOL and by the time he got to the Red Hill was about half drunk. I remember the moment: Momma was drawing a bucket of the smelly well water and laughing as Tolbert began to describe his experiences in the army. He told, for example, how he duped his Yankee superiors into believing he had never worn shoes and told slack-jawed listeners other outlandish tales about what people ate and how they lived in the North Alabama hills. Tolbert soon returned to duty and drew only a few days in the brig for being AWOL. Not many weeks later the Army assigned him to Alaska and the Aleutian Islands. Unlike Elton, who was involved in intense fighting in the South Pacific, Tolbert took part in only a couple of limited skirmishes with the Japanese. On the other hand, he was so impressed by the rich Alaskan farmland that for a time after World War II he talked of returning there to homestead.

Some men were guilty of more than a few days AWOL. Morris Sammons once confided that he took seventy-five aspirins the day he went in for his induction physical. The ruse kept him from military service but probably all that saved him from death was his great size and strength. Cowardly ole Morris, who married Cousin Lena Woods, was quite a bit larger than my father and reputedly one of the strongest men in the area. Another craven big man, Bill Cole, avoided the draft by wearing a dress and hiding in a hole in his parents' pasture. The hypocrisy of the Cole family in covering their son's cowardice knew no limits. I remember Mrs. Cole standing up Sunday after Sunday in church and praying for "all of our brave boys fightin' overseas" and implying that she regularly heard from Bill. (I suppose she did, for he was hiding out on their farm. But suspicions and gossip started when MPs began to scour the country asking about Bill Cole. Neighbors reported that on a few occasions they had seen a very big woman walking in the Cole pasture at dusk. Eventually Bill was discovered and taken away, but in a final ironic twist, military psychiatrists declared him mentally unfit and he was granted a lifetime pension. Everybody was outraged. The returning veterans loathed him and at first some of them threatened to do him bodily harm. In the long run, however, people punished him in a worse way by refusing to have anything to do with him. He bought a new Ford with his pension money, but he was always alone. I remember he stopped once and offered me and several other boys a ride. But we knew who he was and declined. Rather than ride with a deserter and coward, we preferred to walk. I think he finally moved away from the Corn Road community.

My nightmares and spasms had, mercifully, subsided, but now earaches, fevers, and occasional toothaches replaced them. The earaches were the worst and my parents tried all the home remedies they knew to relieve them. Doctors and drugstore medicines were out of the question. Indeed, even if a physician had been available, I would have been afraid to see him. For despite my miseries, I was not ready to die. Of all the home remedies I remember only one: a teaspoon of my own urine poured in my ear. It seemed to work, and I was able to sleep throughout the night.

To protect my ears in cold weather Daddy bought me a pilot's cap complete with leather earmuffs and goggles. This acquisition opened up a whole new area of fantasies for me. Now I was a pilot bombing the Japanese or devastating the Nazis. Airplanes temporarily supplanted my romance with the automobile, and I began to construct them from the few materials at hand.

Not long after the War started anti-Axis propaganda spread over the country. Superman, Batman, and other superheroes were, of course, on our side, so I was sure we would win eventually. The Japanese caricatures, especially, had a long-lasting effect on me. The squinty eyes, yellow skin, and buck teeth—the exaggerated stock features of World War II American propaganda against them—implanted an image in my psyche of an unappealing race. Later I met and became friends with Japanese, Chinese, and other Far Eastern people. I realized that my early impressions were the result of psychologically prejudiced manipulations, but this awareness did not make it much easier to overcome them. But eventually the prejudices faded.

Chapter 11:
A Year at Bethlehem

In late fall or early winter of 1942, we moved several miles south of Battleground to the Bethlehem community where Daddy had rented a farm from Bud Sheats. It was the first and last time we lived away from the Corn Road. And it was the first time we had electric lights. I remember the single, string-operated bulbs hanging from the ceiling in the middle of the kitchen and the other rooms of the old two-story house. The light was dazzling. Our first night there, like a crazed moth I ran in circles around the house exulting in the luminous splendor until I was totally but happily exhausted.

The change of schools was traumatic at first. I had no friends of course, and my teachers at West Point did not know where to place me. Apparently, the transfer of records was a very casual affair in those days. I told them I was in second grade, but after taking a look at me, they decided, much to my annoyance, to put me back in first. Mrs. Hendricks, the first-grade teacher, had me read her class materials. After the reading she left the room to confer with Mrs. Ballinger. Mrs. Hendricks came back and told me I was moving to second grade. I could have saved them the trouble if they had listened to me to start with.

Before long Mrs. Ballinger began using me as an unofficial reading tutor for second—and third grade—students. (The two classes were held in the same room.) She had a habit of leaving the classroom for significant and, most likely unauthorized, periods of time. In her absence I was the "little teacher" and did my best to keep the class working. Not even the third graders were offended that a second grader was helping them. They all acknowledged my reading skills, as they would have a handicap or other peculiar trait, and nobody made an issue of it.

Life was easier for us that year. The land was good and we had much better housing than ever before or, for that matter, ever again. Although I missed Armon and Mary, in many ways I wished we could have lived in the Bethlehem community for good.

For one thing, we had close neighbors. Bill and Lizzy McKenzie lived only a couple of hundred yards across the field from us and their children Jewel, Thelma, and Harold became regulars in our house, and Geraldine and I in theirs. The Blackmons and later the Duttons lived on the other side and son Dalton was only a year or so older than I, but for whatever reason we never became close friends. Bill Mckenzie had older children from an earlier marriage, but eighteen-year old Elton, or Bunk as he was called, and his older sister Evelyn were the only ones still living at home. I remember seeing Bunk only once before he left for the army. He was driving a two-horse wagon and bracing himself in the wagon bed. After the war he would reappear in our life, but that episode comes later.

Harold and I soon became very close friends. He was a year older, but I seemed to be the leader in all our games. Because of the war and my pilot cap my interest had shifted, as I said, temporarily from automobiles to airplanes, and with Miss Lizzy's help, Harold and I carved several fuselages from pine stove wood and made wings from discarded wooden shingles. We finished them off with tiny hand-carved windmills and spent hours holding them aloft in imaginary skies as they blasted German and Japanese aviators. Harold told me years later that when we were children, he felt he had to obey me in everything. The confession both pleased and bothered me, for I wondered if

I had lost some former power over people. For a time, I was afraid I was becoming an unheeded nobody.

What I needed even then was superpowers, and that summer I believed the time had come for me to get serious about becoming a superhero. The country was at war and Superman and the other heroes of my comic book pantheon were doing their duty as loyal Americans. My first problem in joining them was getting off the ground. As I studied the superheroes it seemed to me that their flying ability was a mysterious function of their capes. And, of course, they always wore a mask or disguise. Inspired by this deduction, I took one of Momma's white flour sacks, tied a string to two corners and draped it over my neck and down my back. An old handkerchief with eye holes cut in it served as my mask. Everything was ready; the moment had come to test my theory.

In order to assure myself that no prying, skeptical eyes—Geraldine's, for example—would see me make my flying super leap, I went out into the tall cotton. From a terrace row I spotted a ten-foot gap in the cotton where I could get a running start. When all was in readiness for the flight, I made my take-off dash. The powerful white cape flapped against my back, my expectations rose, my hopes soared, but, alas, my body did not. Instead I fell sprawling against a big cotton stalk. I dismissed the indignity of it all and tried again with the same result. I was discouraged but not totally defeated. After some devastatingly powerful punches and karate-like chops at the Germans and Japanese that were again invading our cotton field, I hid the mask and cloak in the barn, determined to come back tomorrow to work out the kinks after I had consulted my comic books. Maybe I was overlooking something.

That night at supper sharp-eyed Geraldine told Momma what she had seen.

"That crazy Buddy was out yonder in the cotton patch today with a cloth over his head and a flour sack down his back, playin' like he could fly like one o' them things in his ole comic books." (Most people called me "Buddy" or "Jack" back then.)

I was of course mortified beyond words. For a moment I thought about adding her to the list of foreign enemies I had to battle every day.

The exotic laboratories and evil inventions in my comic books intrigued and excited me and I decided to begin my own experiments. Perhaps I could do as much as a scientist as a superhero. I gathered several bottles and filled them in varying proportions with every liquid, powder, and granular substance I could find in Momma's kitchen and Daddy's barn. Then I buried them in the road bank in front of the house. I knew that electricity was vital to many of the experiments, but there was none. So, I decided to "catch" some electricity by running toward the lightning with an open bottle and quickly clamping the lid on when a bolt flashed. But I was always too slow. Like my flying, it was not one of my brighter ideas and if sharp-eyed Geraldine had spotted me chasing lightning in the middle of a storm, she would have had solid proof that I really was the moron she suspected me of being. After a couple of weeks, I dug up the bottles and tasted my invention. The combinations of vanilla flavoring, castor oil, salt, sugar, milk, grape juice, butter, pepper, horse liniment, and other components had congealed and fermented into a truly vile brew. One taste convinced me that my experiment had failed, and I reburied the bottles. They may still be there, and who knows, after decades they may have developed into a cure for cancer or a potential little Chernobyl.

Neighbor Bill McKenzie, "nigger Bill" some people called him behind his back because of his dark oily skin and Indian ancestry, was as loud and flashy as sons Harold and Bunk were easy going and unassuming. Among his many skills, Bill was an auctioneer. Once Harold and I accompanied him to an estate auction. It was exciting watching crowds of men bid on farm machinery, animals, and implements, and I realized for the first time that some people had more money than I had ever thought possible. Bill worked the crowd with his booming, staccato voice, huge personality and presence, and the skillful way he played bidders against one another.

That summer we picked strawberries and did other work for Bill and he entertained us with loud ribald stories and the sheer, irrepressible exuberance with which he lived life. Everybody laughed and whooped when he would boom out his "Hike for the jay!" every time things got too quiet to suit him. I never knew exactly what the words meant, but since everyone else seemed to be in on the joke, I dared not make a display of my ignorance by asking.

Bill was a bee hunter and from him and Daddy—himself almost as skilled as Bill—I learned how to follow the flight of a honeybee to its tree. It takes patience, a sharp eye, and an almost geometric ability to keep undeviatingly on a straight line through brush and woods. The slightest variance from the trajectory will send you wide of the bee tree. Once found the tree has to be cut and the inevitable stings of angry bees endured. But the reward is rich, wild honey.

A minor tornado, a "cyclone" to us, passed close to our place that summer, strewing debris and household items through the field across the road in front of our house. Among the things we found was an electric train. I was salivating with joy when I got my hands on it, but my delight was short lived for we learned it belonged to a boy who lived a few miles away and I had to give it up.

And there were other disappointments. A month or so later

Bill and Daddy gathered a load of vegetables to haul to the Farmers Market in Birmingham. (I think Bill had a truck.) The prospect of going on the road and spending the night in an exotic farmers market in a big city was the most exciting experience I could imagine, and I begged Daddy to let me go with them. At first Daddy said yes and I excitedly made preparations, but at the last minute he changed his mind and no amount of pleading could persuade him. As they departed without me, I was so enraged I threw my new Barlow knife across the cotton field. Later I thought better of my action and went to retrieve it. But it was no use. For the rest of the year I returned again and again to search for it, but in vain. Not even my x-ray superman vision could find it. My little knife must still be there, a victim of my fury, unjustly buried under many years of shifting dirt and accumulated debris.

The saddest event of the summer was the death of ole Ted. He had disappeared and for several days I called and searched for him. Then Daddy announced that he had found his carcass. Ted died from eating poisoned meat that someone, perhaps Archie Rowell, had put out to rid his farm of varmints. I mourned Ted's passing and felt lonely without my faithful friend.

But there were also moments of happiness. One day, Charles Rowell, Harold's friend and Archie's younger brother, but almost too old to be mine, came by on his bicycle. Harold and his older sisters Jewel and Thelma, both now good friends with Geraldine, were there and we all began to play hide and seek and other games. After a while Charles asked me if I would like to learn to ride a bicycle. I thought it was a grand idea and so did the bigger children. For a while they took turns pushing and holding the bike upright as I learned to balance it. Then to my surprise I saw that there was no one behind me. I was riding by myself! I was so thrilled, and it was so much fun that I rode for at least an hour around and around the house as Charles and the others patiently looked on.

And there was a moment of triumph when Thelma and I managed to get Bill's old renegade mule back inside the pasture. The ugly, splay-legged creature was notorious for the wily way it eluded people, sometimes spending days out of the pasture. But somehow Thelma and I were able to head him off as he made a dash for freedom and force him back through the gate. Bill and the other adults were impressed and both Thelma and I received lavish praise for our unlikely deed.

That summer I learned to throw a rock straight up in the air and have it fall back within a small radius of where I stood. Later at school I would show off by hurling a baseball to a grand height and catching it without moving more than a step or two. It was a satisfying new skill, for someone had told me once that it could not be done.

For a few years I had also been experimenting with small bows and weed arrows, but they were flimsy, and I had not learned to grip the arrows correctly, in fact I don't think I ever did. That year Daddy made me a hickory bow, "like the Indians used," he told me. My Grandpa Raley had shown him how to hew the wood to the right dimensions and string it in the Indian manner. I was duly impressed and took up the bow with renewed enthusiasm. The only problem was that I had no arrows worth speaking of, and my effectiveness remained limited.

In late fall of 1942, I noticed that Momma was getting strangely fat and wondered what was happening to her. (In those days, women like Momma never talked publicly of pregnancy, much less to their sons and other male relatives.) In March of 1943 I found out what was wrong with her when my brother Darrell was born on the commotion-filled night of the 23rd. At first, I did not know what to make of the crying presence that greatly changed our family dynamics, but then one day when Momma assigned me the task of watching him while she ironed some clothes, I discovered how playful he was and how much fun I could have with him. Darrell had a bright spirit, and I regretted that we were not closer in age. I suspect that Momma lost a child in 1941. She was gone for a couple of days and Daddy cooked for us. I think she was with Grandma Hooper, but I never knew anything for sure. Perhaps my sisters know. I also discovered many years after the fact that when she was in her late forties, and my younger sisters were small, Momma lost twins. But as I said, she did not talk about such things with males in the family.

About the time Darrell was born all the Bethlehem boys joined to play "follow the leader." And what a game it turned out to be! Under the leadership of a grown boy who had already served a brief prison sentence, we ran through the woods, leaping over logs, rolling down hills, climbing trees, jumping fences, and, finally, plunging into the icy waters of Rogers Swimming Hole. Soon we were shaking uncontrollably from the cold and probably had a moderate case of hypothermia. One or two of the boys got sick with colds and our parents were afraid we would catch pneumonia, but we all survived with a warning never to follow that leader again.

Late that summer the Buckelew brothers, cousins to Harold, came to visit him. We all decided to go to Rogers swimming hole. To get there we had to cross a briar-infested abandoned field, and since I was the only one barefoot they advised me that they were going to run ahead and I could go the long way around the field and meet them later. They took off running and I overtook them, bare feet, briars and all. They were astonished that I snagged not a single briar. I told them I ran so fast that I didn't have time to step on them. I still could not fly but for a while it seemed that a little bit of Superman had rubbed off on me after all.

Even though I enjoyed the swimming holes where we boys romped and splashed in nude abandon, I was never an expert swimmer. According to the custom of the time, Daddy simply threw me in the creek one day when I was about four, after sputtering and swallowing water I survived by dog paddling. The truth be told, I never progressed much beyond that stage. Even though the water was fun, the ever-present danger of water moccasins and other snakes caused me to keep a wary eye on the overgrown banks and murky depths. Someone told me that snakes could not bite under water, a fable that gave me a false reassurance for several years.

My fear of snakes that Aunt Phoebe had first instilled in me was not helped by once witnessing a meeting of snake-handling Christians at Flint Creek near Lacon close to Highway 31. I must have been only three or four when Daddy took me to see them. I remember men stripped to the waist and neck deep in the water groping along the Flint Creek banks for serpents. As I understood it, if one had enough faith the poisonous snakes would not bite, and the occasional fatalities resulting from this bizarre cult were taken as prima facie evidence that those who succumbed were weak in their faith. No doubt I would have been a similar faithless statistic had I joined them.

If I recall correctly, Daddy farmed that year in Bethlehem with Bud Sheats' mule team. I remember once when he and I rode one of them to Bemis's house. Late in the afternoon we started back, crossing Crooked Creek not far below Cook Cove. It was pitch black by the time we got to our pasture and began following the branch upstream toward our barn.

"Daddy, how we gonna see where we're goin'?" I asked fearfully.

"This ole mule can see in the dark, so we'll just let him pick the way by hisself." I was not convinced, but Daddy was right, and we got home safely.

We lost one little animal that year (ole Ted) but gained two big ones. One night, Daddy came home late, leading a team of horses.

"This'n's ole Dock and the big'n's Dan," he said proudly.

I had never seen handsomer animals, even though they didn't match up exactly as a team. Dock, a sleek gelding, was smaller and broader; Dan, a rangy stud, was taller and bigger boned. Both were roans, but Dan had a white spot between his eyes. Oddly enough, Dock was faster than Dan and much safer to ride. Dan had a treacherous quirk; most of the time he was docile, but if there was a mare in the vicinity—or sometimes just for the devilry of it—he would suddenly swerve without warning, throwing his rider and running away. I was his furious victim at least twice.

Chapter 12:
The Walker Farm

After two successful crops as a tenant farmer, Daddy got the happy idea of buying our own farm. He had two in mind: The Walker place a mile or so south of the Corn Road on Bone Road and a farm on Highway 31 close to Longview and only a few miles from Cullman. We saw the Longview farm one day on our way to town and immediately it was my choice. The house was modern by our standards and decent at least by everybody else's. The idea of living in a settlement, close to the highway, bus, and town pleased Momma too, and we tried to persuade Daddy that it was the better choice. A warm house with a good roof sounded almost too good to be true.

And as it turned out, it was. Daddy chose the Walker place, and again Momma was disappointed. At the time I couldn't understand his reasons, but in retrospect they should have been obvious to us. Daddy's pretext—for that's all it was—for turning down the highway house was that the Walker place had better land. Even though the other farm looked good and had good buildings, Daddy said the soil was shallow and depleted. The real reason, I realized later, was that he wanted no part of a settled community at a considerable distance from his brothers and father and without sizable adjacent woods in which to roam and hunt. He was never in love with civilization.

Nevertheless, I soon got over my disappointment in impatient anticipation of living on our own farm for the first time. In December of 1943 we loaded our things on our recently acquired wagon, tied the cow behind it, loaded the chickens in a coop, took the back road from Bethlehem—the church sign was misspelled "Bethleham" for many years—down past Rogers Creek and up through the Panama community, turned off on the narrow road at the Benefield house, went past the Luther Bates farm and Evans place on the left and Walker woods on the right, and reached our place at about three in the afternoon, having covered a distance or five or six miles. Filled with nervous energy, I ran part of the way alongside the slow-moving wagon. Once again, we were living near the Corn Road, this time for good. Daddy bought the farm through the HFA agency for $1,875. He still owed on the mortgage when they sold the place and moved away in 1966.

There was much exploring to do in the following days and weeks. We met the bus and got our mail a mile away at the Hill farm. To get there we took a foot path across our terraced field, entered the woods, forded Bone Creek with the help of some conveniently placed rocks, continued on until we emerged from the woods, crossed another field, climbed under the barbed wire fence and reached the Hill house. In warm weather we waited for the bus beside a huge oak next to our mailbox, but on cold days we waited inside the house. The Hills were neighborly and accommodating.

Mr. Hill, in fact, got a bit too friendly. Geraldine, who was now a pretty and precocious thirteen-year old girl, reported one day that Mr. Hill had met her once or twice in the woods, talked to her, and offered her money. Daddy and Momma were duly outraged, and I think Daddy met and escorted Geraldine home a few times after the episode. There was no more trouble of that sort.

The Sandlins moved into the Panama community about three and half miles from us and soon afterwards learned that Audrey had leukemia. She lingered for a few months, gradually growing weaker until she passed away at age ten. I was used to old people dying but the death of a good friend my own age was an impenetrable enigma that I could not understand.

In those days West Point had no dining facilities, so we all took our lunch to school. One cold winter day I set mine on Mrs. Hill's sewing machine to warm my hands by the fireplace. A few minutes later as the bus came rattling down the dirt road, I grabbed what I thought was my lunch and ran to catch it. To my chagrin, instead of biscuits and meat, or whatever Momma had prepared for me, I discovered at lunchtime I had picked up a sackful of Mrs. Hill's onions. I was mortified, not so much from hunger as from fear that the other students would see what I had brought for lunch. I dutifully returned the onions, retrieved my stale lunch, and endured a good laugh from the Hills about it.

Robert Lee Hill was a rangy, good natured boy about Geraldine's age but in my grade. He was bright enough but had absolutely no interest in school. At fourteen or so he towered above us ten-year olds and was so disruptive that teachers could barely conduct class. Only Miss Gentry, third and fourth grade teacher, learned how to control him. Instead of paddling him as she did at first while he pretended contrition with loud sobs but smirked at us as he returned to his seat, one day she made him sit in her lap. The tactic worked, at least for a time, for Robert Lee was shamed beyond words by her unorthodox maneuver. Not long afterward he quit school for good. Years later he bought the farm where he had lived as a boy and became a respectable and prosperous farmer who befriended my parents as long as they lived. He was a good man but never on good terms with books.

After a few months the Hills moved away and Raymond Powell and his family, also friendly folks, moved in.

Our farm consisted of sixty-four acres, about half of which was in woods. It had four wells, three dug and one drilled, but the latter was the only one we trusted for drinking water. One at the lower end of the pasture was always dry except for stagnant rainwater. For the animals someone had built an extension down into Evans land where there was a nice clean spring that flowed year-round. The Evans family whose well and windows I had helped ruined on another of their farms had a greedy reputation, but if they were aware of the extension into their land, in all the years we lived there they never complained. Before long I had explored nearly every inch of the place, all except the northeast corner. For some inexplicable reason in all the years I lived there I never ventured at all in that direction. Only now do I wonder what was there and why I was never curious to explore it. Occasionally Daddy would go over to our boundary stake on that side of the farm only to discover to his disgust that the hard-drinking Tankersley brothers, owners of the adjacent land, had moved it to their advantage.

1943 was the middle of World War II and many commodities such as sugar, soap, gasoline, and tires were either rationed or in short supply. New car production ceased in early 1942 and did not resume until 1946. Gasoline and tires were of no concern to us, since we had no automobile, but sugar was another matter. With our rationing book we qualified for a small amount and sometimes it was my job to go pick it up. One day, Daddy sent me along with my cousin Gene Johnson to West Point in the road cart, a rubber-tired, one-horse contraption with leaf springs and a soft ride that became fairly popular before and during the war. Gene and I got our quota of sugar and with a little extra money bought several packs of mentholated Kool cigarettes. On the way home we smoked every cigarette, but I was careful not to inhale and suffered no ill effects. I don't remember about Gene.

Once or twice in my life I had eaten bananas and loved the taste. But like so many other products, they were scarce during the war. One day, however, before classes I walked down to one of the stores at West Point and what should I spy but a bunch of ripe bananas hanging in the store window at 5 cents a pound! I had a quarter in my pocket and by the time school started I had so gorged myself that for a long time the very thought of a banana almost gagged me. Eventually I ate them again but never with the same relish.

Because of sugar rationing, candy and chewing gum were also scarce. We chewed sweet gum and even pine resin, but they were, or so we thought, poor substitutes for store bought chewing gum. Geraldine was attracting boyfriends and by a fortuitous turn of events one of them was a Blevins boy whose family owned a store in the Corinth community and therefore had access to sugar and candy. Blevins wrote Geraldine insipid love letters, one or two of which I just happened to see, but even better for me one day he sent her a box of Dentyne chewing gum. I picked it up at the mailbox and knew by the aroma what it was. On the way home through the woods this war-deprived boy could not resist opening the box and purloining a pack for myself. Once she discovered my delinquency, Geraldine let out howls of righteous indignation and demanded my hide. For whatever reason my parents withheld corporal punishment, although Momma lectured me about privacy and taking things that didn't belong to me, advice that without a withe to back it up did not register very deeply.

Part of the problem was that Geraldine and I quarreled incessantly and insulted each other at the slightest pretext. One day I was bemoaning my pudgy, freckled face and wondering if I would ever be a decent-looking man. Geraldine walked by just at that moment and as if gifted with an evil telepathy said to me, "Buddy, you're the ugliest boy in the world." She confirmed my worst fears, for that was exactly what I was thinking too.

The freckles were new. Until age ten or so I was abnormally white and unable to tan. When I was very small Gertrude Sandlin Rainwater once told me that I was so white I should never expose my skin to the sun. I never forgot her words although I could not reasonably heed her advice. In any case, the matter reached a crisis a year or so after we moved to the Walker place. Daddy was plowing and I was busy in the lower field with my pole axe hewing logs to build a cabin for my superhero club— of which naturally I was the president and only member. Suddenly I started trembling and became so weak I could barely stand. After a while I made it to where Daddy was plowing. He stopped Dan and Dock, looked at me, and told me to go to the house and tell Momma to cook me an egg. It helped but I was still unnaturally weak.

That year an over the counter product called Hadacol was very popular with ailing people. It had a high alcoholic content and naïve non-drinking people extolled the almost instant lift they experienced after only a couple of tablespoonfuls. I think there was even a popular country song about it. Daddy and Momma thought it might help me. Instead of Hadacol, however, which had become pricey due to its popularity, Daddy came home a few days later with a similar medicine called Zyrone, a black, viscous liquid nearly as foul-tasting as the evil chemical concoctions I left buried in the Bethlehem community.

But it worked. Rich in iron and vitamins, Zyrone soon brought strength to my body, color to my skin, and freckles to my face. With my new energy I felt like one of my superheroes but resembled Geraldine's dreary description of me. My boundless stamina lasted for months until one day again I got what country people called the "weak trembles." Only now we knew the remedy for it; Daddy brought home another bottle of Zyrone, and soon I was off and running at full speed again.

I think it was about that time that I collected enough money to order a Daisy air rifle. With a little practice I became a crack shot and soon killed nearly all the birds around our house. Daddy noticed the disappearance and voiced his displeasure. "Ye ort not to kill the birds like that. They aint hardly none left. All them little blue birds is gone." Daddy was right and I felt terrible about the needless slaughter. I think that was when I began to lose interest in hunting and started to become a "conservationist," in later terminology, an environmentalist.

The impetus came from readings at school. We saw pictures of the ravages of the Dust Bowl and read about the destruction of forests and widespread land erosion in the South and Southwest. Even though we admired the old frontiersmen, we learned how men like Buffalo Bill Cody had ravaged the wildlife and annihilated the great buffalo herds of the Old West. I took it very much to heart and resolved to do my part to conserve America's natural resources. One day as Daddy and I were cutting firewood, Leon Woods happened by and started laughing when he saw me chopping up the tiny limbs. But when I explained to them that we shouldn't be wasteful with what God had given us, they agreed, and Daddy let me continue. For all his faults, he was always ready to side with those who were trying to do a good work. Unhappily, Momma was often the lone exception to his noble impulses.

I took my conservation efforts a step further. One of our fields was developing a serious gully. I built a dike like one described in a book for erosion control. It worked for a while but had to be reinforced after heavy rains. I was never able to block the gully completely, but at least it did not deepen. In other trouble spots I worked with hoe and shovel to open channels and divert the water. The key was good terrace rows that caught the water and conducted it to the end of the fields. I learned that plowing only a narrow slice of soil with each passage of the turning plow made for a smooth, efficient terrace. Years later one of my final and most satisfying farm projects was the time I hired out to Dewey McCravy, Bill McCravy's brother, to plow his terraces and turn a few acres of land. When Dewey came to the field to check on things late in the afternoon his eyes widened in admiration of my work.

"Them's the best-looking terrace rows I've ever seen," he told me. "How did you get 'em so smooth and reg'lar?"

"Dewey," I confided as though revealing a great secret, "most people take too wide a cut when they plow terraces. You have to be patient and plow them just a little at a time."

In time the birds came back.

Shortly after we moved and before I became a confirmed "conservationist," Daddy decided to clear a "newground," an additional ten or fifteen acres for cultivation. We began with great enthusiasm, sawing down trees, clearing underbrush, and—best of all for me—burning stumps. For days and weeks smoke hung over the land as some of the stumps burned deep under the surface. Several times we chased young rabbits flushed out of their hiding places by our intrusion. When it was all over, we could see our closest neighbors the Johnsons.

Except that the clearing was not and never would be complete. The lower reaches of the new ground had extremely dense underbrush and its slopes were unpromising as farmland. After we had cut down and burned the big trees, Daddy decided to abandon it. Later we put an electric fence around it and used it for a year or two as a pasture, but eventually the saplings became trees and the area reverted to woodland. We farmed the upper part, but many of the tree roots remained and plowing it was always a hard and unproductive chore for us. Thanks mainly to Momma's unrelenting efforts, the only part of the new ground that became truly tillable and productive was her large garden area next to the road.

The summer of 1946 a "faith healing" craze came over our community and Luther Leathers, who owned a big army truck, started hauling people over to Winston County to have their aches and ailments attended to by the Black Faith Healer. More out of curiosity than need, Momma, Daddy, Darrell (I think), and I made the trip. It would be next to impossible to retrace our route. We rode for a long time, hours it seemed to me, on dirt roads through the Bankhead National Forest, stopping only once that I remember to let Daddy take an illegal shot at a huge owl with Luther's 30-30 rifle. The owl got away before he could draw a bead on it.

When we finally got to the faith healer, who lived on a remote dirt road in a house not much better than ours, cars were parked everywhere they could find space. Shortly after we arrived, a limousine drove up and a woman was taken by stretcher to consult the old Black man. Much to my surprise, Momma described several things wrong with me, including a pain in my left side. The pain was real. I called it a "catch" and it would grab sometimes when I took a deep breath. Momma's personal list was impressively longer. I don't think Daddy consulted him. When it came my turn, the kindly old man asked me with a knowing look if I "rassled" a lot. I said, "Yeah, I reckon I do," and was impressed that he would know that about me. He rubbed my side and said I would be all right. "Jist need to cut down a little on th' rasslin' for a time," he said. I was duly impressed to know I had been cured of an ailment I didn't even know I had. But my confidence in the Faith Healer was seriously strained when I saw one of his grandsons with a bad case of what looked like dog mange.

"If he's a faith doctor, Momma, why don't he heal his grandson?"

She didn't know but was convinced that what he told us was worth the five dollars we donated to him. Being a faith healer and all, he couldn't charge folks, he explained.

"Jist whatevah ye feels like donatin', ma'am." He appeared to be taking in a fabulous amount of "donations."

Among the many neighbors who would occupy the two houses closest to us, the first family ranked among the nicest. At a much earlier time the Johnsons had lived and farmed the acreage, but then, if my memory is accurate, they moved away to Indianapolis for many years. Curtis Johnson, son of the owners, returned to the home place for a time before selling it for good and moving back north. He was a kind man and did us several favors. His son Jimmy used to come over to play with me. Jimmy was younger and more delicate than I and knew nothing about country life. Because he seemed bewildered by the sudden change in his life, I felt a need to protect and instruct him. His language was Midwestern "proper" English and so as to make him feel more comfortable and not to appear backward myself, for the first time in my life I attempted to speak the same language I read in books.

Every time we got a good rain a small lake would collect in front of one of our terrace rows below the orchard. Jimmy and I would launch small stick boats with tiny sails and encourage them with shouts and prodding with long sticks to sail across it. For the first time since his arrival in Alabama, shy little Jimmy seemed to be having fun. I felt that I had done a good deed, even though my concern for my little friend diminished my own fun. Only a few months passed before the Johnsons moved north again, and I never saw my friend Jimmy again.

After World War II, Hollis and Marguerite Lynne and their two young sons lived for a year on the Johnson place. Hollis was a nice, clean-cut young man and Marguerite always seemed to me to be too beautiful to belong to our roughshod world. In a sense this was true, for within a few years people like the Johnsons, Lynnes, and other educated people moved on to jobs in the city, leaving behind their slower neighbors and relatives.

Because of Carl Walker's woods, we could not see the house to the south which also had an annual change of neighbors. The Bradfords were among the first I remember. Mr. Bradford was, supposedly, a preacher, but whispers of spousal abuse, bad debts, and gossip about other misconduct caused us to doubt a genuine vocation for the ministry. The most vexing problem, however, was Paul Bradford's infatuation with Geraldine, a romance that my parents wholeheartedly opposed. The matter was resolved when the Bradfords moved away to Arkansas, I believe. There were letters from Paul, but before long Geraldine forgot him in favor of other beaux. As I said, by now she was a precociously mature and pretty young woman. Even I, her ever critical brother, had to admit that.

I cannot sort out which boyfriend it was—it could have been Paul—who invited her to a dance a few miles distant. He had an automobile and my parents refused to let her go unless she was chaperoned. It turned out that despite Geraldine's cries of anger and indignation I had to be the chaperon. Take it or leave it, they told her. She took it, for as bad as having little brother along on a date, it would have been worse to miss the date and the dance entirely. But I paid a price for my unwelcome presence. Never have I been treated more coldly than I was in the rumble seat of that little Model-A Ford. When we arrived at the house, Geraldine told me to wait in the car. I did and the dance seemed to go on forever as the temperature dropped until I was shivering from the cold. The ride home was no better. Geraldine was angry and the boyfriend naturally resentful. I think that was the beginning of the end for that romance.

Chapter 13:
Pursued and Perplexed

When I was fourteen Hubert Denton and his family moved into the Evans house and before long, his daughter Marjorie began pursuing me. Marjorie was twelve or thirteen, not especially pretty, but abnormally precocious in her sexual tastes and development and so brazen in her advances that I was a little afraid of her. I had liked girls before, of course, but assumed that the initial pursuit was my prerogative. I did not know how to respond to her aggressiveness. That year Daddy gave me the small field next to the Evans property and I raised a good crop of corn and peas. But almost every time I worked in the field, Majorie and her little sister would stand across the road in Carl Walker's woods and call out to me. Sometimes Majorie would send the perverse little girl with messages. "Majorie's waitin' for you, Harold. She wants to see ya." Convinced that Majorie was not normal, I ignored the invitations with the excuse that I was busy with my plowing and work.

I was less inhibited when the Dentons came to visit. Then I roughhoused with the girls and gave Majorie a few suggestive hugs as she squealed in delight. One day a dark thundercloud came up while we were playing what we called tag but which was really touch and grope. Momma cautioned us to "be good" while it was thundering and lightning. It was common parental advice in stormy weather.

My indecision about girls led to the worst sunburn of my life. The Hyde family, present owners of the old Bud Sheats store at Battleground, had a sizable fishpond built by the CC Corps before World War II. Before long boys from miles around were coming to swim in it. One Sunday afternoon the Long brothers and I, along with several other boys were swimming—nude as always—when some older girls showed up to tease and taunt us. They dared us to come out and retrieve our clothes. None of us were brave enough to get out of the water, and as a result I was severely sunburned before finally the girls tired of their game and left.

If my little adventure with Majorie Denton was crude farce, a more serious sexual drama played out in the Johnson house when the Dinglers moved in. Mr. Dingler was physically weak and nondescript, and I barely remember him at all, but Mrs. Dingler was a captivatingly beautiful woman with long lashes and dark hair and eyes, a perverse version of Mrs. Lynne, though coarser. Her exotic type was uncommon among our fair and freckled English and Scotch-Irish racial stock. We had never known any woman like her in Corn Road country. For whereas other women, our Woods Cousins for example, were willing and ready to take on men, they at least made a decent effort to hide their trysts and to deny them if confronted. It was the expected thing for women to do, easy or decent, or so we assumed. Mrs. Dingler, on the other hand, openly consorted with a man who lived with them and made no effort to conceal her liaison. But at the same time, she was so disarmingly polite and sweet that nobody knew what to make of her. Momma, of course, was outraged, but then one day Mrs. Dingler came to visit and completely charmed us all, Momma included. The whole Corn Road community was astonished, stupefied, outraged, perplexed, and uncertain how to react. Her behavior was not in our register of normal country psychology.

Finally, the area men reached a masculine conclusion in her favor and put an end to the speculation. Obviously, they reasoned, decrepit Mr. Dingler was inadequate and so his poor wife had to turn elsewhere for gratification. Hence the fault was not hers at all but her ineffective husband's. In this way all the blame fell on him while sloe-eyed Mrs. Dingler went on her sweet way with her lover as long as they lived in the community. There were lewd references, of course, to the unselfish willingness of local men to help relieve her sexual frustration.

Chapter 14:
Other Aggravations

A few years earlier my cousin Gene Johnson, son of Momma's youngest sister Christine, had moved to Cullman where he lived in the most enviable circumstances I could imagine. He had a bicycle, toys, and money for movies any time he wanted. His father Edgar had left farming and now drove a taxi, a job we considered to be upscale work. Once when I was ten Momma and I went to visit them for several days. (I think it was when their son Dean was born). One afternoon Gene and I rode his bike over to the Cullman Theater for the first afternoon movie I had ever seen. It was a horror film starring Boris Karloff. I remember with a faint vestige of my childhood horror how wispy smoke filtered under the doorway and turned into a bloodthirsty vampire. Luckily a cross and silver stake put an end to his vile crimes and the good people were saved from a living death.

Not long after that visit Christine showed up in tears at our house. Edgar, it seemed, had picked up one female fare too many and transferred his affections to her in the process. Daddy and Bufus fixed up a little one-room shack on our property, covering it with imitation brick siding, repairing the roof, and putting in a floor. Soon it was ready for Christine, Gene, and younger brother Dean to move into. Edgar drove by a time or two to talk, but after Momma gave him an earful about what he had done, he did not show up again.

For Gene especially the sudden reversal of their fortunes was traumatic and painful in a way I can only imagine. From being the privileged city cousin whom we envied, he went to being the newly countrified one we pitied. He still had his grandparents, John Thomas Johnson and wife Cora who lived close to us, but after the divorce and Edgar's subsequent remarriage, their relationship with Christine was understandably strained. She accused them, perhaps unjustly, of trying to win Gene over to Edgar's side. As for Dean, they did not seem to take very much interest in him, at least not at first. Gene was the first and obviously favorite grandson whom they plied with candy and gifts. He was short with bad teeth, and it was our conventional wisdom that the candy that stunted his growth and caused his cavities. Actually, Momma said, he resembled his Grandfather Hooper.

Gene and I had always played together very well, but that summer our relationship became strained. Despite our mutual affection, he was mortified that even though two years younger, I was heavier and stronger. We argued and bickered about every imaginable topic though never coming to actual fighting.

About that same time a phase of my childhood ended abruptly. I remember distinctly the day it happened. Gene and I were playing airplanes and cars in a sand pile in front of his little house when all of a sudden, I realized that it was no longer fun, merely silly. I stopped my cars, landed my airplanes, and put away childish things. The absorbing fascination with those particular childhood toys was gone forever. After that Gene and I took to fishing, swimming, and exploring the woods.

Meanwhile Dean and Darrell bonded and became life-long friends as well as first cousins.

Before long Gene and I graduated to bigger toys. I had built a wooden-wheeled wagon, the latest of several over the years since Daddy and my uncles taught me how to make them. They were not good for anything but coasting down hills. But Gene and I decided that instead of pushing the heavy wagon back up the hills around our place we would hitch Dock to it—without asking permission—and let him do the pulling. It worked fine for a while but then the contraption frightened him and before we knew what was happening, he ran away with the wagon, throwing us into the dirt and in my case tearing the only new pair of overalls I had. When we got home wild-eyed Dock and the wagon, Daddy, Momma, and Christine were all waiting for us. "Go git me a withe," Daddy instructed me, while Christine made similar preparations to punish Gene. Momma was angry and berated me about my overalls.

It was the last switching Daddy ever gave me. The punishment was certainly not undeserved, but I made up my mind not to cry like a baby. I had finished playing with kid toys and from now on I was going to be tough. Christine gave Gene a pretty good switching, partly, I think, because of the downward turn in her life, including her frustration over the continual arguments Gene and I were having. As for Daddy, he gave me enough licks to satisfy Momma's indignation, while I kept my promise not to cry. I think he was impressed with my stoic silence, although he said nothing about it.

That same year and for several thereafter our Cousin Aaron Hooper came over from Gadsden to spend the summers with us. Aaron had fallen in love with country life in general and pretty Jewel McKenzie in particular. His third and most consuming love, which ultimately destroyed him, was liquor. By the time he was twelve he would slip away to find whiskey. In his teenage years he was already well on his way to becoming a confirmed alcoholic. To Aaron's three loves probably I should add a fourth: my father. Aaron shifted his affection from his own father to Daddy. He followed him everywhere and became so demanding and proprietary that he resented Gene and me for intruding.

Unwisely Daddy allowed Aaron's adulation to develop into an unhealthy relationship. Momma was not so easily deluded and constantly warned Daddy that things were not right. And she was especially worried about Aaron's hostility toward me.

Not that I made exorbitant claims on Daddy's time or affections. Although we generally had an easy-going father-son relationship, at least until I was in my late teens, our interests and natural predispositions turned us in opposite directions. Nevertheless, Aaron saw me as an impediment to his complete monopoly of Daddy's time and attention and his resentment grew accordingly.

One day his hostility towards me boiled over. Aaron grabbed me and swung me out over the open dug well. I clung for dear life to his leg as he tried to shake me loose and drop me down the well shaft. Momma saw what was happening and ran screaming to my rescue. Aaron denied any intention to harm me. "I was just playing with Harold," he protested. Momma and I both knew better. Even Daddy was disturbed, and Aaron was sent home temporarily.

After that experience I never trusted Aaron again. His drinking got worse and not even his marriage to Jewel, whom he adored, made any difference. Many in the family laughed at his drunken antics and admired his ability to hold a responsible job on the railroad despite his almost constant inebriation. I saw nothing funny in any of it, only a talented, highly intelligent man who was sadly wasting his gifts.

Years had passed since the incident at the well when one night I went with Armon, Aaron, and Jewel to a movie in Cullman. I enjoyed the film, "The Black Rose" based, I think, on the novel by A.J. Cronin. Everything seemed to be going perfectly until Aaron started drinking on the way home. Before long he was drunk and obnoxious, and we had to stop the car.

"Now I'm going to finish what I started with you," he told me with hatred in his eyes. Neither Armon nor Jewel understood his comment, but Aaron and I knew exactly what he meant. Aaron was an ex-Marine in his twenties, but alcohol had eroded his strength and at fifteen I was not the little boy he had once tried to drop down the well. Besides I was sober and infuriated by his remark. It was no contest. I got a crushing headlock on him. He could not break my grip and gasped for breath. "Let him go, Harold, he's drunk!" Armon urged. Jewel pleaded with me, "Don't hurt him, Harold. He don't mean you no harm! It's the liquor talkin'." I knew better but I released him with the warning that he had better never try anything else with me. And he didn't. Aaron remained a drunken but pampered nuisance to the rest of the family until his death several years later, but he and I barely saw each other after that confrontation. I regretted his hostility, for earlier in life I admired him and brother Alan more than any other relatives.

Ever since the loss of Ole Ted I had wanted another dog. Somebody offered Gene and me two cuddly little female puppies, mixtures of collie and Lord knows what else. One was brown and the other was black. I chose the brown because that was Ted's color. Gene was equally happy with "Blackie," as he named her. I called mine "Brownie," and more affectionately "Brownie bang-bang." She loved me with a joyous abandon, and we had great fun together.

But her life was short. A few months later both she and sister Blackie accidentally ran under the wheels of Bufus's truck. Blackie died almost immediately. Brownie lingered and for a time I thought she might survive. But then one day she disappeared, and I could not find her. For days I searched and called for her. It was perhaps two or three years later that I found her little bones in the grass at the far end of a field we no longer cultivated. The thought of my happy little dog dying alone and in agony was almost more than I could bear, and I shed tears for her. It would be many years before I had another dog.

One day on our way to Grandma Hooper's house Gene and I met our Aunt Irene. "Our house burned down last night. Nobody was hurt but everything was lost," she said choked with emotion. Gene and I ran to see for ourselves and found a smoldering pile of ashes and debris from which we rescued a few worthless items. After that Bufus and Irene moved into the log cabin and I think Grandma stayed for a time with Viola before spending her final months with Christine on our place.

It was a frustrating time in my life. I liked Gene but tired of his constant company and endless arguing over everything. Gene was too old for me to dominate him and he was too frail to control me. So for months we lived in constant tension, as inseparably devoted to each other as we were mutually incompatible. After Grandma Hooper died in 1949, Christine moved into Mr. Hendricks's more comfortable renter house close to Bemis and Viola. Distance healed our differences and Gene and I never argued again, but neither did we have much contact afterwards.

Chapter 15:
School and Romance

Even as Gene and I made life miserable for each other, in school and romance things were looking up. Long since cured of my fascination with grown women after the unhappy episode with Marie Cook, I started to notice girls of my own age. Helen Gunter, the daughter of the West Point blacksmith, caught my attention the very last day of third grade. We shared a double desk and had known each other all year, but that day there was something special about her. We spent the day eying each other and giggling. It seemed to be the start of something grand, but unfortunately or otherwise, she moved away that summer and our romance died before it bloomed.

But soon other girls caught my attention. The first was Ellery Elrod. After we moved to the Walker farm, the Elrod family moved into the Bud Sheats house at Bethlehem, and for a few weeks cute little Ellery and I were sweethearts of sorts. But then one day I went back to visit Harold McKenzie and saw a sight that chilled my romantic feelings for Ellery. There before God and everybody was her younger sister playing stark naked in the yard. Now we had been taught that only the trashiest kind of people let their children run naked, and even though we were the poorest of the poor, we never sank that low. The sight was too much for me to accept. So, snob that I was, I dropped Ellery.

A similar shock brought my next romance to an abrupt end. Fourth grade was under way in Miss Gentry's class when Betty Sue Lovell, a little brunette beauty began eying me favorably and giggling with the other girls about me. Soon the other kids were calling us "sweethearts," a relationship that consisted of sly glances, timid smiles, and during rest period after lunch and Bible reading, an exchange of daring winks. On the playground we favored each other in games like "Ring around the Roses." Several times I gave her a few pennies, which she gladly accepted with bowed head and a sweet smile. One day we dropped the pennies in the exchange, and everybody stopped to laugh and jeer. I was mortified but my love endured the embarrassment.

But not long before fourth grade was over, I realized I could not continue to be Betty Sue's sweetheart. For one day as we were playing "Ring around the Roses" her dark hair flew back from her ears and I saw to my horror that they were "plumb rusty," as I told somebody. Duly indoctrinated by my hard-scrubbing mother, I knew that as pretty as she was, Betty Sue did not meet my demanding hygienic standards. I refused to smile and wink at her anymore and kept my pennies to myself. After the briefest puzzlement over my changed behavior she went happily on her way to other interests.

There is a footnote to our breakup. After fifth grade Betty Sue moved away to Florida, I believe it was, and I did not see her for over two years. Then in seventh grade she returned to West Point. This time I didn't notice her ears because the rest of her was too attractive to worry about such trifling details. She was now taller than I, filled out in the mysterious way of women, and infinitely prettier than the dirty-eared little girl I had ditched in fourth grade. She smiled down at me condescendingly, but her eyes were already looking elsewhere, for the older boys were swarming about her like bees around a flower. I mused mournfully about how shortsighted I had been to let her go. Not that it would have mattered; nature and early hormones on her part would have separated us in time anyway. I think she dropped out of school and married early.

After the fiascos with Ellery and Betty Sue, I took a year-long hiatus from romance. Then in sixth grade I got to know Melba Jean Nesmith whom I admired for her academic excellence and even more for her athletic prowess. Melba Jean could catch and hit a softball better than most of the boys, and often at recess as best batters she and I took turns hitting fly balls to the other kids. Several of the boys were bigger, but I tried so hard when Melba Jean was around that I was usually the playground star. I was too inhibited by my circumstances to say anything to Melba Jean about a "special" friendship, for she was from a prosperous family, wore nice clothes and shoes, and was always neat—with clean ears. I wore farm overalls and went barefoot in warm weather. She played hard but always looked pretty and collected. I saw her only once that summer after school was out. I had gone to West Point with Uncle Bufus in his old wreck of truck to pick up a load of pine slabs at the sawmill and was fantasizing about Melba Jean when suddenly there she was, as fair as a sunny day, walking down to Morgan's store. I felt lightheaded at the sight of her but panicky also that she might see me in my dirty clothes and Bufus's disreputable vehicle—to say nothing of Bufus himself. She didn't notice at all.

About the time we started seventh grade Melba Jean moved away from West Point and fifty-odd years would pass before I saw her again at our high school reunion of 1998. Melba Jean told how she finished high school in Sheffield or Florence, Alabama, but in her heart always considered herself "a West Point Warrior." The only other trace I had of her during those decades was the year I attended Florence State College (1957-58). Now a lovely young woman, she had been featured as one of the 1954 yearbook beauties but was no longer enrolled. From her frail appearance in 1998 I supposed she was ill, but she didn't say and of course I didn't ask. She did tell me that upon his retirement her husband kindly indulged her wish to return to her beloved West Point to live out her life. I told her how much I had admired her in sixth grade and how well I remembered her. Melba Jean confessed that she did not recall me at all, but we had a nice visit nonetheless and gave each other a hug as we parted. It was good to be able finally to give her a proper goodbye and so bring a small chapter of my life to satisfying closure. I saw her once more five years later at our next class reunion. We again had a nice conversation. She chose not to attend later class reunions.

At the same time, I was attracted to Melba Jean, I fell once again under the spell of an older woman: twenty-one-year-old Miss Virginia Parker, our sixth-grade teacher. In fact, the whole class was in love with her. Fresh out of college in 1946 and teaching her first class, pretty Miss Parker had a beginner's high spirits and optimism, traits that seemed to epitomize America's postwar euphoria. But she possessed many other excellent qualities to enhance her positive attitude. Vivacious, intelligent, and superbly skilled as a teacher, she captivated us, and we adored her. After lunch she would hold us spellbound by reading heroic "Dave Dawson" books and thrilling tales of the Royal Canadian Mounted Police. As a result, I formed vague fantasies of someday going to the far North in search of similar adventures. Sometime during the year, I won a fight with a playground troublemaker and we were summoned by our teachers. After we had been properly lectured and the other boy and his teacher were safely out of hearing, Miss Parker flashed her beautiful smile at me, rumpled my hair, and with a twinkle in her eye, commented, "Good job, Harold! He deserved it!" At that moment I would have put my hands in the fire for her if she had asked me. As the year advanced, Edgar Will Helton, her future husband, started waiting for Miss Parker to end her daily teaching duties. I recall that at first, we children were not particularly happy that she seemed to be so interested in him, but he was kind to us and eventually we accepted him. After the year ended, we all begged Miss Parker to go on to seventh grade with us and be one of our high school teachers. (Seventh grade was high school to us.) But I have gotten ahead of the story.

If Miss Parker was an inspired teacher, Miss Gentry, who taught me in third and fourth grades, was an unfortunate person who gave the appearance of feeling trapped in a profession for which she had little aptitude and inadequate training. Frustrated by the talkative class, sometimes she would sit at her desk and sob, for even though she finally got the upper hand on Robert Lee Hill, the everyday problems of discipline and instruction seemed to be beyond her capabilities. If I felt sorry for her I cannot remember it. With the customary cruelty of children, we laughed at her size and called her "fatty" behind her back. As I said, obese people were rare in those days.

I became her class favorite. Realizing that academically I was ahead of the others, she put me to working on "special projects" to pamper me and keep me out of mischief. For I could be as disruptive as the other students. She even gave me an assistant, Lindall Gable, to help me. When the class got to a reading section about the Pueblo Indians, Lindall and I offered to build a miniature pueblo structure provided the class would collect the clay for us. Miss Gentry liked the idea and led the class on a field trip to scrape clay from ditches and gullies up on the hill for which West Point was named. The project, its drawings and plans, kept Lindall and me entertained for days on end. Meanwhile our classmates envied us as they read and worked on their assignments and might have turned on us if Lindall had not been two years older and stronger than anybody else in our class. By this time Robert Lee Hill had quit school.

Then a nasty incident occurred. One spring morning in 1945

near the end of fourth grade we saw Miss Gentry huffing her way slowly to class. Some of us gathered under the high wooden steps and as they creaked with her weight, we called out maliciously, "Miss Fatty! Miss Fatty!" She recognized my voice among the others, and when she realized that her favored student was making fun of her too, it was almost more than she could bear. She went to her room to cry. But before long, her grief turned to anger, and she marched out to the principal's office. A little while later the awful summons came: I had to go face the dreaded Mr. Hamner.

Now Mr. Hamner was anything but a softy. A huge athletic man who had been a "science boxer" in his youth, he supposedly had in his desk a fabled rubber hose section that even the toughest boys feared. Mr. Hamner had cut holes in the hose, or so the gossip went, and it would leave great welts when wielded by an arm as strong as his. I knew I was in serious trouble.

I cannot remember now what I told Mr. Hamner, but essentially it was a lie which coupled with a vigorous denial was enough to get me off without making the acquaintance of the dreaded rubber hose. The lie worked so well that I made the mistake of telling it to my parents too. Usually they sided with the teacher in matters of discipline, but on this rare occasion they believed and backed me. The result was that Daddy made a trip to West Point to see whether I was being mistreated. By then I was ashamed of the whole episode but so caught up in my own lie that I thought I had no choice but to stick by it. Poor Miss Gentry was put on the defensive while I escaped with only a blot on my conscience. To this day I am ashamed of having hurt the poor woman. It may have been her last year at West Point and possibly I contributed to her departure.

Besides our teacher-supervised recesses, there were unstructured playground times in the morning and after school.

The meaner boys played marbles "for keeps," even though Mr. Hamner and the teachers forbade it. At day's end some of the boys had a pocketful of marbles, while inept players went home empty handed. I had a maple syrup can full of marbles and even though I shot with either hand as well as any of the boys, I respected the rule and seldom played for keeps myself. Meanwhile the girls jumped rope and played on the swings except for the times we boys decided to raid their territory, enduring their high-pitched screams and angry kicks and slaps. Most of the girls were farm hardy and there was nothing soft in the way they could hit and scratch.

My bus usually made a run on the Dripping Springs Road before returning to pick us up for its north circuit. Other students had a similar wait. This gave us up to forty-five minutes of unsupervised time to play, fight, or do whatever we pleased. In fourth grade I organized an after school "gang" that created a bit of havoc. I got the idea from reading a serial account of a character by the name of Andy Hawkins, I think his name was, and his gang in the <u>Grit</u> newspaper. Andy and his friends had their own clubhouse and every week they investigated the most exciting mysteries. I was especially impressed with an episode in which the gang fired a homemade rocket into outer space. A few days later it came back, guided by an unearthly intelligence. What a thrill! My gang headquartered in a dugout spot under one of the buildings. Our adventures were more prosaic, consisting for the most part in harassing other students, such as chasing and stripping sad little Buddy Brasher of his clothes, or reporting on spy activities and enemy movements. After all, the nation was still at war with Japan. I ran a tight ship and tried to maintain a chain of command, but after a few weeks the gang tired of my highhanded authority and deserted me.

There were plenty of fights and I had my share. Two sets of

brothers in particular, the Dukes and the Gentrys, gave me considerable trouble for years. Monroe Duke was older and bigger than I but weak and clumsy as a fighter. After he threatened me not long after I transferred to West Point, I knocked him over a slide, and even though afterwards he occasionally made idle threats, he never had the courage to take me on again.

His brother Doyle was a different story. A handsome, surly boy, he was younger but stronger than Monroe, and without coming to blows he and I had several tense confrontations over the years. I think we were afraid of each other. In the eleventh grade I finally decided enough was enough and made up my mind that the next time we had words I would slug him without warning. (A ferocious surprise attack won me several fights against bigger opponents.) I waited, having planned my fighting strategy against my rival, but we never confronted each other again. Incidentally, the Dukes preceded us on our farm and lived for a time nearby. Before they moved again one of the smaller Duke boys fell in a well and there were several hours of tense drama before he was rescued terrified but unhurt.

O'Neal Gentry was a bit older but a grade behind me. More importantly, he was a strong, fearless battler. One winter afternoon when the ground was iced over, our simmering feud came to blows. O'Neal decked me once and I knocked him down twice. At least that was the version told around school. In reality, we both slipped on the ice trying to land our punches, but the other boys gave me credit for a win, which was all that counted. His brother Glenn Gentry was a couple of years older and so much heavier and taller that I did not think I could win a fistfight with him. (Later he played guard and occasional center on our basketball center.) Instead, I resorted to my throwing ability and hit him with a piece of copper cable when he came at me. That stopped him temporarily, but Glenn threatened retaliation. Then an older and heavier boy by the name of Duane Shoemake took my side and promised to work Glenn over if he bothered me again. Glenn thought better of his threat and I was free of my most vexing enemy.

Once I threw a fight. It was against a boy named Delos (last name forgotten, may have been Brown or Long). During our struggle over some marbles, I spotted a pocket knife buried in the grass—to replace the one I had thrown away in the cotton patch, I thought—and to get Delos out of the way and my hands on the knife, I let myself be thrown to the ground and the fight was over. Delos strutted off with the marbles and I seized the knife. It was nice, but I never enjoyed it. Instead, because I did not report the lost knife as we were supposed to do, I felt like I had stolen it. Soon I lost it myself, retaining only a guilty conscience for wrongdoing and a negative mark on my good fighting record with a dive.

Fifth grade was a much more rewarding and demanding experience than wasting the year on "special projects" and coasting along in my studies as I had done in third and fourth. Miss Gertie Howell stands out as one of the best teachers I ever had. She taught me—and others—penmanship, mathematics, geography, spelling, and organizational skills. Miss Howell—in reality Mrs. Howell whose husband owned a garage in West Point—took an uncommon interest in all her students and never forgot who they were or what they did in her class. More than forty years after I took her class, I telephoned her to ask if I might drop by her home to pay my respects. "You probably don't remember me, Mrs. Howell, but I was in your fifth- grade class in 1945-46," I began. "Of course, I remember you, Harold, Harold Raley," she responded, to my astonishment recognizing my voice. "Do you recall the section we did on transportation? Well,

I still have your paper." Of course, I remembered nothing about it. She then proceeded to tell me all about my classmates that year, where they lived and what they had done with their lives, including ex-sweetheart Betty Sue and others I had all but forgotten. Although she modestly made light of her amazing gift of recall and complained that she forgot things like everybody else, the truth was she could remember the names and accomplishments of <u>every</u> student she taught in her forty-year career!

Even though I flourished under her kind, cheerful regime, I missed so many days during one reporting period that I received no grades. "Not present enough to receive a grade," or words to that effect, she wrote on my report card. The winter of 1945-46 was especially rainy and for weeks on end the bus could not make its route without sliding into a ditch or miring down hopelessly in the muddy clay ruts. There were no paved roads around West Point in those days. We students thought it was great and a few times took advantage of the calamity by playing softball in Mr. Hill's pasture near one of the slipperiest stretches of road. After playing for an hour or so, Geraldine and I would walk back home. One day the road was so bad and the weather so blustery they brought an army halftrack to get some of us home from West Point. After that Geraldine and I did not even try to go to school until the roads dried out a couple of weeks later. Nevertheless, I would summarize my experience with Mrs. Howell and Miss Parker as my best elementary school years.

My friendship with Lindall Gable continued through sixth grade. Lindall was everything I could admire in a friend. Strong, handsome, loyal, and bright, he teamed with me several times after school in a football contest against several opposing boys. The game consisted in either kicking or throwing the football farther than our opponents and eventually pushing them back and off the playing field. Lindall could throw a perfect spiral and I was not far behind. I recall one particularly hard-fought contest. Ordinarily we won fairly handily, but that day the wind was against us and the other boys backed us up to our end of the field. Determined not to let them beat us, we rallied and slowly gained ground, wind and all. At that moment my bus drove up and I had to leave Lindall alone. When I last saw him he was still battling, a lone warrior against the other team. How I admired his courage and strength! I lost touch with him after sixth grade and learned a few years later that he had joined the Air Force. Someone told me he died of a heart attack at a fairly young age.

Chapter 16:
Free Enterprise

I first became acquainted with the Grit newspaper I mentioned earlier when Armon distributed it for a short time. Grit was a rural American tradition for several generations before falling victim to television, urbanization, and modern tastes. A weekly paper, it had ample sections for women, men, and youngsters of both sexes. In its advertising it sported cures for rheumatism, fevers, and assorted ailments, as well as farm implements and other necessities of rural life. For each fifteen-cent paper sold the carrier kept three cents as his commission. The main problem was that rural newspaper routes were too long and too sparsely populated to be profitable. Add to this the headache of collecting from readers who often did not have fifteen cents and you can understand the main reason why young carriers soon got discouraged and quit.

I was determined to do better. Having been accepted as a carrier, I ordered a whopping thirty issues of Grit which I delivered on horseback. My territory extended from the Corn Road on the north almost to West Point on the south and east and nearly to the Bethlehem community to the west. It took most of the day on Saturday for Dock and me to make our round. Naturally I rode bareback. Mr. White, one of my customers near West Point, told Daddy that I rode bareback better than his boys could sit a saddled horse. The comment was flattering but not quite factual, for I was little, if any, better than an average rider. What happened was that the Whites were my last customers, and in my anxiety to get home after my final delivery, speedy Dock and I would gallop out of their yard as fast as he could take us.

Two of my customers ended up owing me for several past issues. Athel Burney, an old friend of our family, lived in a remote little house west of Crooked Creek. I am not sure Athel could read but his lonely wife lived for her weekly <u>Grit</u>. There was no road on my side of their house so that I had to leave my <u>Grit</u> bag with Dock tied up at the creek and cross a foot log to deliver Mrs. Burney's issue. With considerable embarrassment she would promise to pay me the following week. "I just forgot to ask Athel for the money." Of course, she never paid, for she knew as well as I that Athel didn't have fifteen cents to his name. The nearby Rogers family was in a similar plight. After a few weeks I decided that seventy-five or eighty cents on a good week for such an inordinate amount of riding was not worth it and I ended my association with <u>Grit</u>.

Not long afterwards I hit on a better scheme to make money. We were in the latter stages of World War II, and although militarily things were going well for us in the South Pacific, they were harder than ever for the civilian population. Vehicles were worn out, many commodities were unavailable, and daily battlefield casualties were horrific reminders of the devastating conflict. But amidst the lengthening gloom of war and the debacle of my <u>Grit</u> distributorship, there came a run of better days for me. I cannot remember either the name of the company or the way I learned about their wares—I think it was an ad in <u>Grit</u>—but they offered such products as real soap, genuine vanilla flavoring, honest to goodness candy, and other scarce items. I ordered a supply on consignment and quickly peddled it to neighbors with a fraction of the effort expended during my very forgettable <u>Grit</u> days. In classical capitalist fashion, I sold as high as the market would bear. My soap, a product very similar to the brand name Lava (I think it was called "Pumice"), was an especially hot mover, followed by the vanilla flavoring. But the other items sold well also. I made money for a few months but then sometime early in 1946 my profitable business collapsed when wartime production switched back to the civilian market and my scarce items became plentiful.

Chapter 17:
Too Soon the Victory

Let me back up a bit. Inadequate transportation hampered me throughout my business ventures. Dock and Dan were plow horses and not always available. As a result, often I had to carry my products from house to house in a cumbersome box that left my arms sore and tired. Meanwhile, Daddy had traded for an extra horse, a gaunt equine monster at least sixteen hands high. Happily for me and my business, or so I thought, he asked me if I would like to trade it for a saddle pony. Commercially and aesthetically I was delighted by the prospect, and we set out for Hartselle early in the morning of May 9, 1945, Daddy riding sleek Dock and I mounted high upon his unsightly companion, his bony body and mine separated by a frayed, faded blanket. We must have looked a little like an Appalachian version of Don Quixote and Sancho, except that I was Sancho mounted on the skeletal bag of bones called Rocinante that Don Quixote rode in the story. But I endured the jarring ride comforted by the pleasant anticipation of returning home in grand style mounted on a magnificent saddle pony.

The trip itself was one of the more memorable experiences of my early years. Since Highway 31 with its traffic was out of the question, we took the Corn Road to the Burney Mountain fork then across the mountains to Fairview in the Valley. Everything beyond was unknown country to me. I remember marveling at the lush level fields and the arrow-straight dirt road stretching before us for several miles. Daddy pointed toward Round Top Church just out of sight to the west and told me the Raleys had once lived there on "the old Raley place." I wondered and asked him why they ever left such a fertile land. "Times got hard, I reckon," he answered. He had grown up in the Valley and pointed out landmarks on the way.

We got to Hartselle by late morning and found the town caught up in happy celebration. Germany had surrendered. Stores and businesses were closed, including the mule barns where we had hoped to trade for my saddle pony. In the midst of the general joy I was dejected and—I may as well confess it—angry. Couldn't the war have lasted at least one more day, long enough for me to get my saddle horse? Daddy said there was nothing much we could do but get a bite to eat—if we could find a place open—and go back home. He explained to me that it was good that no more of our "soldier boys" would have to die. Besides, we could always trade horses another day. He was right, of course, but I wanted that pretty saddle horse in the worst way. We wandered around talking to people, for Daddy was never one to hurry. He bought me a hamburger and a cold drink in a little diner on Hartselle's main street. I think it's still there. Around mid-afternoon we started back toward the Mountain, arriving home well after dark. I felt as defeated as Germany. Eventually Daddy traded the old horse, but I never got the saddle pony I wanted.

Chapter 18: Disappointments

As keen as it was for a while, my sadness over the horse was much less grievous than my chronic disappointment with our house. After our year in the Bethlehem house with its decent roof and tongue-in-groove ceilings and floors, it was hard to accept the shell of a structure we now occupied. Except for a few loose boards it had no ceiling at all and when it rained or snowed the moisture would blow in through the cracks. Not long after we moved in Daddy decided to put a ceiling. I thought he meant the whole house, and nothing could have pleased me more at the moment. He put me to lowering the rafters, which I did in record time. But once I had finished the fireplace room, he told me to stop. "We'll leave the rest for some other time," he explained. Twenty-five years passed and the rest of the house was still an empty shell. It was a matter of considerable pain and the cause of much isolation. During my years at West Point I dared not invite classmates to my home, for even though most of them came from farm homes themselves, they would have been shocked at what they saw missing in mine. Many years later I learned that at least one of my classmates had a similar secret about her house. We shared our stories.

"I used to copy off your paper in history class, Harold," she confided. "But why?" I wanted to know. "You were a bright student." "Because many mornings I was too hungry to concentrate. Often there was no food in our house. Do you remember how thin I used to be? Well, hunger was the reason."

Then I realized how needlessly and selfishly I had worried

about my situation. My case was like the fable of the poor man who moans that he only has peeled fruit to eat—until he looks behind him and sees an even poorer man picking up and eating the peelings he has dropped.

Another problem was the roof. Already leaky when we moved in, the wooden shingles decayed rapidly over the next year and the leaks intensified. At first Momma brought out pots and pans to catch the water when it rained, but eventually there were too few to go around and the water dripped to the floor and ran through the cracks. I was often reduced to foot-stamping, impotent rage, Momma and Geraldine were indignant, and all together we created such a commotion that even unconcerned Daddy decided he had to do something to stop our yammering. One of the happiest days of my life was when we finally scraped together enough money to reroof with asphalt shingles. Mercifully, the leaks stopped, though the cracks in floors and walls and open bay window above my bed still let in wind, rain, and occasional snow. Some years later we came by a linoleum rug for the fireplace room. It was an improvement, but I remember it flapping up and down as the wind lifted it above the cracks in the floor.

The fireplace was the only heat we had, and because there was little difference in temperature between outdoors and indoors in our porous house, the water bucket in the kitchen would often freeze over on cold winter nights. Luckily, we had plenty of quilts to pile on, but it took a long time for our body heat to warm them. On cold mornings it took heroic willpower to leave the warm bed and get dressed shivering in the cold. Aunt Phoebe and Geraldine shared a bed across the room from mine. Darrell and later baby sisters Janice and Joyce slept in the other bed in the fireplace room. On the coldest nights Aunt Phoebe would heat an iron by the fireplace, wrap it in a thick cloth, and place it under the covers to warm her feet. In the morning if no live coals remained from the previous fire, Daddy would slice pine kindling to get the fireplace going again. Momma was responsible for firing up our wood stove. None of us complained very much about the cold, heat, and flies; it was just the way the world was in those days.

We had plenty of wood on the farm for fireplace and stove but cutting and hauling it to the woodpile was a major job, though because it was manly and invigorating one I much preferred to field work. From an early age I learned to swing an axe with maximum accuracy and efficiency. "Ye need to swing a axe like Earl Sandlin," Daddy instructed me. "Earl can bury a blade in the wood better than anybody I ever saw." I did the best I could, but Daddy failed to mention that Earl Sandlin (friend Tommy's father) just happened to be a huge man and that brute strength accounted for much of his impressive axe strokes.

With the crosscut we sawed oak and hickory for firewood and pine for stove wood (or "sto wood" as we called it). Luckily for our purposes, we lived in a part of the country where hardwoods merged with the pine forests characteristic of the lower South. Most of the firewood was ready to burn immediately, but all the stove wood sections had to be further split into manageable sticks. We did this by sinking a double-bladed axe in a log, then gripping the pine sections with both hands and bringing them down on the exposed blade, we split them along the seams. I hated the knots because the wood would not readily split around them. We seldom used gloves for other work, but they were necessary for splitting stove wood. Without them the pine bark would cut the toughest hands and long splinters were a constant risk. Naturally one could not get distracted else a lost finger or mangled hand could result.

Daddy was not very good about keeping a supply of stove

wood on hand, and when he was hunting or roaming and I was in school, Momma often had to cut her own wood, sometimes for the fireplace, too. I marvel that she was able to keep food on the table and clothes on our body. Not that she made her heroic efforts with silent longsuffering; she always let Daddy know about his irresponsible shortcomings. Unfortunately for us all, as I said earlier, the more she nagged, the less he tried.

One year this lack of preparation almost turned tragic. In November of 1951—I think it was the 11th—the temperature was so warm that I was barefoot. Bufus helped us gather some late corn and we all commented on the unusual weather. That night a cold front came roaring through and temperatures dropped to six or seven degrees below zero, some exaggerated it to eleven or twelve. We were caught off guard. Only a family or two in the region had primitive television sets and even with them weather forecasting was in its infancy. We huddled around the fireplace the next morning freezing behind and scorching our clothes in front. The woodpile was nearly bare, and we had to spend the day cutting and hauling firewood, something that should have been done a month sooner. We heard stories about children and older people almost freezing to death in houses like ours, but I think most of the tales were exaggerated. At any rate, Daddy, as usual, learned nothing from the experience and did nothing until it had to be done.

Chapter 19:
Mr. Carl Walker

Unlike our shell of a dwelling, the nearest house on the left side of the south road was complete down to the last detail. But until the 1940s no one ever lived there. For many years it stood as a sad monument to a lost love. Bachelor Carl Walker built the house around 1917, intending to marry his fiancée and live there after his military service. But while he was serving in World War I his sweetheart, a Reid girl if I remember correctly, married another man. For more than twenty-five years the house stood empty until Carl finally sold the farm to the Nichols family in the mid-1940s.

The Walkers kept sheep and his two spinster sisters spun wool on old-fashioned spinning wheels. The woolen garments they produced for sale were highly prized. Carl himself was a thrifty, hardworking farmer. He never owned a car and declined to have their house wired for electricity. He had another peculiarity: he claimed that he still had his baby teeth and never cut a second set. Maybe he had forgotten, but it was true that his teeth were much smaller than normal.

Carl never married but instead lived the rest of his life with his sisters in the ancestral Walker home a mile from his former dream house. For all his romantic disappointments, eccentricities, and semi-solitary life, Carl was a friendly, congenial man who loved company and conversation, especially my father's. Nor did he completely lose hope of finding a wife. Late in life he confided to Daddy that he was smitten by Mrs. Long, an attractive neighbor lady. Newly divorced, considerably younger, and mother of four young children, the lady rejected his attentions as impractical for all concerned. Mr. Walker, she reasoned compassionately and sensibly, would not know how to deal with teenage stepchildren. Besides all that, she was Catholic and could not remarry as long as her former husband was alive. It was rumored that Carl had accumulated money which he kept in trunks and boxes in his house, but apparently that was not a factor in Mrs. Long's decision. Later she and her family were to be important in my life.

Eventually Mr. Walker's sisters died almost simultaneously, and Carl was left completely alone. Daddy would drop in on him from time to time to see how he was faring. Years passed; one cold winter day he and my sister Joyce went to his house and found him dead. Daddy said Carl apparently died trying to put a log in the fireplace. Looking around, Daddy and Joyce discovered the money rumors were true. He had it stored in shoeboxes and other containers about the old two-story, twin-chimney house. Daddy told us that it had always been Carl's intention to leave his money to the American Legion, for he despised his closest relatives, Ithamar Duke and his family (which included my old enemies Monroe and Doyle). Unhappily, he never made a will, or if he did none was reported. Whereupon the Dukes swooped down on his property, piled the spinning wheels, old books and papers, and other possessions in the field and burned them. Some of the papers were hundreds of years old, according to Carl, going all the way back to England. The Dukes were interested only in the money. Ironically the antiques and other ancient possessions they burned might have been more valuable than the cash. I once asked Daddy, "Weren't you a little tempted to keep some of the money?" "No, it was his, not ours," he replied. For all his faults and indifference to family needs, Daddy was an honest man. Only one book escaped the bonfire. On our last visit Mr. Walker lent me an old book about John Wesley and his Coadjutors (I think he was a non-active Methodist) but died before I could return it. I still have it and remember him with cordial respect every time I see it.

Chapter 20:
War and Renaissance

In the winter of 1944-45 we had planted a few acres in clover. I cannot remember why except that during the war years we sometimes varied our normal rotation of corn and cotton to grow peanuts and a few other crops that the government encouraged. That spring, not long after the debacle of our horse-trading trip to Hartselle, I was scouring the field for four-leaf clovers when Momma came to tell me that President Roosevelt had died in Hot Springs, Georgia. I had never known another president and now somebody named Truman occupied the office. It was as if a piece of the sky had fallen or a quadrant of the familiar horizon had suddenly vanished.

A few months later came even more world-altering news: American pilots had dropped something called an "atomic bomb" on Hiroshima, then another on Nagasaki, and in a matter of days the South Pacific war was over. I remember the euphoria of final victory in World War II, but also the unprecedented stupor and unfocused fear we felt about a weapon that seemed to be of an incredible magnitude of destructiveness. Even Superman and Batman seemed to pale in comparison. On one of his infrequent visits Uncle Hays explained to us how the chain reaction started and spread inside the bomb. All at once it seemed to me that the very ground we stood on could no longer be trusted, for Uncle Hays, who was much better informed than we were, either gave the erroneous impression or I misunderstood him by taking his explanations to mean that the atomic reaction might continue to expand with unimaginable fury until it consumed the whole world. Indeed, some apocalyptical preachers were already saying that the end of the world spoken of in Revelation was now at hand.

But if on the one hand there were gloomy predictions about the end of humanity, on the other, the victorious soldiers now streaming home from the ends of the earth caused a resurgence of American life. To our great joy, Tolbert and Elton were among them. As I recall, for a few weeks Elton's skin was yellowish from jaundice or anti-malarial quinine, but Tolbert's condition was even more bizarre. Accustomed to the subzero temperatures of Alaska and the Aleutians, at first he could not tolerate the Alabama weather. One cold winter day in late 1945 when Grandpa Raley had a roaring fire in the fireplace and the rest of us were huddled around it, Tolbert sat in the back of the room sweating in his undershirt. As I mentioned before, for a time he talked of homesteading in Alaska, but then he met Sarah Huffstutler, married her, and settled down in Alabama.

The return of the veterans was like a human springtime after a bleak winter. Many girls—not all—had waited impatiently but loyally for their sweethearts, and now that they were back couples were marrying in record numbers. My 4-F Uncle Athel, the future minister, acquired a certain reputation and had more girlfriends than he could accommodate during the war years. In those days, church weddings in our part of the world were a rarity and in fact I cannot remember ever attending one. The most impatient couples drove over to Mississippi where blood tests were not required, or else went to a preacher or Justice of the Peace for a simple and inexpensive ceremony. Long honeymoons were out of the question for most. They simply set up housekeeping and got busy raising families.

Geraldine was among them. Only sixteen but a mature and beautiful young woman, she caught the eye of several suitors, among them Pete Ball. Pete was older than the average veteran, and instead of asking Geraldine or the other girls out on dates, he would sit by the fireplace with us and regale the family with his lurid tales about the war in Germany. He told about cutting off the fingers of dead soldiers and searching through stacks of frozen corpses for rings, watches, and valuables. The stories, some of which we doubted, horrified us and the brutality repelled Geraldine so completely that she would have nothing to do with Pete. After a while he stopped coming around and turned his attention to other girls. Eventually one consented to marry him, and neighbors said they heard her screams far into her wedding night as Pete brutalized her.

Bunk McKenzie, whom you remember from the year we lived at Bethlehem, was a more acceptable suitor despite the fact that he was eight years older than Geraldine. One morning she announced to my startled parents that she wanted to get married. They objected that she was too young, but she insisted and with some reluctance and misgiving they relented. Bunk was, after all, a good, solid man and totally devoted to Geraldine.

Their relationship had to survive at least one tense moment. I call it "the runaway Pontiac." Bunk owned a 1937 Pontiac that had been converted into a truck. Nobody in our family, including Geraldine, really knew how to drive, and to make points with her, or so I suppose, Bunk began teaching her. One day she drove solo between our house and the Johnson place. Unfortunately, when she tried to put on the brakes her foot hit the accelerator instead. In panic she pressed all the harder, lost control of the steering wheel, and bounced the Pontiac down across the cotton field until it flew over a terrace row and buried its wheels in the soft ground.

Geraldine was unhurt but embarrassed, angry at herself, and almost in tears. We all came running but before we could get there, Tootsie Russell happened along and attempted to get the car out of the field. He revved the motor to a high whine and rocked it back and forth alternating the clutch and low gear. By the time Bunk arrived blue smoke was everywhere, and the clutch was almost burned out. As patient as he was, Bunk was angry, luckily not at Geraldine but at Tootsie for the needless damage he had done to the vehicle.

I approved of Geraldine's approaching wedding much more readily than my parents—but partly for the wrong reasons. She and I were often at odds with each other, and I thought it would be good to get her out of my way. But after she left, I missed her terribly. The family seemed reduced, as indeed it was, and the old house was too quiet and empty. From then on Geraldine and I never had a cross word, but I have always regretted how often I treated her badly when we lived under the same roof. It took a separation to reveal to me—and hopefully to her—how much I loved her.

Without being a substitute for Geraldine, for Janice would soon display her own personality, her birth in May of 1946 changed the family dynamics again. Instead of a midwife, this time Momma gave birth in Dr. Cornelius's clinic at West Point. I had a good opinion of his doctoring skills for he had once treated me successfully for my painful big toe crushed by a heavy iron vessel. It was the first time I had ever been to a doctor, and it alleviated—but did not erase—my irrational fear of doctors. We must have left Darrell with relatives, for I remember Daddy and I drove our two-horse wagon to West Point. He gave me instructions to stay with the team while he went to see about Momma and the new baby sister. The hours dragged by and I got hungry. There was a fine mist and the humidity put a chill in the air. Then just as I was feeling my forlorn worst, Mrs. Howell saw me and brought over some cookies. Naturally, she wanted to know all about the new baby, information which she filed away never to be forgotten.

Janice would turn out to be a psychological stalwart, quick to express indignation over wrongdoing, fearless in her opinions, and a steadying force in times of trouble. It has always saddened me that I have been unable to live near my sisters, for every time I see them, I am comforted and reassured by their wholesomeness and strength of character. My hope has always been to be a brother worthy of their confidence and trust. More on all my siblings later.

Chapter 21:
Labor, Lightning, and the Lord

At twelve I was a full-fledged dirt farmer, able to do just about any work a grown man could do. In the spring I would occasionally cut school when we had heavy plowing or planting, but Daddy never pressured me to drop out as other fathers did. Many still had the nineteenth-century idea that once a boy learned "readin' an' figurin'" he had enough schooling. And the same old-fashioned philosophy applied to daughters, too. Once school was out, the hard summer work started. I enjoyed the stalk cutting in early spring, for I could ride on the thumping horse-drawn machine and pretend I was driving a tank and knocking down trees in Europe. The plowing and planting were harder, but the job I dreaded was chopping and hoeing the cotton. Throughout the summer the crabgrass aggressively tried to take over the cotton rows, and we, particularly Momma and I, were just as determined to defeat it. Picking cotton and gathering corn were also hard work, but by then the weather was cooler and we had the satisfaction of seeing the reward of our labors and in good years the anticipation of a little money to spend. By late July we "laid by" the crops, which meant the hoeing and plowing were over and we had a few weeks of relative rest before the harvesting commenced.

Some farmers found themselves losing the crabgrass war. The year I was twelve it was Morris Sammons, he of the seventy-five aspirins. Morris and Lena were farming the Hale place where I was born, but he knew very little about cotton. For years he had driven a big semi, spending his leisure time boozing and, by his own admission, womanizing. Morris sent Daddy a frantic request for help with his cotton. Daddy was already busy with several tasks, so he told me to go help Morris hoe his cotton. Later Morris confessed to Daddy that when a twelve-year old boy with a short-handled hoe showed up he thought for sure his cotton was lost. But once we started to work, he had trouble keeping up with me. By afternoon of the second day we had the grass just about whipped and Morris was convinced of my hoeing ability.

But about three in the afternoon a towering black thundercloud formed with a curious yellowish-green rain band. We knew the signs: probably a hailstorm. Sure enough, before long we saw sheets of rain and hail lashing Bufus's fields to the north. We ran to the house and not long after we got inside big hailstones started crashing on the tin roof. I was standing by the fireplace when suddenly lightning struck it, hit me like a hammer, and sent tongues of fire throughout the house and out into the yard. I remember the ends of my hair snapping and popping and my ears ringing from the thunderous pop. For a moment the air around me was filled with tiny exploding stars. Morris was concerned but I assured him I was all right, even though the ringing continued for a few minutes. The cotton was ruined so I took my little hoe and went home. In later years I would tell people, exaggerating a little for effect, that I had been struck twice by lightning and that it would not be wise to stand next to me in a thunderstorm.

The lightning, atomic devastation, and loneliness I experienced after Geraldine married turned me more introspective the summer I turned twelve. I was reading more than ever, particularly two histories of the United States written with a strong pro-Southern bias. At about age ten I became fascinated with the Civil War and imagined myself flanked by brave Confederate cavalry whom I would someday lead to glorious victory. Years would pass before I discovered that my Great-Grandfather William Raley and his brother James actually fought on the Union side (1st Alabama Cavalry, USA).

In any case, my thoughts ran deep and troubled that summer and when yearly revival began at Dough Ball the message resonated to my searching spirit. One night I went up and knelt before the preacher's podium—there was no altar to speak of— and with several of my neighbors, young and old, gave my heart to Jesus Christ. My Christian life would take many odd turns and suffer many reverses in times to come, but of all the decisions I ever made in my years on the old Corn Road surely that was my finest.

But I confess now after all these years that there was an element of disappointment in my conversion. I was expecting an enrapturing, mind-sapping emotional flood to sweep over me, as they had taught me to expect "getting saved" to be. Instead, my mind became clearer as I experienced a measured, enlightening perception that took me outside and above my primal feelings and caused me to understand the significance of my conversion much more acutely than I felt it at first. And it was this understanding that gave rise later to appreciation and feeling. I said nothing about the experience, afraid that others might think I had not really been saved. Without being a congregation of Holy Rollers, Dough Ball was sympathetic to them and had its share of shouters and even a few tongues-speakers. Our religion was primarily emotional.

The two preachers who had run the revival baptized their crop of converts in Flint Creek close to Lacon. At twelve and all of ninety pounds, I posed no problem to the preacher whose name may have been King. I remember he had a tiny black hole just behind his right ear. The lady in front of me, though, was a different matter. She probably more than doubled me in weight, and when the preacher took her under, he could not lift her. The other pastor rushed to his aid and the two of them managed to raise her as she gasped and spat out muddy creek water. We changed our clothes in separate bush patches for men and women and rode back to Dough Ball on the back of a big truck. For a few weeks after that I read the Scriptures with all the zeal of a new convert. My parents respected my new condition and did not complain when I left pea-picking to read the Bible. Since I was a precocious reader, they soon asked me—at twelve—to lead the teenage, or "Young People," group. I did the best I could and since Mary and Armon were solidly behind me, had no trouble with a class older than I was.

Momma did not share our Dough Ball faith and her rejection of Baptist doctrine and similar beliefs caused deep resentment on Daddy's part, especially after he became a Church Deacon. Consequently, although both my parents were believers in their own way, they kept their beliefs to themselves and as a family we had no religious life to speak of. The Hoopers had been Methodist, but over the years Momma had come to believe in the teachings of self-proclaimed "Apostle" Herbert W. Armstrong and the Worldwide Church of God. She was won over, it seems, by the accuracy of some of his early predictions about Germany, particularly its resurgence after the devastation of World War II when many thought it would never again be a major economic power. (But if he was perceptive about global matters, Armstrong was apparently far less so in personal matters. In his old age he married his secretary who sued the Church for its assets after his death and helped plunge it into a destructive schism. Before Momma's death, however, the contrite and courageous new church leaders publicly acknowledged Armstrong's errors, repented of the church heresies, and led their followers back to mainline Protestant theology.) Momma kept her beliefs mostly to herself during Daddy's lifetime but did allow me to read some of the strange tracts she received through the mail. For some reason I remember several called "News from Belgium and the Belgian Congo." She told me that before their marriage she made it clear to Daddy that she did not choose to worship as he did.

Although he talked very little about it to me, or anyone else for that matter, I think Daddy always took her attitude to be disloyalty to him and, much to her resentment, finally stopped asking her to go to church with the rest of family. Not that she wanted to go, but I suppose she wanted to be asked. I am sure it was one of several differences that soured their marriage and caused both much unhappiness. Although I sided with Momma on several points, on this one I think she was in the wrong. Tolerant flexibility for the sake of family harmony would have been better for us all. After all, East Battleground theology was generally in line with the teachings of other Protestant churches and there were many solid Christians in the congregation. Momma, however, had the dogmatic nature of the "true believer" who would no sooner yield on the smallest point than she would on the greatest. But let me add this disclaimer: I was not privy to their arguments about church and religion, for in so many ways they were very private persons. Therefore, anything I say or any judgment I am tempted to make stands a good chance of being wrong, or at least uninformed.

Speaking of misguided Armstrongs, it was about that time that Ed Armstrong started attending Dough Ball. Probably in his forties, but with a teenage mind, Ed was the lusty, tongue-tied, repulsively ugly, and dimwitted nephew of the Hendricks family, neighbors to Uncle Bemis. My cousin Mary, now a beautiful, happy teenager, soon became the unwilling object of his attentions. Well, to be truthful about it, pesky, affection-starved Ed lusted after any girl who would look twice at him. So obnoxious and persistent he became that the neighborhood girls concocted a plan to deflect his unwelcome attentions.

They dressed one of the short, slender, and willing Gatlin brothers in female attire, outfitted him with wig, heels, and makeup and took him/her to church. Ed approached and was delighted when the new "girl" smiled and responded to him. She even agreed to let eager old Ed walk her home after church. He was delirious with delight and asked for another date. The girl demurely declined, stating that she did not want to rush things, or words to that effect. Mary and the other girls followed at a distance, dying with laughter. The charade did not last very long, and when Ed discovered that he had been duped, his feelings were hurt, and he did not pester Mary and her friends again. Ed was unaware of his mental and physical limitations, but his hopes were essentially those of a normal man. He dreamed in vain but talked incessantly of finding a wife and leading a normal life. I felt a great rush of pity for him and befriended him as best I could. A few years later he had to be confined to a rest home.

As we often did in early fall before our crops were ready to harvest, we hired out to pick cotton that year, this time for Bill McCravy, whose farm lay across the Corn Road from Brasher Sheats' place. My hope was to pick enough cotton to buy a dark red Schwinn bicycle complete with basket that the McCravys had priced at six dollars. I had longed for a bike ever since Charles Rowell taught me to ride at Bethlehem. Cotton was three dollars a hundred that year, so with two hundred pounds I could close the deal. Not an easy task, for I was not the best cotton picker around. Momma believed the cotton should go into the sack picked free of burrs and debris, and she instilled this meticulous habit in me. Other pickers were not so picky, including Bunk who could easily top three hundred pounds and his father Bill who, people claimed, could weigh up over four hundred in a day.

I made a good start and by dinner (lunch) had well over a hundred pounds on my ledger. The bicycle was getting closer to reality. But by mid-afternoon my energy was running low. The picksack strap had rubbed my shoulder and neck raw, and without kneepads my knees were almost too sore to touch the ground. (Because I was never able to pick for hours stooped over in the classic cotton picker stance, I spent much time on my knees, which slowed me even more.) By four o'clock though, I had broken my personal record with a hundred eighty-three pounds. Only seventeen more to go! But when we went back to the rows for the last time, I was too tired to do very much more. I picked as long as I could, but then despite encouraging words from friends and family, in utter weariness I lay back on my sack and looked up at the sky. Just before quitting time I rallied for a last little flurry; then as the sun was setting, we threw our sacks across our shoulder and headed for the scales. Bunk, Geraldine, and Daddy had bulging sacks; mine was ridiculously puny but I was too tired to care. When it was all over, I think Bunk had picked three hundred twenty-five pounds, Geraldine and Daddy totaled around two hundred fifty each, and I had—with exactly seventeen pounds at final weighing—two hundred! Hallelujah! We closed the deal and the bike was mine! I held it all the way home on the back of Bunk's old Pontiac.

Chapter 22:
Driving and Peddling

For the briefest time we owned an automobile, a four-cylinder 1928 green Chevrolet, which like Bunk's Pontiac had been cut down and converted into a truck. I was enthralled, for I had never given up my childhood dream of owning a car. I have forgotten exactly how Daddy came into possession of the vehicle, but I do remember driving it a few times. Two events stand out. The first was the day I drove the old Chevy down the Corn Road to Ebenezer community. Daddy, Tootsie Russell, and perhaps one or two other men were my passengers. Everything went fine until we got to Ebenezer. By then I was negotiating the bumps and ruts with an emerging expertise and feeling pretty sure of myself. But just as I was about halfway across the lane on a left turn onto Highway 31 a car topped the hill and I let the old truck roll back down the grade. I was too shaken to drive any further that day, so Tootsie with his toothy grin and horse laugh took over the rest of the way.

A few days later we gathered beans, corn, peas, and other vegetables for a peddling run to Hartselle and Decatur the next morning. The logistics involved hauling the vegetables to Uncle Tolbert's house that night. Everything went according to plan until I rounded the curve at Brasher Sheats' house (I was driving again). Then motor went dead as I let up on the accelerator and the old truck coasted to a stop. We pushed and cranked for an hour or so, but it was no use. I think we walked on to Felton's house and he came back with us to inspect the Chevy. A slipped timing chain was his correct diagnosis. We lost most of the vegetables and not long afterwards the truck as well. Daddy traded or sold it to Bufus and we went back to the horse and wagon era for five or six more years.

Just before we got rid of the old Chevrolet, Cousin Mary and I drove it over to Uncle Tolbert's to help him hoe his cotton. We worked two and half days and it was during that time that I got to know Grandpa Raley better. After all their children married and moved out, Grandpa and Grandma Raley left their place in Athel's care and moved in with Tolbert. He came out to help us hoe and we had long conversations about life. Grandpa seemed wiser and gentler than I remembered, and I enjoyed the time with him.

We finished the hoeing and Tolbert paid us seven dollars apiece. Tired of grassy cotton, Mary and I cranked up the old Chevy and happily started home, but on the way to Battleground we had to ford Kid Branch, a shallow stream without a bridge at that time. My wadded bills apparently worked their way out of my pocket, fell out during the bumpy crossing, and dropped through gaping holes in the floorboard. I got home and searched frantically for my money, but it was gone. Later I heard that some local boys had found money at Kid Branch, mine no doubt.

After we traded the Chevrolet, I continued to street peddle in the summers for several years but only in the company of Uncle Bufus. The day before our run the family would pick and gather the several varieties of peas, beans, roasting ears of corn ("roseneers"), cucumbers, okra, and whatever else was marketable in Hartselle and Decatur. Bufus would show up around daylight in the green Chevrolet and we were off, stopping for a few minutes here and there to take on more vegetables or to talk with friends.

You rode with Bufus at your own peril. His eyesight was dismal and to the panic of his passengers and frequent outrage of other drivers he strayed back and forth across the highway. "By gannies, I pay taxes on both sides of the road," he explained. "By gannies" was his favorite preface to all his strongly felt statements. He compensated for his erratic steering by driving so slowly that the highway patrol ticketed him twice that I remember, though not on our peddling runs. He was also a chain smoker, but because he was busy driving and could not roll his own cigarettes, that job fell to me. I became quite the expert, though of course I never smoked myself. And there were other hazardous peculiarities about his driving. Bufus always waited until the last possible moment to shift gears going up steep hills, and as a result the engine often stalled, and the truck would roll backwards into trees or ditches. It did no good to advise him to shift sooner; that was just the way life was with Bufus. Many swore "never again" after one of these harrowing experiences, but most of us relented and took our chances anew. After all, he had a car and we didn't. Going down an incline, he always cut the engine off and coasted, "to save gas," he explained. I got into the same habit because of him and discovered that in mountainous country I could almost double my gas mileage. Of course, coasting was illegal and could result in a fine if the police caught you doing it. But while we were concerned with right and wrong, we considered legalities without obvious links to these absolutes to be mere nuisances that we avoided.

Flats and mechanical breakdowns were everyday hazards with the decrepit old Chevrolet. Gasoline fed by gravity into the carburetor from the gas tank located just in front of the dash. (Imagine the safety implications of a similar placement today.) The floating gauge was primitively accurate, for you could see the fuel sloshing around it as it bobbed up and down like a fishing cork in the water. I left out a pertinent detail: there was a quart-size slave container next to the carburetor that first received the fuel from the main tank. On at least one trip the main gravity line got clogged and every four or five miles the truck would sputter and die. Whereupon Bufus would siphon off a quart from the tank, refill the slave container, pour a little in the carburetor to prime it, and hand crank the engine to life again. With his snail-like highway speed and frequent stops we were only a little swifter than a good team of horses.

Later Bufus traded "up" and got a bigger truck, a 1931 ton and half Chevrolet. But there was a problem: it would not stay in high, or fourth, gear. Bufus devised a simple but comical solution. He cut a stick the length from the dash overhang to the gear lever and when it was time to shift into high, he would insert the stick as a prop. It worked for as long as he kept the truck. Needless to say, Bufus's stick was the subject of much derision. Of course, Bufus was indifferent to criticism and interested only in what worked for him. For him aesthetics always took a back seat to pragmatic practicality.

But if Bufus was innovative in a rudimentary way his temper often clouded his intelligence. Once when the Chevrolet failed to crank, he beat the carburetor with a hammer for its obstinacy. Remarkably enough, the chastised truck then started but so did rumors about Bufus's mental stability.

One of Bufus's frustrations may have been the crude way he was discouraged from attending Dough Ball. For a short time after his marriage to Irene he became a pillar of the congregation. But before long, his divorce and remarriage became an issue and Bufus left in a huff never to return. Exactly what his beliefs were, I cannot say, but I remember one little indictment he made of Christians in general. "By gannies, if we really believed in the life hereafter we wouldn't mourn when Christians die. The truth is, many people really don't believe in the next life when you get right down to it." He had many peculiarities and endured much gossip, but I spent enough time with him to know his heart, and it was good.

He was at his entertaining and profitable best in the streets of Hartselle and Decatur. Ringing a cowbell, yelling out the virtues of our vegetables, and dancing a jig for the housewives, he brought them out in droves to laugh, banter, and buy. One of my jobs was to knock on all the doors of those who did not respond to his street antics. That part I hated, but I have to say that Bufus knew what he was doing, for many of the women were, I suppose, persuaded to come out by my childish looks and practiced good manners. The other job of moving the truck to a new location was more to my liking.

We usually ate at the Farmers Café in Decatur and invariably ordered the beef stew. It was steamy and spicy and since we rarely had beef at home, I considered it a real delicacy. Bufus would top off his meal by drinking a quart of whole milk from the bottle. Then with a hearty belch, a thunder of flatulence, and a fresh cigarette he was ready to hit the streets again. He explained his fart philosophy: "By gannies, they's more room on the outside than on the inside." By three o'clock or so we had only odds and ends left from our produce. Then Bufus would negotiate the remainders with groceries or storekeepers. Any leftovers he took home for Aunt Irene to cook, or if they were too far gone, for the hogs. He never discarded anything, no matter how stale.

Nor did he ever forget or forgive any money owed him. Eventually times got too hard even for thrifty Bufus and Irene and they sold the Hooper farm and moved away to Chicago. There they saved every penny they could and ten years later had enough money to come home to Alabama and settle in Hartselle. Upon his return he asked L.E. Shaneyfelt, Mary's husband, to drive him to a certain address in Hartselle. L.E. reported the incredible conversation he overheard. "Do you remember the vegetables I sold you that time?" Bufus asked the man of the house. The former customer recalled the transaction and Bufus dunned him: "You owe me thirty-seven cents." The startled man paid him.

On the other hand, Bufus could be a bit more forgetful about what he owed. Once I picked peas all day for him. Late that afternoon his brother from Mississippi came to visit, and in his excitement Bufus forgot to pay me. But his generosity more than offset those oversights. He gave me free room and board one summer in Chicago where I was working to raise money for my second year of college. Because his own children were not interested in education, he said, he wanted to help me with mine. He went on to tell me that if I ever needed money to continue my studies, I had only to let him know. I was moved and thanked him, knowing that for Bufus a promise made was a promise he would keep.

Bufus himself had an almost mystical reverence for learning. Illiterate until he was eighteen, he provoked consternation in an elementary school teacher by showing up one day and asking to start first grade. "But you can't come to school," the teacher protested. "You're too old!" "Is there a law against it?" Bufus wanted to know. "Well, no, I reckon not," the teacher admitted, "I just never heard of such a thing." Bufus insisted and persisted and the teacher finally relented. He studied with a vengeance and in six weeks progressed all the way through sixth grade, at which point he had to drop out to return to work. He asked me many questions about college, in particular about my chemistry classes. When I told him that common table salt (NaCl) was a combination of two chemicals that consumed separately were hazardous to human health, he started to look on me not as the little boy who had picked his peas and rolled his cigarettes but as that special kind of human being called a "college-educated" man.

But his dark side also emerged from time to time. About the time of the carburetor beating, Bufus chained wayward Bertha to a tree, or so my Uncle Athel Raley reported. In fact, the two temper tantrums may have been products of the same rage. To a certain degree, Bufus had good reason to be exasperated with Bertha. For the older she got, the more delinquent and immoral she became, finally reaching the point of running off with men. Her behavior probably reminded him of his first wife's immoralities. As soon as she was released, or worked free from the tree, she left home for good, like her brothers before her. I saw her only twice after that. On a March morning several years later, she knocked on my door in Chicago. Shivering from the cold and hemorrhaging from an unaided childbirth, she asked me to take her to a doctor. The office was still closed, and I left her there reluctantly but at her insistence, trembling and half dead on the steps. The last time I saw her was at Aunt Irene's funeral in Hartselle in 1975. She had survived everything abuse, an immoral life, and bad judgment had brought her—treacherous lovers, broken marriages, multiple pregnancies, miseries—and seemed to be finally at peace with herself. She even said respectful words about her stepmother and chatted pleasantly with me about the old days back on the Corn Road.

Chapter 23:
From Empire to Romance

Even though I enjoyed my bicycle immensely and took proud care of it, there were only a few places where I could ride it. After Gene moved away and Daddy traded the green Chevrolet to Bufus, I started spending more of my free time fishing and exploring the woods for miles around. My air rifle had long since worn out and I graduated to a Springfield .22 squirrel rifle that Daddy kept in addition to his shotguns. Not that I did very much hunting with it. Occasionally I would shoot a rabbit or squirrel if I just happened to spot one, but for the most part I carried the rifle for the feeling of power and protection it gave me in my wanderings, especially against snakes. Once when Gene and I were roaming in the woods I shot into a nest and killed a mother squirrel. I felt terrible about what I had done, especially when I climbed up and discovered two little squirrels in the nest. Gene and I took them home and fed them peanuts. I taught mine to ride like a little opossum in the bib of my overalls. There he would sit head out alert to everything that was going on. Everybody was impressed and I was delighted and vowed to keep my unusual pet, but when Bobby Huffstutler's older brother offered me several dollars—either $3 or $5—for him as a gift to Luther Bates's daughter Rosalee who was to become his wife, greed overcame my affection and I sold him. I think Gene sold his squirrel at the same time. From then on, I took no more pleasure in killing wild animals and hated myself later for selling my little friend.

Besides the rifle, I also had come into possession of a

homemade Bowie knife which I carried in a holster strapped to a wide, double-buckled belt. I spent hours trying to throw the knife the way the cowboys did in the movies, but the handle was too heavy for the blade and I was not very successful. But it did serve to clean fish—and as a backup weapon should my rifle fail. I meant to go down fighting against my mythical enemies.

We lived well south of the normal range of birch trees. On maps they barely extended south of the Virginia border. But apparently no one told the birch trees and in ages past a few had marched down the Appalachian slopes and one or two were left on Burney Mountain and surrounding hills. The inner bark of the smaller branches has a tart, sugary, mint-like taste that we highly prized. We would cut short sections and carry them in our pockets until the bark was gone and the sticks were dry. Once after a "birch bark" run on Burney Mountain I stooped to drink from a small spring. Looking up after slaking my thirst, I saw with a thrill of terror a black snake staring at me not more than three feet away. I grabbed for my rife, but the black racer was swifter and was gone before I could aim. I fired randomly a couple of times anyway to relieve my fright and frustration.

Immense perils surrounded me in my imagination. I fanced myself not wandering through the relatively tame forests of Morgan or Cullman County but in the dangerous uncharted wilderness of the Northwest Territories or in case civilization had come too close, the even more primitive vastness of Siberia where weapons were essential for survival. I drew up a map of an imaginary realm and made periodic visits to inspect its boundaries. These I marked by tying strings to certain trees and with each visit extended my territory like an aggressing Roman empire. Eventually one boundary stretched westward almost to Bethlehem and another to the Burney Mountain several miles to the north. I claimed only pockets of territory to the east and south because of too many intrusive farms and dwellings. One criterion for the unity and cohesiveness of my mythical kingdom was the ability to traverse it without crossing open fields or pastures and exposing myself to human view. On those days set aside for my secretive imperial inspection I was careful not to let people see me.

Although I was the ruler of my kingdom, deadly imaginary enemies, dangerous beasts, and perplexing mysteries filled it. I read books like Jack London's <u>The Call of the Wild</u> and many Western and Canadian adventure stories and toward the end of my imperial period came across the Conan series which stimulated my imagination to an even higher pitch. Under the influence of the savagely strong Conan I began to wander around the countryside at night, sometimes running long distances on desperate quests, and my imperial vision underwent a significant shift. If placid farmers toiled in the fields by day with their puny plows and dumb mules, by night the land reverted to its real nature: a domain of vile monsters, exotic beauties, and sinister mysteries. Sometimes I would be away for hours and my parents would ask where I had been. "Oh, just out wandering around a little," or "just out possum hunting," I would answer unconvincingly as they looked skeptically at each other.

Then as quickly as it began, my interest in empire building waned and vanished. I went on to more interesting teenage activities, but some of the places that I had especially cherished, like the Seven Falls and Sharprock area where Daddy had also played and explored as a boy, continued to attract me long after I abdicated my imperial claims. On a nostalgic whim years later—I must have been about twenty-five—I revisited one of my old "boundaries" on Burney Mountain. The markers were gone, rotted away. My empire was history.

About the time the Dinglers moved away, a man and his wife from Hartselle started showing movies on Thursday night at

Battleground school and for several months I dutifully walked the four or five miles through the woods to see them. I usually went early to have to have time to visit Geraldine, Bunk, and little nephew Larry. My back route took me by the Cook house, past a former neighbor, Enos Brown, across a creek, and along Bill McCravy's place. The old road emerged at Brasher Sheats' place a half mile or so from Geraldine's house near the schoolhouse. After the movie, admission a quarter, I went home along the Corn Road, hoping someone would give me a ride. Usually, not always, they did. The movies included a twelve or sixteen-week serial. I remember the story line of only one film. A young woman worked for a handsome executive who never noticed his mousy secretary. Meanwhile she pined away in hopeless love for him. One day for some reason he removed her thick glasses and noticed to his surprise and astonishment how beautiful she was. Before long the transformation was complete and mousy girl became lovely lady. He declared his love, she confessed hers, and all ended happily. The sweet romanticism gave me much to dream about as I walked home along the moonlit Corn Road.

The more interesting teenage activities included a new romantic interest, for unlike Mr. Carl Walker whom Mrs. Long and her family rebuffed, I was accepted and for a time became something of a regular visitor in their home. The main attraction for me was Mrs. Long's older daughter Carol a couple of years younger than I, but Doug and Larry, both close to me in age, were also good friends. Martha was younger. Carol was the all-American girl, and many of the qualities I had admired in Melba Jean I found in her also. Athletic, bright, pretty, energetic, and good natured, Carol—and indeed all the Longs—took the breakup of the family in a way I can only describe as noble. All the children pitched in to help their mother whom they loved and respected with a greater tenderness than I had ever experienced in a family.

Doug, Larry, and I spent many hours swimming and playing ball outside, and inside amusing ourselves with monopoly and other games. One night the boys and I camped out in a tent near the house for an all-night monopoly game. Once or twice Mrs. Long came out to check on us and bring us food. My infatuation with Carol soon cooled but not so much that I was indifferent to her emotionally. Besides, not only were we good friends but she was becoming prettier by the month during the time they were our neighbors.

It was about that time that a party was announced at the Shoemake house near Panama and all the young people for miles around were invited. Carol naturally wanted to go and hinted that she would like for me to escort her—on foot of course. I was delighted but had to clear things with Mrs. Long. That dear wise lady neutralized me with trust. "Harold," she said to me, "I know that I can trust you and that Carol will be safe with you." Carol's safety was not exactly the first thought that came to my fifteen-year-old mind, but it became my dominant concern, for there was no way I was going to betray that great lady for whom I had limitless respect. Carol and I enjoyed the party and I saw to it that she got home safe and sound. We had a few other fun-filled dates and an exciting but innocent kiss or two, the first for me and, so she confessed, for her too.

Around the Fourth of July that year Douglas, Larry, a couple of other boys, and I somehow got our hands on a few sticks of dynamite complete with fuses. We cut the sticks into quarter sections, inserted a fuse in each, and proceeded to have the noisiest and most dangerous fireworks display we had ever seen. On a dare we slipped to within a few yards of Floyd Bibb's grist mill at the Burney Mountain intersection and set off a quarter stick, running unseen through the tall corn before it exploded. When it did, it almost brought down the near corner of Floyd's mill. He was, reportedly, infuriated, but we were long gone down the Corn Road towards Battleground by then. Eventually and luckily, our dynamite ran out without injury to any of us, and we were reduced to dueling with giant firecrackers and roman candles. Doug caught me stomach center with a candle shot, burning a round hole in my shirt but causing no injury. I chased him with two giant firecrackers exploding at his heels.

After our spectacular fireworks battles were over, we had started home from Battleground when we spotted an obviously drunk man lying under an apple tree near the road. Approaching with some trepidation and peering into his face, I announced that it was Garland Ball, one of Pete's kinsmen. We spread the rumor and a few days later got word that a very angry Garland Ball was refuting the slander right and left and threatening to get even with the liar that accused him. Daddy told me that Garland didn't drink at all. "Well, it looked like him to me," I answered defensively. I was probably wrong, but it was an honest error that came from looking at the man's face from an odd angle. People assured me that it was probably Bill McCravy, he of the bicycle, known like his brother Dewey for occasional alcoholic binges.

Although I was never aware of her plight, nor did her children speak of it, her husband's desertion must have left Mrs. Long in financial straits. After a couple of years, she got a job in the West Point High School lunchroom and moved there to be close to her work. Eventually she found better work and moved to Cullman where Carol and Martha finished high school. Doug was graduated with me in 1953 and I am not sure Larry completed high school. I was destined to have a few more contacts with Carol and Mrs. Long, one of them a truly bizarre experience. Even though it took place several years after the events described here, let me tell it anyway. In 1960 I was in

Mexico City, perfecting my Spanish skills. I knew absolutely no one, and spent my time wandering the streets, reading, going to movies, and absorbing the culture. My last day in Mexico I noticed a crowd of people gathered around an automobile illegally stopped on a busy boulevard. Moving closer, I could see that the occupants were Americans and that the car had an Alabama tag. You cannot imagine my astonishment when I recognized Mrs. Long, Carol, and a young man, Jerry Desoto, who was Carol's new husband. They were lost; Jerry was half blind because he had broken his glasses and the brakes on their car were worn to the metal after the long trip over the high Mexican mountains. To add to their miseries, their hotel reservations turned out to be bogus and they had no place to stay. They were tired, hungry, and none of them knew Spanish. Even though Jerry's surname was Spanish, his family had lived for generations in Louisiana and knew only English.

Mrs. Long was a woman of great faith, and she was convinced, as were Carol and Jerry, that my appearance at that critical moment was providential. I found them a hotel, got the car parked in its garage, and ushered them into a restaurant for a long, excellent meal. I was scheduled to return to the United States the very next morning and did not see them again in Mexico. But years later I met up with Carol and Jerry at a West Point class reunion and learned that everything had gone well with them after my help. That was the closest I ever was to being a hero. I thanked God that I was there for them. It had to be by divine intervention. Mexico City had at the time 15-20 million people. What are the odds, then, that a neighbor and friend would show up—by now fluent in Spanish—to help them? Every time I think about it, I can only agree with Mrs. Long, Carol, and Jerry that it was nothing short of miraculous. I guess it taught me that God can use anybody for his purposes.

Chapter 24:
The Unraveling Years

Despite Daddy's lackluster farming habits and frequent diversions, we did relatively well on the farm until 1949. He was right about the land; it was fertile and mostly level enough for easy cultivation. In 1946, I believe it was, Daddy gave Geraldine and me the last six rows of cotton in the east field. As it turned out, these were the best rows of all, and Geraldine and I ended up with several hundred pounds of cotton. But Daddy was a man of his word and let us keep the money we made.

Even though 1948 was a good crop year, it marked a turning point in Daddy's health. He had been bothered by bad teeth for several years, and one day he unhitched the horses and announced that he had to see a doctor. The diagnosis was not good: his abscessed teeth had introduced toxins into his system and would have to be pulled. That summer he lost all his bottom teeth except one. Not only did his facial appearance change but his weight suddenly ballooned to well over two hundred pounds. Until then he had been tall, slender, and handsome. All at once he became pudgy around the midriff and at thirty-nine his face began to take on the shrunken appearance of a much older man.

Not long afterwards another calamity overtook him. Attempting to lift a heavy crate with a squirming pig inside, he hurt his back. The condition became chronic and only visits to the chiropractor would relieve the pain. On certain days he was bent nearly double and could barely walk leaning on a staff. It was painful to see this once powerful man reduced to near helplessness. As for me, I made a vow never to do the foolish things he and his brothers did to ruin their back or rupture themselves, as several of them had done. That vow and a physiology more like my mother's than his has kept me, thanks be to God, so far free of similar problems.

It was about that time that I got together enough money to buy a motorbike from my friend and classmate Edward Cornelius, of the West Point Cornelius family. As I recall, I paid Ed thirty-five dollars for it and Tommy Sandlin and I walked to West Point to pick it up. At first the bike exceeded my expectations. It was powerful enough to haul Tommy and me up the steepest hills and before long boys from miles around gathered at my house to ride it. They were impressed, and I was fairly bursting with ownership pride. But before many weeks had passed, the bike began to lose its power. Uncle Felton said it probably needed rings. I bought the rings, took the motor apart, and rebuilt it as best I could. But the problems continued and before long, it would not start at all. A new sparkplug did not help. I spent many hours trying to discover what was wrong but finally decided that somehow the magneto had gone bad. Eventually I removed the motor and rode it as an ordinary bicycle. My earlier bicycle had worn out years before.

I had a chance to trade the bike and motor for a sleek, saddle-broken filly. I made the deal, thinking that at last I had the saddle pony I had wanted since World War II. The only problem—but an irreparable one—was that she was half blind from a whiplash that previous owner Dude Gray had given her. It angered me so much that I wanted to take a whip to him. Daddy felt the same way. But even with her handicap she was a gallant little horse that did her best to please. But she would fix her imperfect vision on anything moving in front of her—car or horse—and run at stumbling, breakneck speed to follow it. After she did this a time or two, I admitted sadly that she was too blind for safe riding.

Ed Powell, Raymond Powell's son, expressed an interest in the horse and offered to trade me a suit for her. Wilburn Blackwood and I took the little mare to his house to consummate the deal. But then strange things started happening. Ed came out and talked for a few minutes, indicating the trade was in order. But then abruptly he went inside. We waited nearly an hour with the horse, but Ed did not come out again. Finally, I overheard his older brother cursing and saying, "Are they still here? Didn't you tell them we aint gonna trade?" I got the hint and we left. Some people said that Ed was a little off, but that was the first and only time I had ever seen him behave oddly. Eventually we traded away the sad little horse, but I cannot recall for what. It may have been to old friend Donald Cheatham.

Or it could have been for a very old mule. At any rate it was about that time that Daddy told me to finish plowing the cotton on the lower west side of our farm while he went off somewhere. There were two or three rows left when I noticed that the mule was beginning to lose her balance. Suddenly she fell and for a long time could not get to her feet again. I unhitched her and when finally, she lurched to her feet took her to the barn. When Daddy came home, I told him what had happened and that I was unable to finish the last few rows. He looked her up and down, patted her gently, and said, "She's gonna die purty soon. She's done all the plowin' she can."

Despite his prediction, however, the old mule rallied and lived another week or two. She even seemed sturdy enough to plow a little more, and I think I hitched her to the same plow I left in the field the day she fell. She held up fine and we finished the plowing. Afterwards I took her back to the barn and was preparing to lead her down to the spring when Wilburn Blackwood showed up. "Let me ride the ole son-of-a-bitch," he said with his customary profanity. "You can't, Wilburn, she'll fall on you," I told him. "Naw, hell no, I can ride her!" he insisted. Daddy told him the same thing, but Wilburn was determined to ride her. "Let him go," Daddy told me with a shrug. Then turning to Wilburn, "But you be careful. It's steep down yonder by the spring."

Wilburn left—and didn't come back. After a while I went looking for him and found the old mule on the side of the hill against an oak tree with her feet in the air. Wilburn was nowhere to be seen. Daddy and I managed to get her back on her feet, but she died that night. We disposed of the carcass in the customary way by hitching our mule Red to a long log chain looped around the mule's neck and dragging her to a deep ditch between our land and the Evans place. There we covered the carcass to keep out dogs and varmints and let nature have its rotting way. Winter rains washed away the dirt and revealed her white rib cage.

I ran across Wilburn a week or two later and asked him what happened. He spat out a long stream of brown snuff juice and explained. "That damn mule fell, and I thought I'd killed the ole sonuvbitch. So, I run off through the woods."

The Blackwoods were a family of degenerates who were neighbors of ours on several occasions. Some of the more malicious gossips said that redheaded Wilburn, the only son and child, had incestuous relations with his mother Nellie. That part I didn't believe, but I witnessed other things that caused me to be always on my guard around Wilburn and his father Algie. The latter, a tall, lean man with intense black eyes was obsessed with knives and cutting people. He would giggle whenever he thought of the prospect. "He-he, I reckon I'd jist take my knife and cut a feller's guts out, he-he!" I was always on my guard around him. Perverse where sex was concerned, he believed that any woman who even said hello to him was advertising her availability and he was prone to act accordingly. For his part, Wilburn also lusted after females—animal or human—but preferred arson as an everyday pastime. As we walked through fields and woods, he would secretly toss matches into the leaves and grass and smoke would rise behind us. No amount of threats or scolding deterred him. People accused him of burning a neighbor's barn. As for Nellie, she slipped around like a ghost. Sometimes we would look up and there she was, at almost any hour of the day, standing in the doorway. And once there she would not leave until Momma fed her. Feeding the Blackwood's, however, was no simple or small affair. All three, especially Nellie and Wilburn, had bottomless stomachs and although Wilburn was slender and Nellie almost petite in size, they could put away amazing quantities of food. Indeed, they did not stop eating until everything on the table was consumed. Their normal diet was much cruder than even our simple fare. One day, Wilburn showed up unannounced for dinner (lunch) at Aunt Irene's house. Unfamiliar with mustard, Wilburn reached a long arm across the table for the jar and emptied the entire contents in his plate. We suppressed our laughter and waited to see what he would do. As I recall, he lopped it up without grimace or comment and moved on to other dishes.

One year the Blackwood's moved into the Evans house south of us where the Bradford's and Denton's—among others—had lived. Their first night there it was stormy, Algie was gone, and Nellie and Wilburn were terrified to be alone not only because of the storm but also they were "afeerd o' haints," they said, and "they might be some in this ole house." Over my protests Daddy sent me to keep them company until Algie got home. Everything was all right until Nellie made up an evil concoction that she called supper and invited me to eat. Even possum looked better as far as I was concerned. I pleaded any number of indispositions so as not to have to partake of her vile cooking. They took no offense and proceeded to eat everything on the table with hearty belches and occasional possum-like grins in my direction.

Speaking of vile things, I remember vividly a frightening experience with another mule carcass, dumped at the back side of Bud Sheats' pasture in a much cruder way than we disposed of them. I think I was on my way home after spending the day with Harold Mckenzie. I already knew the dead mule was there, for I had located it by smell on my way to his house. Only this time the body had come back to life. I heard noises and as I approached to investigate, I saw to my horror that the mule's legs were moving in rhythm to a loud thumping noise. An animal was inside the body. I was transfixed by repugnance at what I saw. For then a huge opossum emerged from the rib cage its snout covered with gore. Not that I needed more proof, but it was another confirmation that possum meat was not for me. I must have run the better part of a mile to get away from the scene, but that was easier than getting the gory vision out of my mind.

1949 was a disastrous crop year. A warm winter with frosts so light they did not kill the cotton stalks from the previous year allowed boll weevils to move north from South Alabama and Mississippi. They decimated much of the cotton crop. Instead of our normal seven or eight bales, we had only two or three that year, not enough to pay off our debt at the bank and have money left over for our needs. A yellow tee shirt was the only new clothing I got that fall.

Other farmers were in a similar plight and thus began a mass exodus to find work in the North, primarily Detroit and other Michigan cities. Over the next five years families left farms by the score, leaving hundreds of acres abandoned. For several years nearly all the farms on the Burney Mountain Road were fallow. Idle fields quickly reverted to pine forest and houses and barns soon deteriorated and many of them collapsed within a few years. Powerful weevil poisons flowed into streams and creeks, killing most of the fish and creating an ecological disaster. But many people thought it was simply a great opportunity and ate the contaminated fish. At least we knew better.

The late forties were years of family loss as well. Grandma Hooper's health, never robust, took a turn for the worse in 1949 and she died that summer. We buried her beside my Grandfather William Hooper at Friendship Methodist Church. A year earlier Grandma Raley had died suddenly either of a stroke or a heart attack at sixty-three. She was buried at Ebenezer Baptist Church on the West Point Road. Grandpa Woods attended the funeral, and I wondered what it must be like to outlive one's child. A few months later Grandpa Raley remarried, this time to Mrs. Effie Huffstutler, Uncle Tolbert's mother-in-law. By our calculations this made Grandpa both father and father-in-law to son Tolbert, and we made jokes about the complex relationship. Country singer Grandpa Jones had recently popularized a goofy song titled "I'm my own grandpa," and we modified it to fit the family situation.

Miss Effie, as we called her, had a startling resemblance to Grandma Raley and we felt sure that was what attracted Grandpa to her. They moved into a little house on the far back side of Tolbert's farm. A few months later Grandpa got up one morning and walked all the way back to Burney Mountain and the Valley to see places and people he had known in younger years. We were all impressed by his stamina, not realizing that he was tying loose ends of his life together. I saw him a few more times that winter. Our cow had gone dry and Grandpa told us to come over for milk if we wanted. I made the trip several times across the woods, crossing near the Cook place and fording two creeks to get there. On the last trip I had on two thick flannel shirts to ward off the freezing wind and they made me appear probably ten pounds heavier than I really was. Grandpa looked at me approvingly and remarked how much I had grown lately. We talked about school and life in general, and a few days later he died in his sleep, probably of a heart attack. He was sixty-nine, the same age approximately at which his father William "Bill" Raley had died in 1900.

Daddy briefly joined the northern migration in 1949 but stayed barely two or three weeks. In the summer of 1950 he went back, this time for nearly two months before homesickness and the alien city life in Detroit brought him back to Alabama. In his absence I managed the farm and finished the crops. A year earlier Daddy had traded away ageing Dock and Dan for a mule team, Red and Nigger. (This was long before the age of political correctness.) Red was larger and more placid while little Nigger was as dark of character as he was in color. From the first we disliked each other. Neither animal had been broken for riding, although Red would nervously endure a rider without bucking if he had to. Given Nigger's fiery, treacherous temperament, I never tried to ride him. Our fences were in their customary disrepair and clever little Nigger soon discovered that he could crawl under them on his belly like a dog, the only mule I ever saw do such a trick. I became so accustomed to hearing Daddy's hounds barking at him loose in the cornfield at night that for many years I was instantly awake whenever a dog barked.

One day while plowing I became enraged at Nigger's antics and foolishly hit him with my fist. At that he reared up and as he came down, he put his hooves against my chest and slammed me into the ground with such force that it left the imprint of my rear in the plowed ground. Even though no harm came from it, I was shaken by the experience and unlike his nose, my knuckles were sore for weeks. After that I decided I needed to control my temper and try to be at least as intelligent as that little black mule.

I took pride in my oversight of the farm convinced as I was that I could do a better job than indifferent Daddy. But the work was demanding, and one cornfield almost got away from me. By midsummer the crabgrass had a vicious grip and the corn was stunted with yellow leaves. Lack of help and time made hoeing out of the question. Resorting to heroic measures since Daddy was not around to stop me, I more than doubled the amount of fertilizer we usually applied to the corn at laying-by time. Next, I buried the grass with a "middlebuster," a sort of double-edged turning plow. I was in the midst of my radical remedy when a county farm agent showed up to conduct, as I recall, a survey of cotton acreage. He frowned when he saw what I was doing and remarked, "I wouldn't give you a quarter for this field of corn." He pointed out that I was ruining the root system by deep plowing that late in the season. I listened politely but continued what I was doing after he left. What good was a root system anyway, I thought to myself, if the grass sucked up all the nutrients? I lucked out, for just as I finished plowing there came a good soaking rain. The buried grass died, the fertilizer kicked in, and within a few days the corn turned dark green and yielded a bumper crop. "Whatja do to it?" Daddy asked admiringly upon his return. "Doubled the fertilizer, just like I been tellin' you we ought to do. And got lucky with the rain." Daddy shook his head and bragged about my corn to neighbors but never changed his farming ways. For him the only way to farm was the failing way he and his father always had.

One summer Cousins Mary and Armon rented a parcel of land from Daddy to make a small crop of their own. Their own farm just over the line in Morgan County was desperately poor, and Uncle Bemis barely eked out a living on its rocky hillsides. One day I was plowing in the west field when Mary came down to tell me the communists had invaded South Korea and America was at war again. It sounded like an ominous replay of 1941.

The weevils were still and probably forever with us, but by 1950 and 1951 the poisons I mentioned helped most of the remaining farmers increase their cotton yield. We bought a two-pronged, hand-cranked dust sprayer that covered two rows at a time. I think the Farm Bureau made them available at a reduced price. The dust itself was stifling and our masks were rudimentary. By the end of 1951 I had something resembling arthritis in one of my knees and my joints creaked in odd ways. It took time for the poison to work its way out of my body. For the dusting I wore the same pair of vile smelling pants which I kept in the barn. No amount of washing would remove the stench. Aside from dusting, the only other dubious purpose the clothes ever served was to mask the smell of alcohol on my breath at breakfast a couple of times after I went drinking with Cousin Lonzo.

Rural remoteness, the Great Depression, and World War II had kept modernity at bay along the Old Corn Road, preserving many features of the 19th century until the 20th was half gone. Then the unlikely combination of boll weevils and the postwar Boom brought it to an end with a suddenness characteristic of things that have outlasted their natural time.

As a consequence of this economic growth, the gap widened noticeably between progressive, adaptable farmers and those like Daddy and Uncle Bemis who clung to the old ways and ignored new techniques. The differences were becoming embarrassingly evident at school. Many of my classmates not only had spending money and better clothes but also new homes and shiny, late model cars or pickups. By early 1952 a few families had television sets. In contrast, the postwar economic boom passed us by. People were buying tractors and beginning to joke about those who still plowed with mules. Horse manure and wagon ruts on major roads, once common features, were becoming rare and within a few short years were gone.

As a result of this growing economic slippage, which left us ever further below the rising standard of living, our younger siblings—Darrell, Janice, and Joyce, and double-cousins Dot (Dorothy) and Arvil—grew up even poorer in an odd way than Geraldine, Armon, Mary, and I had been. My sister Joyce was born in 1949 at Dr. Clement's clinic in Falkville at a time when my confidence in our way of life was—without my conscious awareness—ebbing away and my resentment against our willful poverty was growing. When Momma showed cute, blonde little Joyce to me and asked me what I thought, I answered dryly, "Just looks like another Raley." Momma laughed and told the others what I had said but did not catch the embittered undertow of my words.

I had grown up proud to be a Raley and tried to emulate Daddy and his brothers in their brash talk and manly claims of physical strength. Now, however, I was beginning to see that I would never really be like them and, furthermore, that much of what they had stood for no longer seemed to matter. Progress and poverty were making these strong men weak and obsolete. Besides, it was plain to see that I would never be as tall and imposing as my father, and even though I was strong for my size, in the world they came from men were appreciated mostly by how far their head was above the ground, not what was in it. I was bookish and showed only modest interest in hunting, dogs, guns, and related activities. Great Uncle Am Woods once cautioned Daddy about my reading. "Ye better watch that boy. That Phillips feller down yonder other side of Panama went crazy from readin' too much and they had to put 'im in the asylum." Daddy asked me about my books but decided they had not damaged me too much yet and that I still had enough sense to manage. "I reckon some readin' won't hurt you none, but just don't overdo it," he cautioned. Daddy believed in moderation and minimalism in most things.

In my growing resentment I turned away from Dough Ball and became indifferent to my faith. In my mind it was all part of the same old-fashioned, failing way of life.

Chapter 25:
Arkansas Traveler

Daddy came back from Michigan later in the summer of 1950 and with some little unspoken resentment on my part—for I had enjoyed being the man in charge of the farm—he resumed control.) I wandered about restless for a few days before hitting on a daring plan. I would hitchhike to Arkansas to stay a while with Bufus and Irene! Bad times had finally driven them off their farm and Bufus decided to try his luck in Arkansas, where he had lived as a young man. His old friend and former employer Mr. Burfoot rented him a farm, and Irene wrote us that there was a lot of work and good money to be earned. I mentioned it to a friend, penniless John Chaney, and he eagerly agreed to accompany me to Arkansas.

Even though John was twenty-two, he was smaller than I and looked to me for leadership. As best I remember, John's education was limited to being able to write his name. In any case, he willingly did what I suggested, and we got along famously. John's main interests were women and alcohol, which for him constituted the sum of masculine amusements in the world, but he was a jovial person of remarkable moderation and patience if neither was available. Moreover, he knew a thousand jokes and stories to pass the time.

Momma objected to my plan, but when I assured her that I would be staying at Irene's, reluctantly and with an endless number of cautions she relented to the journey. Daddy was again away at the time. In later times it was told that I "ran away" to Arkansas. I may have said so myself. But it was not true; my parents were fully informed of my plans and my destination and I wrote to them once we got to Arkansas to let them know I was all right.

John and I left early in the afternoon, walking along the Corn Road until somebody gave us a ride out to Highway 31. We each carried a bare change of clothes. By late that afternoon we had hitchhiked to Sheffield-Tuscumbia in Northwest Alabama. There sitting under a bridge we decided that a can of beer would be a good thing for our trip and being of age John went to fetch it. He came back with two malt liquors—"all they had"—he explained, and we drank them down in manly gulps. The alcohol gave me a rush and a rise in false confidence. I was sure we would get to Arkansas in a breeze, make lots of money, and have grand adventures.

Two more rides got us to Iuka, Mississippi, well known to eager or anxious Alabama couples as a place to get a quickie marriage without the hassle and delay of blood tests. What a thrill I felt as we crossed the state line riding on the back of a pickup truck. My first time out of Alabama! It was dark when we reached Iuka and we slipped into a crowded movie theater to catch the last part of a western movie. In those days you could often slip in and see the second half of the movie free. We caught only a few minutes of the movie and then unwilling to pay to see the whole film, walked back to Highway 72 and started hitchhiking our way west. Finally, a friendly man took us to Corinth, but there our luck ran out. It was about ten at night and traffic had died away. We walked around the town a bit, but Corinth was as dead as an old graveyard we passed. It was getting chilly. I was hungry and sleepy and my old bed back in Alabama now seemed so much finer than our forlorn circumstances. As usual in small cities in those days, everything in Corinth was closed and dark and there was nothing to do but wait for sunup and more traffic. We hunkered down under a storefront awning for the rest of the night, dozing a little now and then and hoping the Corinth police wouldn't spot us and take us to jail.

Our spirits rose with the sun. We found food, I have forgotten whether in a restaurant or elsewhere, and soon were back on the road. I still had three dollars. A dump truck driver with a load of rocks stopped to offer us a ride. Informed of our plans to get to Arkansas, the gaunt driver responded, "I'm goin' all the way to Memphis and you boys can ride if ye'll help me unload these here rocks."

We agreed and got in. But we had not gone many miles when the driver began to shake so badly that he could barely steer the truck. "Boys," he informed us, "I got to get me a drink. Now I'm gonna stop and you boys got to help me look fer a bottle I got hid out there in the pine woods." We agreed, afraid not to, and he rolled his rig to a stop. Then we fanned out in the spot he indicated and started kicking around in the pine needles until he found the bottle of moonshine. "Here 'tis!" he shouted gleefully. "I found it!" Then he uncorked the bottle and gurgled down the whiskey without stopping for breath. In a minute or two his trembling stopped, and he regained his calm. "I'll be fine now, boys. Don't y'all worry none."

He was right. We made it to Memphis without further problems and as we had agreed, helped him unload the truck. The rocks were heavier than we thought and by the time we finished it seemed like they weighed a hundred pounds apiece. Then he drove us to the Mississippi River Bridge and pointed to the other side. "Over yonder's Arkansas. You just walk across that bridge and you'll be there." We said much obliged for the ride and walked out of Tennessee and across the Mississippi River into Arkansas. The dump truck driver was still steady the last we saw of him.

I had only a vague idea of where Bufus lived. "I'll know it when we get there," I assured John. The truth was I had forgotten the name of the crossroads Irene had described—Hicks Station—and hoped I would recognize it when we came to it. Meanwhile I was hyper. For some inexplicable reason that morning I had bought a box of No-Doz pills and after taking several was as nervous and keyed up as a squirrel. A woman stopped to ask us the way to St. Louis. "Is it west or north?" She asked. "Well," I told her, "it has to be north because it's up in Missouri, thatta way," I pointed northward. "You sure?" she responded doubtfully. "Somebody told me it was to the west." "Well, somebody's nuts," I snapped back, and the startled woman drove off the way I pointed. Old backwoods John had never heard the word "nuts" used that way and thought I was making an obscene suggestion to her. His respect for me ticked up a notch or two after that for he was sure I could be counted on to proposition women for us. "Goddamn, Harold, ye talk to women that way," he said approvingly, "And they's some of 'em bound to let you have some!" (In the language of that time, it was a euphemistic way of referring to sex.) I decided it was better to accept John's nasty-minded admiration than to explain what the expression meant. "Yeah," I lied as offhandedly as I could manage, "it's worked for me a lotta times." At fifteen I thought I needed me some reputation even if it was completely unearned.

We had no luck hitchhiking in Arkansas and after a while I flagged down a Greyhound bus. I still was not sure of our destination but after about twenty miles I spotted Hicks Station and we got off. Luckily it was the right place. We inquired in a store about a "Mr. Burfoot" and the storekeeper told us he thought he lived a few miles north and advised us to take the dirt road and ask along the way. We followed his directions and people pointed out the Burfoot farm. Bufus's two-room frame dwelling was only a short distance across the cotton field from the bigger Burfoot home.

Needless to say, Irene was surprised—and probably dismayed—when we arrived at her door. It had not occurred to me earlier that she might not want a stranger in her house, especially one of the trashy Chaneys they had known only briefly before leaving Alabama. But because John was friendly and polite when he had to be and I was probably her favorite nephew, she quickly warmed up and prepared us a bed in the back room. Bufus came back from the fields a little later and seemed genuinely happy to see us. The Burfoots were now too old to be active friends; and left with a choice of ignorant Black neighbors and trashy white tenant farmers they seemed to have little company.

We had not eaten since leaving Corinth and Irene, always a splendid cook, outdid herself that night with delicious chicken, green beans, fried okra, and other vegetable dishes. The powdered milk, however, which we were condemned to drink during our stay in Arkansas, I downed with a repugnance approaching my old dislike for 'possum. At first, I was still high on No-Doz and we talked a long time about things and people back in Alabama. But later after the caffeine wore off, we slept like dead men and the next morning were ready to see about work.

Irene was right; it was plentiful. It had been a rainy year in Arkansas and cotton fields were a riot of grass and mosquitoes. We went to work for a white tenant farmer a couple of miles from Bufus's house. Even though the man had money to pay us, the family members were the most abject people I had ever met, worse than any I had seen in Alabama. The whole family, including the emaciated, dirty-haired blond children, was covered with scabbed-over mosquito bites. "Why don't you screen in the house?" I asked him. "What the hell fer?" he responded, expertly spitting a long stream of snuff juice. "Them mosquiters'd jist cover you anyway soon's you stepped outside." He sensed my disapproval and took a disliking to me; I felt the same about him and was glad when we finished hoeing his field and got our cash money.

I must admit, though, he was right about the mosquitoes. Unlike the few I had experienced in Alabama these were not deterred in the slightest by sunlight. Instead they came at you in dark clouds in broad open daylight, so that we had to carry leafy branches to fight them off. In the late afternoon thousands of birds crossed the sky on the way to their roosting spots.

All the houses had water marks on them. "Floodin' from the St. Francis River," Bufus explained. One Saturday afternoon he took us canoeing on the river and explained that according to a local legend anyone who drank from its waters would always want to return. I took a sip and, sure enough, did revisit the place briefly on two occasions even though I felt no compelling urge to do so.

The next day Bufus walked with us to a small Baptist Church located three or four miles down the road towards Hicks Station. The sermon and service were nothing special, but on the way, we walked by a house where a beautiful young girl was standing on a porch. "She's got herself knocked up, I hear tell," Bufus said, "just like her sister before her." "Wish I'd come out here sooner" John said wistfully. On the way home we saw a big farm with lots of tractors and farm implements. "Y'all see that new John Deere over by the edge of the field?" Bufus asked. "Well, by gannies, they say that man and his boys drove up to Missouri one night, loaded that tractor on their truck, and brought it back to Arkansas. Real lowdown people. Folks 'round here don't put nothin' past 'em."

On Monday of the second week we contracted to hoe twenty acres for Bufus's black neighbor, a tall reserved man with startling blue eyes. "White blood mixed in somewhere back in the line" Bufus explained, "but he'll keep his word and pay you." John was a hard worker and with a little help from Bufus we finished the hoeing by morning of the second day. Ten dollars apiece seemed like a lot of money for such a quick job. Bufus would not accept any pay for his help.

We did a few other jobs and accompanied Bufus on trips to Forrest City and Parkin, I think the name was. I remember the latter community as an expanded plantation community with a cotton gin, store, and another business or two. In any case, it was the closest I came to seeing for myself the uglier side of plantation life in the Old South. We had no Black folks on the Mountain and my experience with them was limited to a few brief contacts in Hartselle and Decatur on our peddling trips. As we were waiting for Bufus, an old, white-headed Black man and his wife drove up in a two-horse wagon loaded with furniture. At that instant a white man of perhaps forty or forty-five ran out of the store, jumped up on the front wheel, grabbed the reins, and began to curse the old man. "You turn this goddamn wagon around and git yore black ass back yonder to the house! You owe me money and you aint gonna move till I tell you ye can move. You understand me?" The old man dropped his head, murmured a feeble excuse, tapped the team with the reins, and slowly turned the wagon back in the direction he had come. "Out here they say the rule is that if a man has to kill a black," Bufus explained later to my questions, "the law'll take his word for it and there won't be legal trouble, providin' he sees to the buryin' of the body."

Even though there was still plenty of work, after a little over two weeks we had our fill of Arkansas and its mosquitoes and decided to start back to Alabama with forty dollars apiece in our pocket. Early on a Saturday we walked back to Hicks Station and caught the Greyhound bus to Memphis. There we decided not to return by way of Mississippi but to take the long way on Highway 64 through Tennessee. That way we could see a little more of the world and who knows, John reminded me, maybe run across some friendly girls. Actually, he put it in cruder anatomical terms that got his idea across in an unmistakable way.

The bus let us off on the east side of Memphis where 64 and the Nashville road divided. There we waited for a considerable time before a girl about eighteen or so stopped her Chevrolet and offered us a ride. She was not a beauty, but friendly and well developed, and to John's lascivious delight, wearing shorts. Even though I was nervous sitting next to her, she and I carried on a friendly chatter, much too upscale to suit John, who spent most of the time silently looking at her bare legs. He complained after she let us out that "all we'd've had to do was ask her. Man, she was ready as ready can be!" He believed that any girl wearing shorts was advertising her sexual availability. I had been around enough girls in high school to know better. I told him to be patient and see what the day might bring.

It turned out to be an unforgettable day. After another ride that got us about fifty miles into Tennessee, John was still salivating over the girl in shorts when a mature woman in a shiny new 1950 Ford pulled over and invited us to jump in. John gave me a knowing look and we got in. Things were looking up until I realized that the woman was half drunk and determined to put distance between herself and something she kept looking for in her rearview mirror. "My mean ole husband keeps me locked in," she explained. "Don't want me drinkin' and havin' fun. It's not the money, he's got plenty of that with his damn lumber business. He's just a mean ole son-of-a-bitch. But today I got loose with the car keys and, boys, I'm aimin' to do me some catchin' up! He'll be a-comin' after me, but I can outrun him." Meanwhile we were careening around curves and weaving worse than Uncle Bufus back and forth across the lanes. "Where'd you boys say you were goin'?" "Uh, ma'am, we'll just get out over here in Bolivar, if it's all right with you" I told her. "We got to see our uncle about some business." John looked at me in white-faced agreement. She dropped us off and sped away in a cloud of dust and a screeching of rubber. I expected to see her wrecked car later but didn't. John cursed in relief and made crude but admiring comments about "these here crazy Tennessee women."

We had no more wild rides, but late that afternoon we made it to Selmer, Tennessee where we saw more pretty young girls than we ever thought possible in one spot. "Hell, I'm gonna come back to this town first chance I git," John said. I thought it was a good idea, too, and we talked about a return visit. Meanwhile, John made a nasty proposition to a couple of them and was soundly rebuked for his efforts. Nevertheless, he was pleased. "Long's they talk to you, don't much matter what they say." A couple of girls smiled at me and I thought how nice it would be to come back to Selmer some day and get to know them. Many years later in winter I drove through cold, deserted Selmer and wondered what happened to those pretty summer girls of 1950.

We made it across the Tennessee River and through Savannah. Near Waynesboro we saw a summer revival gathering for a sweaty meeting. I remembered with a momentary pang of troubled conscience my own conversion and how far I had fallen away.

Somewhere east of Waynesboro darkness overtook us. We were considering our options when a salesman in a big car—maybe a Buick—stopped to offer us a ride. Informed that we were headed to Pulaski, he said he was too. We settled in, tired and relieved that the next to last leg of our Tennessee odyssey was nearly over. The salesman stopped briefly in Lawrenceburg and while he was inside a store, I opened his glove compartment. There I saw a seriously large pistol. We were both tempted for a moment. "We could grab that pistol and be down yonder in them woods 'fore he gits back, "John observed, stroking the barrel. "Yeah," I agreed, "and it might be smart to do it. He might be dangerous or crazy. He may shoot us before we get to Pulaski!" We debated what to do and finally decided to stay in the car. The man returned, and we spent the rest of the trip in pleasant conversation. But I kept a nervous eye on the glove compartment just in case.

We arrived—alive—in Pulaski around ten o'clock at night and the salesman let us off at the intersection of highways 64 and 31. But instead of heading south towards the Alabama line, we saw blazing lights and traffic to the north. We went over to investigate and learned that it was a Tennessee Walking Horse competition in a local stadium. Neither of us had ever seen such beautiful animals, so we slipped in under the bleachers and watched the program. To me the event seemed to belong to a finer, more elevated world than I had ever dreamed of. What kind of people were these beautiful ladies and handsome men with their magnificent horses? It must have been after midnight when the competition ended. We rushed back to Highway 31 hoping somebody in the crowd would give us a ride down to Ardmore and the Alabama state line.

Sure enough, we caught a ride to Ardmore and walked over into Alabama. But then it was like Corinth all over again. All of a sudden there was no more traffic and we had to sit on the sidewalk by the Greyhound bus stop the rest of the night. Morning found us tired and hungry and with our fill of hitchhiking. Before long a Greyhound bus drove up and for fifty cents, we rode all the way down through Athens, Decatur, Hartselle, Falkville, and finally to Cotton Hill. As we drove through Athens, a town I did not know at all, I glanced idly at the stately buildings of Athens College and wondered what sort of strange things went on there. I was destined to find out years later.

From Cotton Hill we walked up to the Corn Road, taking different roads at Friendship Church and pledging to get together soon. We did but never in the same way or to the same degree. And we never made the trip back to Selmer to see the pretty girls. I reached home around ten in the morning and began to tell Daddy and Momma of my travels. "Daddy, the best cotton I saw anywhere is what we have right here. Too much grass and rain has mostly ruined it out in Arkansas." He was pleased by my observation and both my parents were glad I had returned safely. So was I.

Chapter 26:
Empty Pockets

With some of my Arkansas money I bought a basketball and goal which I erected with considerable effort down in a level place in our pasture. I had a notion to improve my shooting skills and maybe try to make the basketball team that fall. For a time, my friends were quite impressed with my Arkansas adventure, which I embellished for effect. I also spent most of my money to impress them. By the end of summer and time to begin my sophomore year at West Point I was broke as always.

But if economically I fell farther behind most of my classmates, my academic standing remained impressive. Luckily, I was absent in seventh grade the day the class took a round of IQ tests, but the teachers put me at the head of my class anyway and from then on my assumptive position as a brainy student went unquestioned. Grades came easier for me than for many of my classmates because of the "smart" label I wore. Other students had to earn their marks; in my case, the teachers tended to give me the benefit of the doubt.

It turned out that I was not quite finished with Arkansas. After my sixteenth birthday in November Bufus and Irene came home for a visit and announced that they were moving back to Alabama. They asked me to return to Arkansas with them to help load their things. I agreed and we started out in a newer version of the old green Chevrolet, perhaps a mid-30's model. In Arkansas we spent a day or two taking care of business and loading the vehicle. Finally, we were ready and planned to leave early the next morning. Then it started to rain and Bufus was afraid the river would rise over the road. "We better leave tonight," he said, looking out the window at the rain and lightning. Irene agreed and we started out.

We had not gone many miles, however, when it became apparent that Bufus could not see the road. Several times he almost ran in the ditch and only Irene's screams saved us from muddy disaster. "Let Harold drive!" she insisted. "He can see better!" "Jack, do ye think ye can handle the drivin'?" asked the chastised Bufus. (Like many people where I grew up, Bufus called me by my nickname "Jack".) "Yeah, I think so," I answered confidently and slid behind the wheel.

And I did, all night, no license and all. I had the eyes and Bufus, the experience and together we made a passable driver. Luckily, traffic was very light, except in Memphis where I worried the police might pull me over. Even at sixteen I could still have passed for fourteen. But everything went well. We got through Memphis, Corinth, and Iuka, and as the sun was coming up were nearing Tuscumbia, Alabama. "Pull over, Jack," Bufus instructed me. "I can see now." He drove the rest of the way in his normal way, that is, slow, erratic, and in whichever lane he pleased.

The lack of money bothered me more and more, and toward the end of the school year 1950-51 I was seriously ready to do something about it. A new highway to replace old 31 was being cut through the mountains south of Lacon and word was out that they were hiring all the men they could get. One day my friend J.L. Cobb and I left school to check out the rumor. We got to the work site after a lot of walking and hitchhiking and sure enough the foreman was ready to hire us. "How old are you boys?" he wanted to know. "Eighteen," we assured him. "Well, bring your birth certificates and social security cards and I'll put you to work tomorrow." We were out of luck. We both had social security cards, but J.L. was seventeen and I was only sixteen. We returned the next day and confessed our ages, hoping he would let us start anyway. "I figured you boys might be stretching it a little yesterday. I wish I could hire you but if they catch me working underage boys, I'm the one in trouble. They won't let us do that no more."

A few days later Douglas Long came by with the news that work was available in Birmingham. It consisted, so he claimed, of hosing down cars for a chain of big used car lots, locking the vehicles at night, and performing certain other chores. The red dust from the iron mines settled on the cars overnight, he explained, causing them to lose their fresh luster and appeal. The pay—unspecified—was good, the work was easy, and he was on his way to Birmingham to get in on it. Easy stuff, he claimed. Several of us eagerly joined in the quest.

Unfortunately, there were too many of us to catch a ride easily, and it was afternoon before we finally reached Birmingham, tired and hungry from walking and waiting in the hot sun along Highway 31. Then and there, reality hit us. It turned out that Doug didn't know the location of the fabled car lots. For a couple of hours, we wandered aimlessly up and down the Birmingham streets. Then, thoroughly disgusted with Doug, who under our threats of rearranging his body parts hinted he had dreamed up the whole thing, and angry at ourselves for our gullibility, we started back towards Cullman.

Maybe the military was the answer. Not long after the Birmingham fiasco, several of us—Doug included—went to Cullman to talk to the Army and Air Force recruiters. There was fighting in Korea and armed forces were recruiting aggressively. A lot of older boys I knew had already joined and some of them had come back on furlough with cars and uniforms and as many dates as they wanted. The recruiters gave us a test. We all passed. I got forty out of forty questions correct on the Army test, and thirty-nine of forty on practically the same Air Force test. The recruiters were impressed by my scores and mentioned Officer's Training School. The problem, however, was the same one as before: being underage. I asked Daddy to give me permission to join the Air Force, but he refused to sign. "Wait till ye're eighteen and you can join then if ye want to." In my anger I tried altering my birth certificate but botched it so badly than anyone could see it had been tampered with.

One Sunday afternoon my financial frustrations culminated at Bibb's store at the Burney mountain junction of the Corn Road. Sometimes area boys would gather there and for want of anything better to do, drink a coca-cola and watch the cars pass. Billy Woods, friend and trading partner in comic books, and several other boys were there with me when a shiny 1949 V8 Rocket 88 Oldsmobile pulled up. It was my old buddy Tommy Sandlin. Tommy had dropped out of school and gone north to work for Cadillac Motors in Detroit. The Oldsmobile—and the pretty east Cullman girl sitting next to him—were the payoff to his initiative. We were fairly drooling with envy. Tommy was friendly but aloof. He had moved on; we had not, and he was trying hard not to show his disdain for our backwardness. On the way home I vowed that it was only a matter of time until I followed in Tommy's footsteps.

Not that dropping out of school was an option. Despite all my frustrations it never occurred to me to stop short of graduation. I still enjoyed my classes and my grades had not slipped very much even though I no longer studied, and my frustrations were building.

Chapter 27:
Geraldine, Darrell, Janice, Joyce

My siblings and I were born over a 19-year span: 1930-1949. This extended time created several family oddities. Geraldine and I—1930/1934, respectively, belonged to an older generation of cousins, some of whom I mentioned earlier. More than eight years passed after my birth before Darrell was born in March of 1943, then Janice arrived in May of 1946, and Joyce in March of 1949. These long intervals meant that Geraldine was married and raising her own family when Janice was still a toddler and before Joyce was born. By the time Janice was in first grade and Darrell in fourth, I was a senior in high school, and Joyce had not yet started school. I have reasons to believe that Momma lost a male child in 1941 (the log cabin year), and either Janice or Joyce—or perhaps both—told me many years later that she lost twins in the 1950s. As I said earlier, Momma's generation did not discuss pregnancies and birth matters with their sons.

Despite these age differences and with only the fleeting frictions common in nearly all families and human relationships, we five have always been compatible and united as a family, even though in my case geographical distance has prevented me having the closer contact with my siblings than I would have liked. But close or far apart in geographical terms, my love for them never wavers. And it is out of that abiding affection that I offer the following verbal portraits of my sisters and brother.

A. Geraldine

Although all five of us were born into a poor family, I think Geraldine probably had the easiest time of it growing up. In 1930, her birthyear, Daddy was still healthy, and Momma was still hopeful. From what I can piece together from the happy tales and anecdotes they told of those early times their married life retained much of its youthful exuberance. By today's standards, the whole society was poor, which meant that theirs was an egalitarian poverty, that is, nearly everybody was equally poor or equally rich, depending on how you look at it. This meant that if times were hard, life was socially easy. No one—or few—claimed social superiority based on wealth or suffered social inferiority for lack of it. People were judged for who they were, not by what they had. With few variations, they were all in the same boat, and even those families that were beginning to prosper still kept the simple country brand of hospitality and friendliness.

But these conditions are generalizations. On a personal level, Geraldine had other qualities and advantages, at least in comparison to the rest of us. To begin with, she was a healthy, beautiful little girl, the firstborn family darling, especially to her father, younger uncles, and Raley clan in general. Daddy doted on her, and I am sure Geraldine thrived on the attention. In fact, supposedly she asked Daddy to "send him back" when she saw me for the first time. (As things turned out later, I wonder if he was tempted to comply with her request.)

Geraldine not only resembled Daddy's side of the family more than the rest of us—brown hair in contrast to three blonds—Darrell, Joyce, and myself—and a redhead—Janice—but also had his easy, popular way of making friends. She and our double-first Cousin Mary Raley enhanced these qualities in each other and were without question the stars at Raley and

Hooper family gatherings. Geraldine was, hands down, the healthiest member of our family. As I recall, she was rarely, if ever, sick as a child, had perfect teeth and skin, and seemed immune to the childhood diseases that plagued me and some of my siblings. Whereas I suffered often from toothaches, earaches, sores, colds, colic, anemia, and the nightmares I mentioned earlier, Geraldine seemed to sail unscathed through childhood. I envied her, and I can see now what I did not understand as a child: it was probably the underlying cause of our frequent spats.

I mentioned Elton McKenzie in an earlier chapter about our year at Bethlehem. Geraldine was twelve at the time and already a precociously mature, pretty girl. Elton—"Bunk," as everybody called him—surely must have noticed her even at that tender age. For when WWII was over and he returned in 1945 or early 1946, it was not long before his attentions became seriously focused on her. I described earlier in this writing the morning Geraldine showed up at the breakfast table and announced her wish to marry him. Momma protested mildly because of her age: 16, compared to Bunk's seasoned, war-tested 24. On the positive side, Daddy recounted Bunk's solid qualities: hardworking, honest, trustworthy. The debate was short and favorable to Geraldine's petition; permission to marry Bunk was granted, and the wedding took place not long thereafter. They took up residence soon afterwards south of Cullman near Good Hope where Bunk farmed the first year of their marriage. Our nephew Larry was born there, on Geraldine's birthday if my memory serves. Judy came along a couple of years later, and I remember accompanying Bunk to the Cullman hospital to pick up Geraldine and beautiful little Judy, for whom I have always had a special fondness. It was a happy time for all the family.

As I reflect on these events from today's distant perspective, I think Geraldine left home at an optimal moment, that is, just before the family fortunes began a downward slide that was to define and diminish our family for nearly twenty years. I cover a lot of these misfortunes in telling my own story.

As the beauty she had become by her teenage years, no doubt Geraldine could have chosen a husband from among several worthy men. But from all we knew and saw regarding her marriage to Bunk, she not only chose early but well. The best came first, for Bunk was devoted to her, and we discovered him to be kind and generous to us all. He was especially fond of our parents, and as he confided to me many years later, saddened by the simmering conflicts that denied them happiness. He did not take sides and placed no blame on either. He simply loved them both and wished they could be happy with each other. By all accounts, Bunk's own family life was unfulfilling, and if not a waif, at least an oft-neglected child. Obviously, it pained him to see some of those conditions repeated in our family.

Bunk was a man of few words, but those he spoke went to the heart of matters, as the truth always does. I will venture to say though—perhaps in error—that his taciturnity may have had an effect also on Geraldine. As a mature woman she was—and is—an engaging conversationalist, but with less of the girlish exuberance I remember when she and Mary were the young stars of both families. How much the change was due to Bunk or simply the deepening of maturity, I cannot say.

In any case, Geraldine has done it right in her life. I think I speak for all her siblings when I say that we love her, admire her, and wish her all the best in this world and the next. (And I hope she has forgiven me for stealing some of her chewing gum long, long ago!)

B. Darrell

As I said earlier, the night of March 23, 1943 was filled with noise, movement, and voices. At one point, I think somebody, probably Daddy, picked me up and carried me downstairs, but I was too groggy to ask what was happening. The next morning, I discovered the cause of all the commotion: a baby brother. With Darrell's arrival, instead of a duo, we were now a trio of siblings. Like Geraldine and me, Darrell was born at home. By the time Janice and Joyce came along there were local clinics and they were born with a medical doctor in attendance: Dr. Cornelius at West Point in the case of Janice; Dr. Clements of Falkville when Joyce was born.

Momma was especially solicitous where Darrell was concerned. She feared that a kidney infection she suffered during the pregnancy might have affected him also. Whether it did or not, I have no way of knowing. What I do know is that Darrell, like me, suffered for years with a series of ailments. He seemed especially susceptible to lung problems, and I recall that he had Whooping Cough for what seemed like nearly a whole winter.

My particular regret where Darrell is concerned is that we were too far apart in age and temperament to share the common experiences of boyhood. By that time, I was living half my life through the books I read and tended to supplement my increasingly impoverished circumstances with escapist, make-believe adventures and imaginary heroes. Although I played with him when he was a baby, later I generally neglected him when he was old enough to venture out into the world. It was selfish of me, for I could have helped him through childhood, especially since our father was losing interest in both farm and family and increasingly distancing himself from the responsibilities they presented.

I think it is fair to say that the world beyond our local realities and circumstances was a much greater factor in shaping Darrell's life than mine. Even World War II, no doubt our country's greatest event and effort of the twentieth century, was remote from us, a story of far-off things rather than something that was taking place all around us. But whereas anything short of total victory was unthinkable in WWII, Korea and Vietnam began the era of wars that we chose not to win, and, further, instead of confining them to foreign shores, we imported the conflicts to our own shores in the form of ideological and political contentions and dissensions. Seen from my perspective, Darrell's generation bore the full brunt of those unhappy times. I also think it is fair to say that the combination of our failed family circumstances and the unhappy mood of the nation were conditions that Darrell had to face and overcome. For Geraldine and me our circumstances were hard, but the sides were cleanly drawn; by the time Darrell was born they were even harder, and now sullied by doubts, accusations, loss of faith in the national ideals. A new generation came to believe that America was the enemy of mankind and must be dismantled and rebuilt. They proved to be good at tearing down; we have yet to see an equally vigorous constructive side. These were conflicts we could not, or would not, win, and the best we could hope for were not clean-cut triumphs but fragile compromises that mocked our history and often betrayed the people we were supposed to protect. Our soldiers were as brave as ever, but our politicians were feckless and weak-willed.

Darrell did two tours in Vietnam, and the country rewarded him and thousands like him with sneers and disrespect, including the 50,000 American soldiers who died there. Happily, in recent years the country has repented of its ungrateful attitudes and begun to acknowledge the bravery and sacrifice of those who served in those pointless wars.

Darrell's struggles were not over. He came home to a family that had slipped too far down the poverty scale for any hope of recovery. Daddy, who unbeknownst to us siblings was already too ill with emphysema to do the hard work it would take to restore the farm. Both Janice and Joyce were now married, or soon would be. Like Geraldine, they married very young, probably in part to get way from the financial straits and emotional poverty of our failed family. At any rate, our parents were left nearly penniless and without any real hope of improvement in either a financial or human sense.

Darrell married Rosea and had two children with her, Scotty and Tracy, both bright, handsome youngsters. Scotty spoke with me years later about his wish to study law. I encouraged him, for it was obvious that he was intellectually capable. In the end, other influences, not all of them good, caused him to go in a different direction. I never got to know Tracy very well, but the few contacts we had showed me that she was a bright, pleasant girl. By that time, however, my contacts with the family were few and far between and I did not see her again for several years.

Darrell outlived most of his childhood miseries. Because he was a bit smaller than I, naturally I assumed that I was the stronger of the two. But one day in 1975, I learned differently. I was reroofing Momma's house in the Bell Springs Community. Darrell and Rosea had built a new house across the field—in reality the Bell Springs Cemetery—and Darrell came by to lend a hand. I had been carrying the new shingles, one bundle at a time up a makeshift ladder. It was all I could manage. I asked Darrell to being me another bundle. Lo and behold, he comes up carrying two bundles on his shoulder. I realized then and there that he was stronger than I was. Adversities greater than mine had made him strong. It lent some proof to the old saying that if it doesn't kill you, it will make you stronger. As for me, I had spent years in university classrooms, which may keep the mind in shape, but it does little to build bodily strength.

Darrell was, and no doubt is, not only strong but as intelligent as anyone in our family. He reads quite a bit, but as far as I know, he was never academically inclined as I was. But we are alike in one way, or so I believe. From our father we both inherited a considerable dosage of wanderlust. But unlike Daddy, who travels seldom took him more than a few miles from home, Darrell is a long-distance traveler. He told me recently that as a semi driver, he has been in nearly every state in the Union. Although I have traveled a good bit geographically myself, my wanderings led me acquire other languages and learn other cultures. I realize now that my particular way of escape was part of our shared imperative to get away from the restrictions of our poverty-stricken childhood. We all did so in our individual ways.

In recent years and with advancing age, Darrell and I have grown closer and communicate better than we did in the past. The age difference that separated us earlier is not a factor now. We have had very different experiences, but in the end we both feel the unbreakable brotherhood that unites us. I pray daily for him, his family, and his circumstances. We both have our friends, and our circumstances may be different, but I think we both realize that there is no substitute for a brother. And I know that our sisters feel the same way.

C. Janice

Give or take a few months, as Geraldine was leaving, Janice was arriving, which profoundly altered the family dynamics. For one thing, her birth coincided with a pause in our downward slide into poverty. We missed Geraldine—I as much, if not more, than anyone in the family—but we had no reason to worry about her. On the contrary, her marriage was solid, her visits frequent, and in character she was strong enough to grow and prosper in her new status. In fact, she came to exert a greater and more positive influence on the family as a married woman and mother than she had as an unmarried girl subject daily to our family problems and limitations.

For me it meant first of all that instead of being the junior sibling, all of a sudden, I was the senior child. In a way I feel but cannot fully explain, I thought of myself as a holdover from a previous, prewar generation, while my younger siblings belonged to a new family generation and perhaps a new America.

Janice was a darling: cute, cuddly, and with curly, reddish hair. As she grew, she proved to be stalwart, frank, honest, and direct in her views. She had a keen sense of humor, but we learned that if we did not want to hear the truth about things, we should stay away from Janice. In some ways she was like Momma, but whereas Momma was often tense, worried, and probably desperate about things, Janice had about her a psychological calmness that Momma lacked. To say it another way, Momma was a faithful but troubled servant of truth; Janice was, and is, its unruffled master. When she speaks, Janice gets her point across in no uncertain terms. Geraldine, Joyce, and I are relatively soft-spoken, Darrell and especially Janice have stronger voices and maybe stronger views. At least Janice does not seem to be beset with second thoughts and contingent reservations as Joyce and I seem to be. Some of us see the world in all its complexity; Janice sees it in all its simplicity.

In another way, I think Janice was like Daddy would have been if he had married a woman who encouraged him to be himself instead of demanding he be the kind of man he was never suited to be. Momma spent her married life trying to remake our father in the image of what she thought a man should be—probably her own father. It was not a bad image—just not who Daddy was born to be. Janice became to a certain degree the sort of person Daddy really was, honest, uncomplicated, direct, caring. But as I reflect on his life, I think none of us realized at the time how much of himself he kept hidden and suppressed (or at least unexpressed) because of Momma's endless carping and complaining. He was more sensitive than any of us realized, and he never learned how to work out his hurts and frustrations in a positive way. Momma was very intelligent, but she was not very sensitive to, or even interested in, other people's feelings, including most of all, Daddy's. To say in other words something I wrote earlier, she was almost devoid of psychological insight. I think some of Daddy's brothers sensed this deficiency in Momma and wrongly accused her of failing to care for Daddy in his final days. She bitterly resented the accusation, and with good reason. For despite her disappointment in Daddy, she never failed to care for him as best she could. It was not in her nature to do anything less. She was dutiful above all else, and she never dodged her responsibilities.

Because of our age differences, I have always thought of myself as a sort of combination older brother/uncle to my younger sisters, especially so after Daddy passed on at 59 in 1968. I was concerned with Janice after she married John Powell, whose family we knew well and in fact to whom we were distantly related. For a time, it looked like Janice had jumped from the frying pan of poverty to the caldron of misery. John did not have steady work and on a pair of visits I perceived that they were living almost at a subsistence level.

But in the end, Janice's steady character prevailed. But not without a couple of incidents—that I know of—that demonstrated just how strong she was. Once when they were living in a small house in Falkville, the entire ceiling fell on them. (I don't remember whether their children Robin and Mark were born.) John was naturally dismayed and reportedly asked Janice, "What do we do now?" Calmly she replied, "Well, John, the first thing is we're going to clean up this mess." Later, as I heard it from John himself, he had left another job and was once again without a wage. Tired of their constant moves and uncertain finances, Janice told john, "Either you get a steady job and stay with it or I'm going to leave you." John's saving grace was that he truly loved Janice and said so in his own words: "I couldn't live without her." He took her warning to heart, and from that time forward their fortunes improved and their marriage has stood every trial and test of time.

Here let me repeat and expand on something I said earlier: our family situation was progressively harder on my younger siblings than it was for Geraldine and me. The gap between our family situation and that of many of our neighbors grew progressively wider. WWII put a damper on economic improvement for millions of Americans. In a sense, in our region it meant that we were still living in the mode and manner of the 19th century until the 20th was almost half gone. We lived, farmed, and thought more or less as our grandfathers had. Then once the war was over and industry turned its attention to the civilian population, the old way of life began to melt away like snow in August and with a suddenness that characteristic of things that have outlived their time. Tractors and new automobiles replaced mules, wagons, and jalopies. Change and prosperity finally began to reach our region.

But not us. We and a few other families did not change, but the world around us did, and by not participating in the new and standing still, the old became even older, poorer, and more outdated. This is why I say again, Darrell, Janice, and Joyce grew up poorer than Geraldine and I had been. As children, Geraldine and I were not ashamed of our circumstances because they were, generally speaking, the same as everybody's. Now, however, the family and others who failed to change with the times had sunk to the financial bottom where they could see only the ugly, humiliating underbelly of life.

Yet even though our family bent but it did not finally break. Despite all, they endured, life went on, and their spirit was not crushed. Oddly enough, in that problematic time for America, it was the prosperous youth who most often stumbled, lost hope, and numbed their souls with drugs and poisonous doctrines. A hard life had so toughened Janice that she could keep her hopes alive when many of her generation were letting theirs die.

(I cannot resist adding something here that comes from my university experience but applies to Janice and the world where she grew to womanhood. Many of our intellectuals scorn that world and its people, but when the chips are down—and they always are sooner or later—they are the people who save nations, who stand tough, who win wars, who keep the faith.)

Sometime around 1980, I believe it was but have forgotten the exact date, Janice was diagnosed with breast cancer. We were all concerned, and John was all bur frantic with worry. But Janice took it in stride, recovered nicely, and as far as I know, has had no recurrence. She is, always has been, a woman without guile or vices, of good habits, and an abiding faith in God. She and John are firm believers and model Christians for the rest of the family to admire and emulate. I know the whole family would repeat with me: I love my little redheaded sister and her family dearly.

D. Joyce

I have always thought—and have said so to Joyce—that she is the one most like me. (I hope she doesn't resent the idea.) But I hasten to add: not in looks. Joyce has always been movie-star beautiful. In fact, I think of her every time I see a picture of actress Donna Mills. Blonde with perfect figure, hair, and features, Joyce is, so to speak, the blond crown jewel of the family. No, the comparison to me I had in mind is more mental and psychological. Joyce has areas in her mind and imagination that are not readily apparent to others. I do not mean to imply that she is devious or given to misleading others, only that there is a depth in her being that requires a degree of patience to appreciate it. What you see is not all there is to see in her. For this reason, I absolutely love the times—much too few—we can talk person to person. In some ways, I think we mirror qualities in ourselves that we can only see in the other sibling. For this reason, I always sense an instant intimacy even though we may not have seen each other in several months. And for that same reason I always come away from our conversations feeling that there was not enough time to say everything that needed to be said.

Joyce and Janice grew up together and still stay in contact and communication more than the rest of us. Like her sisters, Joyce married early while still in high school. Her first husband, D.L. Haynes was a tall, slender man who naturally put on more weight as he grew older. (He passed away in 2019, still on amicable terms with Joyce and the rest of the family.) As it turned out, he was a better friend to Darrell than he was a husband to Joyce. I dare suspect there was never a compelling love between Joyce and him, for she confided in me that as the lone child left at home after Janice married, she was anxious, if not desperate, to get away herself. By that time Daddy's emphysema was so advanced that he could barely work at all, and there was hardly any income for the barest necessities. She told me that she once had to go to school with a hole in one of her shoes, and I recall that on my way back to Oklahoma where I was teaching at time, I stopped to see her at West Point High School She came out to the car prettier than ever, but dressed in a way that put a lump in my throat, especially a sweater that was frayed and almost threadbare. By then she had stopped asking for clothes and other things because there was no money at home to buy them. The family was at ground zero, and when D.L. asked her to marry him, she readily accepted.

As I recall, not long after our meeting at West Point, I invited Joyce to Oklahoma where she could live with us and attend Oklahoma State University where Vicky and I were both teaching. To my disappointment, Joyce rejected the invitation, perhaps because she did not want to be under my supervision in a place that was distant and alien to her, or more likely, because she already had it in mind to marry D.L. Even though her marriage did not last many years, it produced two excellent children: Amanda and Jason.

Although Joyce now had a family, she also completed her education, attending the University of Alabama in Birmingham for her B.S. degree, and nursing school subsequently. She worked many years as a nurse in Birmingham. During the time, she developed the Guillaume-Barré Syndrome. She recovered to a considerable extent and continued in her profession, but not without lingering effects that were both physical and emotional. Always gifted with a keen sense of humor, she once told me that someday I would find myself in her unit and under her care (the cardiac section, as I recall) where she would get even with me for real or imaginary abuses by me that she had endured in childhood. It never happened, but had it occurred, I knew I would have been safely cared for.

On the other hand, I am not so sure I would have been as safe if Joyce had been my chauffeur. By all accounts, she has a lead foot when it comes to driving, and I even have a bit of corroborating proof. A few years ago, perhaps a year or two from her retirement, she asked me to follow her through a series to twisting roads on our way to a restaurant in east Birmingham. I made a manly effort to stay within sight of her, but it was a challenge. In fact, once or twice I lost her. We made it to the place and had a pleasant dinner, but it was not something I would want to do every day, maybe not even once a year.

In 1956 when Joyce was seven, Janice, 10, and Darrell, 13, Daddy decided to move with me to Chicago. We stayed there for nearly eight months, and all three attended school there. I lived some twenty blocks from their neighborhood, a small Southern enclave with several families we all knew, including Uncle Bufus and Aunt Irene. In October I got a job back in Alabama with a chance to resume my college studies. I jumped on the offer at once, and despite having no prospects in Alabama, Daddy decided to return to the farm. Momma had a job in a department store cafeteria, I think it was, a small but steady salary, and opposed going back to her dreary, isolated life in Alabama. But Daddy, citing abuses his children had suffered at the hands of a inner city black gang, was adamant and declared he would not stay a day longer in Chicago than I did. So we all returned together. In a few months, I was working and back in college, but Daddy and the family were as destitute as they were before the Chicago interlude. I think I mentioned that Bufus and Irene lived ten years in Chicago, accumulating enough money to retire comfortably in Hartselle. I had mixed feelings about Daddy's leaving his easy job with General Motors, but inner city-Chicago even then was very dangerous and no place to raise children. I once asked Joyce if the transition back to lonely farm was difficult. She said that it took some getting used to, especially having to walk so far to the store. Of course, the children got to see their friends at school. I can only imagine how hard it was for Momma (which is to say I cannot imagine it). Not only did she have to give up her job and the companionship of her sister Irene, but once again had to face the bleak certainty of a grim future.

Based on my own experience, my family's, and others caught up in destructive poverty, I get angry every time I hear some naïve person—I was about say, some fool—say that money is not all that important. That kind of baloney is easy to say if you have food in your stomach, clothes on your back, and shoes on your feet. Experience with real deprivation will teach you a different lesson. Just ask Joyce or anyone else in our family.

But Joyce survived all that I have written—and much more that I have not mentioned in this context. Today she manages her life and loves her God with grace and the balance of good values and virtues. She does it all admirably, and so it seems only right that I should love and admire her with a boundless brotherly love.

(I mentioned 1956, which takes me beyond the context of this writing—1934-1954. The Chicago episode (March-October of 1956) came after Joyce Adams and I were married. Our son Robert Landy Raley was born in the Chicago Presbyterian Hospital (September 5, 1956). Joyce developed an infection that the Chicago doctors seemed unable to cure. Joyce was frightened and after a few weeks wanted to consult her doctor back in Athens. We made a trip to Alabama, and the old Alabama doctor cleared up the infection. While there, I got the job offer from Flanagan Lumber Company, and moved back to Alabama. My parents and siblings came back home at the same time. If I get around to it before mortality gets around to me, I hope to write the second—and longer—part of my autobiography.)

Chapter 28:
Random Recollections

Some memories just seem to float like lint in the air, never settling into any pattern or place. Here are a few of mine:

You just never know about some people. For years an old white-haired couple lived in a two-room frame house close to a sharp curve on the Powell Road Cutoff. I don't remember their name, if I ever knew it, but they always sat on their front porch and waved cheerfully to occasional travelers on the lonely back road. Finally, the man died, and people were stunned to learn that he did not intend that anything was to go to his wife. Wasn't it philosopher Ralph Waldo Emerson who said that most people lead lives of quiet desperation? Maybe he should have added: and some have hidden hatreds.

Strange Creatures Roam Among Us. On summer around 1950 we heard from neighbors that an animal of unknown size and description had broken into several houses, taking meat, flour, and other food staples and leaving big, claw marks on walls and cabinets. It was a hard summer and food was scarce after a couple of lean crops. I suspected the creature was the two-legged human variety.

Odd ailments. When I was four, I saw a man with a huge wen on the back of his neck. I wondered what caused it and asked Momma. She was distracted and did not answer me. I still wonder.

Under Siege. Around 1951 several classmates and other youngsters my age came down with rheumatic fever. There were also cases of polio. Every morning I wondered if I would be the next one stricken. To prove I was still healthy, I would run at full speed down through the pasture, jumping over the old terrace rows.

Secret Sorrows. Probably Grandpa Raley's closest friend was Mr. Hamilton who lived over on the Burney Mountain where the Raleys once lived. (Some in our family called it "the other mountain.") His children were happy and fun-loving, but later one of his daughters committed suicide.

The Things Parents Tell Their Children. When I was four or five Daddy told me that if you plucked hairs from a horse's mane and put them in water for about a week they would turn into little black snakes. He showed me several down close to the Seven Falls Creek and said that's where they came from. Although I knew logically that it couldn't be true, I believed it in spite of myself—and still wonder about it.

This Tricky World. Even though I knew—or thought I did—the woods for miles around like the back of my hand, one day I got lost not far from Billy Woods' house. When I got back to the road, everything felt like it was in the wrong place and familiar things seemed alien. Hours passed before the world resumed its old patterns. Do we really know the world as well as we think we do?

Forbidden Love and Loyalty. A girl from the Bell Springs Community near Lacon Mountain turned up pregnant one summer. Under pressure from her family she finally confessed that her lover was a local married man. But no amount of persuasion could get her to say his name. Speculation was rampant and every likely husband was a suspect and every wife was suspicious.

Man's Inhumanity to Woman. On Flint Creek near where I was baptized some men picked up a girl with a reputation, got her drunk, and passed her around for sex until they were tired of her. Then they tried to give her to some boys who drove up, but nobody wanted her. So they pushed her out of the car and left her by the side of the road the way some people disposed of unwanted dogs.

Animals Can Be Stupid Too. One day as I was walking across a field a rabbit jumped out of its bed and ran headlong into a tree. It was addled but got up and wobbled off into the woods.

For No Good Reason. A couple of times Mr. O'Rear Smitson gave me a ride on the Corn Road. One day for no good reason his younger daughter told people that I was drunk when they picked me up. First I knew about it.

Check Your Traps. One winter I built a rabbit trap, set it up, but didn't check it for several days. When I finally went back to take a look there was half-starved rabbit inside. It had suffered enough, so I released it, hoping it would survive.

Unneighborly. One day Daddy came home mad because Luther Bates had shot at one of his hunting dogs. He never cared much for Luther anyway, and after that incident, even less. Nevertheless, occasionally we hired out to pick beans for him.

Nothing to Say. As far as I can remember, in all the years she lived with us, Aunt Phoebe and Daddy never said a word to each other. There was no animosity between them that I knew of, just nothing to say.

Double Checking. At night after the dishes were washed and put away, Aunt Phoebe always touched each one to make sure Momma had put them in their proper place in the cupboard (we called it a "safe"). It was a great annoyance to Momma but a duty for Aunt Phoebe.

Weak Magic. Magic doesn't always work, but sometimes it's all we have left. In order to conjure up some company one lonely day, I took a different pathway home from the school bus. When I got home sure enough there was company! Afterwards, when I wanted company, I would take that different path. Sometimes it worked, more often it didn't.

Warts and All. One summer when I was about eight, I had a huge wart of my left hand. I tried to get rid of it the standard way: trying a pebble in a handkerchief and leaving it in a crossroads for someone to pick up and catch the wart. Sure enough, somebody picked up the handkerchief, but the wart stayed on my hand. Exasperated by the whole thing, a few days later I tried a more draconian method: I bit it off. It bled a little but didn't come back. I considered it a lesson learned about taking matters into your own hands, or in this case, my own teeth.

Winter Wonderland. In 1947 we had a spectacular ice storm. Walking through the woods I could hear the tree limbs breaking from the weight. Some of them sounded like screams. Do trees suffer pain?

World in the Distance. From certain places along the Burney Mountain Road you can see smokey-blue mountains in the distance. As a child I thought how lonely it must be for the people there to live so far away. Still intrigued as an adult, I tried to go there in my car to see for myself. But the blued distance always receded before me and I could not reach it. All I found instead were ordinary farms and people on ordinary roads. Still, I know the blue mountains are out there somewhere ever out of my reach. Some things, it seems, were created to exist only in the unreachable distance.

No Silver Lining. As a small child, I was convinced that all dark clouds were evil and dangerous. They terrified me as much as snakes. Once on my way home from Cousin Gene Johnson's house, about two miles east on the Corn Road, a tiny cloud turned dark in the shadow of another above it. I ran in panic, desperately trying to get home to the Red Hill before lightning struck or something equally terrible happened to me. Momma asked me why I was out of breath. I didn't tell her.

Casting Spells. I had certain rituals for causing rain when I wanted to rest from working in the field. For two days straight one summer it worked, and I was exulting in my power. But on the third day the spell failed, and Daddy said he reckoned we needed to finishing hoeing the cotton. Sometimes even Daddy chose work over pastimes.

City Lights. After hitchhiking home from Cullman or Hartselle, usually after midnight, I would stop for a while and look back at the city lights. Even though I was tired and hungry, I felt a strange urge to turn around and go back to them. Their glow symbolized all the happy things I went there to find, but never did. The magic of cities is their lights, and we are like moths addled by the illumination. So I would stand there in our dark field, tempted to fly back to the lights. Happiness seemed to be hiding from me somewhere out there where the lights were, and I wasn't. We spent much time in darkness, but I knew instinctively that we were creatures of the light. After a while I would go in the house and have a glass of milk and cornbread. Momma was always awake. Our existential darkness is no match for a mother's love.

Preaching Fool. They told the story of how Uncle Tolbert once began a mocking sermon to some of his friends. (He had his share of Raley sarcasm.) But when he tried to stop, he couldn't. Not until he was chastened, scared, and exhausted did the Spirit release him. The moral of the story? Do not tempt God; he is dangerously good.

Eyewitness. They said that Uncle Bemis once came upon an orgy in the woods. Some local men and women were romping in a silvan sexual pandemonium. As he watched them from his hiding place, I can imagine he had the same little grin on his face and hummed the same toneless tune as always. It took a lot more than such idiocy for him to alter his calm manner.

Time Sweeps All its Sons Away. According to an 1887 newspaper account, a Hartselle man was arrested for killing his wife, who had recently returned home after five years in the insane asylum. He planned to marry his mistress who, he claimed, urged him to commit the crime. The whole town turned out for the trial, and many Morgan County people came to his hanging. He was convicted on the testimony of his ten-year-old daughter and later confessed himself. He died repentant, praying under his black hood for forgiveness and salvation until the rope cut short his words. It was the crime of the century, people said, and would serve as a lasting warning to evildoers. It didn't, of course. In general, we remedy our wayward lives based only on our own painful sins, never because of anyone else's wrongdoings. After reading the account, I had the forlorn thought that we are all like people in unmarked graves. In a generation or two the memory of us will fade and no one will recall our time in this world. As the Issac Watts' hymn goes (original version), "Time, like an ever-rolling stream sweeps all its sons away/ they fly forgotten as a dream dies at the opening day." I don't recall the Hartselle man's name. I wonder if anyone does.

An Attack of Maturity. When I was barely fifteen, I had what I can only call "a premature moment of maturity." I was walking home through the woods from my Aunt Irene's house—the same upgraded log cabin where we had lived back when I was six—when all of a sudden, I felt that I had stepped into a different time and was a different person. I found myself summarizing the meaning of my life and experience from a mature philosophical perspective. I even recall describing it as "philosophical," a word that was not a part of my usual lexicon. It was a pleasurable experience that did not frighten me at all, yet I knew that the moment was out of place that I was not ready for the mature perspective such thoughts required. I think of it as a brief vision of my life that lay many years in the future, a stray moment of mature contemplation. Yet I knew that my life was heading in the direction of those brief insights. The sensation, though not the memory, of that odd moment soon faded, and I was again who I was at that time: a fifteen-year-old boy not yet out of the woods.

Chapter 29:
Misadventures

Not long after I turned sixteen Cousin Lonzo Johnson started coming around in Uncle Am's 1940 Chevrolet. Lonzo always had access to a car but sometimes not enough money for gasoline. I was making a little money working for neighbors like Paul Pitts who lived near the Panama community. Paul was one of the nicest men I knew and I worked hard for him. "I wouldn't mind one of my daughters marrying a hardworking boy like you some day," he once told me. He had four daughters but no sons. I was flattered by his esteem but unexcited about his daughters. They were pretty enough, but the one nearest my age was sullen and bad tempered. I had several arguments with her on the school bus. The others were too young to attract my attention. Later a tree fell on Paul and killed him, and that was the end of a good friendship and a reliable source of income.

At a more sophisticated level Lonzo had the same philosophy about girls and drinking as my old friend John Chaney, and for a year or so with our pooled money and his car we paid both considerable attention to them. Carol had moved away to West Point and I had no consuming romantic interest.

Lonzo and I were second or third cousins but looked like we belonged to different races. I was stocky and fair; he was lean and dark. Despite our differences we never had a cross word and always agreed on our strategies, which, I should add, usually came to naught.

Even though Lonzo had lost nothing of his great cursing eloquence that impressed us so much as children, he now had a nice manner, handsome appearance, and good manners, a lot like his Uncle Leon. Nevertheless, he had a dark embarrassing secret: he was illiterate. As a child their parents saw to it that he and neighbor Wilburn Blackwood boarded the school bus. But at the very next stop they would jump off and play hooky in the woods behind Shorty Cook's house. As far as I know, neither of them ever went to school a day in their life. But unlike Wilburn who was probably a middle-level moron who could not have learned, Lonzo had remarkable native intelligence. He masked his illiteracy by memorizing everything, from road signs to complicated instructions. Indeed, he learned to compensate so well for his educational deficiency that later in Chicago he worked for ten years as a factory foreman, able only to sign his name but keeping all the necessary information in his head.

One day as we were cruising the Corn Road the two Tankersley brothers, who were always moving our boundary markers, flagged us down and asked us to take them to buy whiskey. We agreed but since the brothers were already half drunk, with signs and whispers Lonzo and I worked out a scheme to keep part of the whiskey for ourselves. We picked up a gallon of moonshine and brought the now drunken brothers back to a wooded area not far from their house. While I talked to them, Lonzo opened the truck and poured a pint or two in another bottle. They were too drunk to miss it and we had enough of the fiery liquid to go on a small spree ourselves. We met up with Leon Woods who laughed about our duplicity and talked us out of a generous swig or two for himself.

One night, Armon and our Cousin Owen James came by in Armon's 1936 Ford to invite me to the movies in Hartselle. We collected Cousin Lonzo on the way, took in the show, and spent a couple of hours cruising around Hartselle and outlying areas. Late that night as we were returning home along the Valley roads, the car headlights suddenly flickered and went out. The night was pitch black but instead of stopping as we yelled for him to do, Armon drove on and after a hundred yards or so landed us in an eight-foot ditch. Nobody was hurt but we had to leave the car and walk the rest of the way home. Armon and Owen got home about four in the morning, Lonzo half an hour later, and I made it around five.

My parents disapproved of my keeping company with the Woods in general and Lonzo in particular, but he had a car—and a girlfriend. Joyce Ann Smith was a pretty girl obviously in love with Lonzo and sure they were headed for marriage. As I said, I had no steady girl at the time. Carol and I double dated with them a time or two, but I still felt protective of her and Lonzo and the Woods family did not seem to me to be a proper environment for her. There were other girls but none I really liked. A year later Lonzo left Alabama for Chicago with his mother and stepfather Charlie Milligan, leaving Joyce Ann bewildered and heartbroken. She waited for his reaffirming letters, but, of course, none came because illiterate Lonzo couldn't write them. Finally, Joyce Ann moved on with her life. Briefly it included me, but that episode comes later.

Chapter 30:
Roads Not Taken

In ninth grade I made the decision to skip shop with kindly Mr. Edleman and take English instead. Building milk stools and mailboxes held little interest; I knew that someday I would leave the farm anyway. Usually the boys who chose English over shop were looked on as Caspar Milquetoasts, and in some cases they were. As for me, however, I was strong enough to keep the respect of my classmates. My English teacher Mrs. Bettina Higdon was a beautiful lady, slightly irreverent, witty, very outspoken for that era, and demanding in her standards. Her husband Raymond was a prominent undertaker who later became the Cullman County Tax Assessor. She taught me geometry, two years of algebra, and one or two English classes. I consider her to be the best high school teacher I had. I have never forgotten a backhanded compliment she paid me in geometry class. Wanza Heard, herself a bright girl, complained one day after a reprimand, "Harold doesn't work much and is always cuttin' up. How come you don't do somethin' to him?" "I don't know what it is about Harold," she said to Wanza in the hearing of the class. "He never seems to study very much but he always has the right answers. But, the rest of you have to work. So get with it!" It was true of geometry, which I understood instinctively, less true of algebra. English was easy, primarily because I had comparatively good writing skills.

Not that Mrs. Higdon let me do as I pleased. Far from it. One day as I was horsing around at my table with Glenn Gentry, my former enemy now on friendly terms, and Hugh Kilgo, a very bright boy a grade ahead of me, Mrs. Higdon became annoyed with the disturbance and swatted me in the palm of the hand with a ruler. I cherished the stinging sensation for, as you may guess, I had developed a respectful crush on her and admired her immensely.

Even though Carol liked me a lot and, unlike me, wanted a closer relationship than the romantic friendship we enjoyed, she unselfishly stepped aside as I went through a couple of my short-lived romances with other girls. The first was Claire Vaughan, probably the only time I was ever attracted to a blonde girl. Claire and Carol were good friends, and Carol befriended us both when it became obvious that Claire had developed a crush on me. Her face told the whole story. She was extremely fair and would blush pink in my presence. We never dated but that year at the West Point Fair we went around together to some of the booths and afterwards were considered a romantic item by our classmates. Once I got up the nerve to go to her house near the Bethlehem community but got cold feet before I got there and returned home without seeing her. Shortly thereafter her family moved back to Oxford, east of Birmingham, and even though we wrote a few times, I never saw her again. In her last letter she told me she had married a soldier off somewhere on military deployment, but feeling lonely, she wanted to continue our friendship. I did not think it was a good idea and did not write her again.

I soon returned to my normal tastes and was attracted to Majorie Collins, a petite brunette a grade behind me. Nothing ever came of our mutual attraction, but it was obvious from the flurry I caused in her presence that she liked me also. But like Claire and other girls I liked, Majorie and her brother Troy soon moved away from West Point.

My decision to skip shop had unforeseen consequences. The

altered schedule meant that I could not practice basketball under Coach Lovell's supervision. When it came time to try out for the team in my junior year, I was too ignorant of the game—to say nothing of being short—to have a chance for the varsity. The coach sent word that he wanted me on the B team, but by then reality had hit me and I realized that for lack of transportation I could not make the practices or get home after the games. It was a bitter realization that I let sour not only my relationship with the Coach but also my outlook on school and life for the next year and a half. The rebellious anger would cause me several serious problems.

To begin with, my grades began to suffer because of my spotty attendance. Basketball was not my only disappointment. To the amazement of my classmates, I announced that I wanted to study Latin and asked Mrs. Hidgon if she would be willing to teach a class. She agreed in principle but said that we needed six to ten students for Principal Earl York to approve it. (Mr. Hamner left West Point when I was in seventh grade.) I could round up only three, Hubert Tolbert, Edward Cornelius, and myself, so Latin became a dead language again.

Add to these frustrations the indignation I felt when Mrs. Lee, my junior-year English teacher, accused me of plagiarizing an essay about the Korean War. I denied the charge with an anger that startled and frightened her. She did not know, of course, that I was protesting a lot more than the essay. The accusation was settled in my favor—perhaps when Mrs. Higdon and others spoke on my behalf—but the larger issues about the direction of my life remained.

My interest in girls had not disappeared, but now that nearly all the boys had cars and dating presupposed movies and food in popular drive-ins like the Globe in Cullman, I was unable to participate unless by chance I was asked to double date as an emergency stand-in. I hitchhiked occasionally into town and sometimes saw my friends driving around. Asked what I was doing walking around town by myself, I would answer with a laugh, "just waiting for somebody." I felt that the world had passed me by.

Eventually the age of farm mechanization even caught up with us, at least temporarily. Daddy traded for a giant one-cylinder Farmall tractor with several plows and attachments. It burned just about any fuel available, gasoline, kerosene, and petroleum products in between. We soon discovered, however, that it was no real improvement over our animals. To begin with, it took real muscle to keep it aligned on the sloping fields. As for preparing the land for planting, it had only one turning plow and was impossibly slow. We used it for a while before trading it. The tractor was devilishly hard to hand crank, so to start it we usually left it parked in the sloping pasture behind the barn. There we could let it build up speed and then start it by letting out the clutch. Darrell tells of seeing Bufus trying to crank it this way but apparently forgot to put it in gear. By the time he realized it, he could not engage the gears and the tractor had practically no brakes. Darrell says Bufus rode the tractor as it sailed over the old terrace rows, bouncing him high in the air. But again, the fates protected Bufus from his own follies and he came out unscathed.

My main experience with the old Farmall happened near Round Top in the Valley. Coyd Flowers, Daddy's cousin, had a field he wanted turned. So Daddy sent me over the Backbone (a western extension of Burney Mountain) to Coyd's farm. It took me hours to get down to the Valley and nearly two days of almost non-stop plowing to finish the field. Coyd had a job with Morgan County and probably thought I dawdled away the day when he came home the first afternoon and found the field only half done.

We worked a few times for Coyd and I liked him. He died of a heart attack at 46 in 1970.

In my senior year I was almost completely estranged from school activities and missed many classes. Once a class leader, I had become not so much a class rebel, which was not my style, but a silent dissenter and no-show. I had spent much of my life alone, but whereas before I had been comfortable in solitude, now I craved company just when I had so little of it. John Chaney and I renewed our old acquaintance and a couple of times while I was out with him a cousin of his stole items from a farmer's barn. I did not really enjoy John's company any longer, for he was forever stuck at age fifteen, but I had nothing better to do, it seemed. I stopped going to church altogether unless it was to flirt with the girls.

But in the midst of my sullen, rebellious turmoil, Daddy announced that we were going to buy a car. Crops had been fairly good that year, but the truth was we couldn't afford an automobile. I think the real reason was that he was worried about me and wanted to find some way to deal with my odd withdrawal, sullen attitude, and disreputable activities, some of which had gotten back to him. Of course, I denied everything when asked about them.

We went to a Cullman used car lot one Saturday in October of 1952 and bought a shiny 1940 Ford, V8 and black of course. I had a license by then, having taken the test in Lonzo's car, but the car had no license plate. I drove home by the Dripping Springs road to avoid the highway patrol and felt that maybe life was beginning to turn the corner for me.

Since Daddy did not have a license and did not really know how to drive, the Ford effectively became my car. And I proceeded to make up for as much lost time as I could with girls and dating. After a couple of tentative moves that got nowhere, to my misfortune my eye fell on a girl a grade behind me but a year older. A smoker, Joyce Fincher seemed more sophisticated than the other West Point girls and talked to me about books, art, and poetry. She was a gifted artist as well. I was captivated by her flattering attentions and pretty soon we were dating, and she was talking ominously of marriage.

Now that I think about it again, my chronology is a bit off, for she had caught my eye even before we bought the Ford. A couple of times Lonzo and I double dated with Joyce and her cousin (he was tiring of girlfriend Joyce Ann) and experienced a couple of embarrassing problems. The first time the timing chain went out on his car and Joyce's father had to take us home. The next time, a Sunday afternoon in late November, we ran out of gas near the forest watchtower in southern Cullman County and barely had enough money between us to get the girls and ourselves home. As we were leaving, Joyce whispered to me, "Come back tonight, Harold. Come in your car and don't bring Lonzo."

It was my birthday and that night Joyce told me how serious she was about our relationship. This led her to confess things to me that I was unable to handle. I was the boy she wanted to marry, she told me and that all the other boys who had been in her life now meant nothing to her. "What other boys?" I wanted to know. Unfortunately, she told me. There had been many, mostly in Florida where she had lived. Her main boyfriend had a motorcycle and she had broken a collarbone on the machine and her heart in the romance. For even though he promised to marry her, he left her for another girl. Afterwards, there were others, in Florida and Alabama

I tried manfully to understand her, to accept what she was telling me, but in the end, it was no use. Her history and experience frightened me and put a cold end to my romanticized notions about her. After a few more dates she was more eager than ever to get married, but the more she talked about it, the less enthusiastic I became. I dated other girls, including Joyce Ann Smith, who had now given up on Lonzo. The other Joyce found out and made a tearful, jealous scene. I knew then I had to end the relationship, but for a time lacked the courage to tell her.

In one thing, at least, maybe I should have heeded her advice. In November of 1952 it was time for me to register with the Selective Service. And at Bunk's urging, as soon as I became eligible, I also joined the Army Reserves. "Don't do it, Harold," Joyce pleaded. "Don't get involved in that military stuff." But I did anyway, primarily for the few dollars in pay I received each month. Every Monday night I had to attend the Reserve meeting in Cullman. It did not seem like a big deal.

Finally, one day in March of 1953 she and I met in the school hallway. I had been avoiding her. "Do you love me, Harold?" she asked. I hesitated and looked out the window, thinking this is as good a time as any to break it off. "What do you think?" I responded in an icy tone, averting her stare. Tears came to her eyes and she responded softly, "I understand. Goodbye, Harold. I won't bother you again."

Except it was not quite the end. The school was getting ready for its annual festival and the teachers asked Joyce and me to make several posters. Neither of us knew we would be working with the other. It was a tense, yet tender time for us both. I came to appreciate once again the qualities that had attracted me to her in the first place. She was marvelously talented, and her tone was subdued and considerate, and not without her occasional flashes of humor. But the hurt was still in her eyes. I wished we could have started over again as friends and nothing else. I saw her only once after that, a year after high school, at a church revival at Jones Chapel near her home. "Hello, Harold," she said to me. "Is that all you have to say to me?" I asked her with as flirtatious a smile and tone as I could manage. By then I had forgotten much of the hurt and disappointment in our relationship and that night was impressed anew by her gorgeous looks. Perhaps we could at least have a final summer fling, I thought. But she, undoubtedly reading my selfish thoughts and wiser than I about the heartbreak it would lead to, smiled tenderly, said nothing, and walked away from my life for good.

Chapter 31:
Michigan, Military, Misery

Graduation was approaching. My life became a chaotic blur of activity. My plans were made to head for Flint, Michigan with classmates Marlon Alvis and Waymon Rutherford as soon as I had my diploma in hand. Tommy Sandlin was in Alabama on vacation and offered us a ride to Detroit. In the meantime, I hardly showed up at home anymore. The night before I left for Michigan my father and I had words about my behavior that turned into an angry shoving match. Luckily Armon was there to mediate. The graduation itself was a bit anticlimactic. My grades had slipped my final year and I ended up in third place behind Ruby Clay and Yvonne Anderson, but they conferred the title of Class Poet and Vice President on me. Both girls, and especially Yvonne, had remained my steadfast friends throughout all my personal turmoil in high school. I remember them both with special affection. All the goodbyes were, of course, both happy and emotional.

After the bitter scene with Daddy and some anguished words from Momma, which I brushed aside, Armon took me to Junior Heck's house on Highway 31 where I was to meet Tommy early next morning. He was on time; Waymon and Marlon were in the back seat; and we headed for Michigan.

It took all day and part of the night to get there. Meanwhile Tommy informed us about Northern ways and what to expect. We stopped only a few times, once when the Oldsmobile began clattering not long after we crossed the Michigan state line. We could find nothing wrong and the noise soon stopped. We drove on into Detroit without incident. In that pre-interstate era we went through many towns and countless red lights. On the other hand, in 1953 traffic was probably a tenth of its present volume. After we passed Pulaski, Tennessee I was in virgin country. But because our destination held out the promise of fabulous money, we could not wait to get to Flint.

Tommy dropped us off at the Detroit bus station, a crowded, bewildering place. Our plan was to take the first bus on to Flint, about sixty or seventy miles north and the heart of General Motors country. We had heard there was a hiring frenzy. But before we left Detroit, Waymon almost fell victim to his country boy naiveté. A man approached him, introduced himself as a California doctor, and asked if he would be interested in driving a new car to California for a truly handsome sum of money. Waymon ran to report the offer to us. Marlon was interested, but I took one look at the man and warned them to stay clear.

"That man's a queer," I told them.

"A queer? I don't believe there's any such thing as a queer," Waymon responded. "I aint never seen one."

"You have now," I replied, "and there are lots of them around, more than you'd think."

"How would you know?" Waymon asked skeptically.

"Because I've done a lot of hitchhiking and been picked up by several. They look just like any other man. But you can tell." (Remember that all this took place before the age of "political correctness," and our language reflected it.)

What I told him was true. I had been propositioned at least twice during my hitchhiking days, once in the company of Douglas Long by a large middle-aged man in a Hudson automobile, and again by a clean-cut young man in a new Ford. The first time, Doug and I were shocked almost speechless, for we had barely heard of such men. We got out of the Hudson trembling with anger and disgust. Later in college I saw the older man again. He was a prominent citizen of Athens, Alabama. The next time I handled the situation better, if for no other reason because I was probably stronger than the homosexual and could have defended myself easily.

Marlon and Waymon were impressed by my experience and rejected the California offer. A few hours later we boarded the bus for Flint. Foolishly, I decided to check my small suitcase. We arrived around midday as I recall, and I went immediately to retrieve my luggage, which contained my clothes, birth certificate, and high school diploma. It was nowhere to be found. I went back over the next few days but to no avail.

Meanwhile the rumors were true. GM recruiters had booths set up at the bus station to hire people as they got off the bus. You can work here in Flint, or we can send you to Lansing, they informed us. We signed up for Flint. Waymon and Marlon decided to go with Chevrolet Division, but I had to delay a decision because of my lost papers.

We took lodging at Ma Britt's place on the west side of Flint. I cannot recall how we came across the place, most likely by chance and a big sign that read "Rooms for Rent." Ma and her family were originally from Arkansas and had not lost their Southern speech and manners, so we felt that at least we were with our kind of people in this strange Yankee city. We were put off by the odd accent and brusque manners of the Northerners but eager to take their money. Not long after we got to Flint, we went out to an amusement park where we met some girls. The girls were receptive, and we spent some time and money with them, but they laughed when we asked in good Southernese if we "carry them home."

"I'm kinda big to carry," one of them said with a cute giggle.

After that experience and a few other sarcastic comments about my speech I decided I would amend my English so that my Southern origins would not be so obvious. It worked and within a few weeks no one would guess I was from Alabama. The transformation was not as difficult as it seems. Unlike the deep and noticeable accent of South Alabama, our Appalachian speech was not that far removed from standard lower Midwestern English, needing only a few tweaks here and there in its cadence and phrasing, a little work on its rough grammar, and an increase in tempo.

I should mention that the day we got to Flint a terrible tornado hit the north side of the city. Reports made it sound like the whole city was devastated, and when my relatives heard the news, they were afraid I had been killed. I slept through the storm, remembering in my sleep only something like the rumbling of a train that did not quite awaken me.

If only my financial situation had been as easily remedied as my English. My papers were irretrievably lost, it seemed, and without them I could not work. My friends and I conferred about my plight and decided that I would use Waymon's papers to get a job. It worked and for a few weeks I hired in at Fisher Body as Waymon Rutherford. It took a while to get used to the name. No doubt some of my coworkers thought I was retarded when they called my "name" and I did not respond.

Meanwhile I was nearly out of money, and my friends were not much better off. Payday was still nearly two weeks away. I decided to go down to Wyandotte to find Cousin Armon and Uncle Tolbert who had moved there shortly after Uncle Felton. Armon had spent some time in the Army when his National Guard unit was called up, but after he got out there was no work for him in Alabama, so he went north with our uncles. I bought a ticket with almost the last of my money and ended up back at the Detroit bus station. I knew vaguely that Wyandotte was south or southwest of Detroit not far from the river. I set out walking in that direction, naturally without Tolbert's or Armon's address. All I knew was that they lived in a certain trailer park in Wyandotte. After walking for an hour or two a city bus came along going my way and I rode it to the end of the line but still had a long way to go to get to Wyandotte. Finally, late in the afternoon I spotted a trailer park not far ahead and by a miracle it turned out to be the right one. I found Armon and then Tolbert, and when my uncle saw me, he hugged me with tears in his eyes. "We thought maybe you might be dead, killed in that tornader. We wuz worried to death about you, son. Ye need to write ye Daddy and Momma, too."

I thought my problems were over. Armon lent me the few dollars he had and fed me lavishly. That Sunday, replenished, I went back to Flint and to work the next day.

But I underestimated the inflated price of things in prosperous Flint. By the Tuesday of the following week three and a half days before my first payday, my money was gone. I spent my last dollar on bread and a few slices of bologna and went out to eat them in a city park. I recall that a particularly obtrusive, obsequious man—probably a homosexual—came up and asked me any number of nosy questions about my background and life. I gave him only evasive answers. On top of my other problems, I thought, the last thing I need now is another homosexual pestering me.

After work on Tuesday night I was hungry, by Wednesday seriously so, and by Thursday so hungry that I was becoming desperate. I said not a word to my friends, for it had become a matter of pride and shame to me. Not thinking very clearly, I walked into a bank to ask about a loan. Any collateral? the young banker wanted to know. No, I admitted, thinking to myself that if I had collateral, I wouldn't need a loan. He was gracious but unhelpful and I was again on the street, wondering if I would be able to work two more days without eating. I thought of stealing food and even robbing somebody. I was hardy and used to hunger and minimal diets, but the factory work was hard and hot, and I was getting close to my limit. Probably I had lost ten or twelve pounds of my original hundred and forty-five. My belt was in its last notch and tough as I thought I was my tank was on empty.

This and similar experience taught me that truly hungry people will do almost anything in their desperation. Morality, ethics, and honesty sound like empty, pious words that collapse as real hunger takes over. As a consequence, I understand and even sympathize to a degree with those who break the rules to feed a starving family or themselves.

Determined not to crack, I made it through my shift on Thursay, and got back to work on Friday. Then I began to count the slow minutes and hours until my first check. I worked second shift (3-11 p.m.) and four hours into it at the break the foreman came down the line with our checks. I took mine with a trembling hand. "Want to work another shift, Waymon?" he asked me. "I need some extra men." Instead of screaming "NO!" at the top of my lungs as I felt like doing, I answered calmly, "I'd like to help out, and ordinarily would, but I've already promised to do something else after work." He shrugged and walked away. I felt like I had won a battle, but one I would never want to fight again.

The promise I had made was, naturally, to eat as quickly and as much as possible. I cashed my check at one of the quick cash stations just outside the factory and fairly ran into the first open restaurant I could find. It may have been the small diner just around the corner from Ma Britt's, but my memory is hazy on that detail.

I overdid it and almost got sick. I remember wolfing down a large meat pie and loathing them for months thereafter. But with a full stomach and a good night's sleep I was all right. I recall going out to a movie the next evening and being in especially high spirits. The ordeal was over. Within a few days I was back to normal weight and strength.

The next time the foreman came around asking for extra time, I obliged him and since it was on a weekend earned time and a half for my efforts. I had never made so much money. After sixteen hours I was tired but anxious to see H.G. Wells' <u>War of the Worlds</u>. I got home, cleaned up, and went alone to the movie. My friends had gone elsewhere. Despite my enthusiasm about the movie I fell sound asleep halfway through and slept through the rest of show.

My job at Fisher Body was spot welding fenders and supports on 1953 Buicks. My partner and I had to wear safety glasses and gloves because of the hot metal and flying sparks. Today robots do my old job. My partner was a local boy some years older than I who lived on a farm outside of Flint, and except for his Michigan accent could almost have passed with his country ways for a rural Southern boy. We quickly became genuinely fond of each other.

After a month, however, the inconveniences of my Reserve affiliation became apparent. I was called for basic training and had to quit my job as "Waymon Rutherford" and return to Alabama. My partner, whose name I have long since forgotten, had a 1937 Buick for sale, a huge straight-8 monster with salt-rusted fenders but, he assured me, with a good engine and fair rubber. We agreed on a price of $30.00. Waymon—the real Waymon—who had bought a 1939 Oldsmobile in the meantime, drove Marlon and me out to the farm to pick up my rusty old Buick. A couple of Cullman County boys heard I was leaving for

Alabama and wanted a ride. They offered to buy gasoline. Naturally I accepted, and the next day we headed south.

It was early morning the next day when I finished delivering my friends to their respective homes in Cullman County. Both were, I think, leaving the factory scene and joining the Air Force. Groggy with fatigue and lack of sleep, I misjudged a curve in the graveled road and the old Buick slid into a ditch. I left the car and walked to Uncle Am's latest residence a few miles north on Highway 31. We retrieved the Buick and I made it home. A couple of days later, in uniform, I had to leave for Fort Jackson, South Carolina.

I went by train from Birmingham. It was only the second time in my life I had been on a train, having once ridden the mail train from Lacon to Cullman. Regular military men met the recruits in Columbia and escorted us to Fort Jackson. They assigned us to our barracks, gave us our bedding and other equipment and told us to be ready for duty early the next day. In the meantime, we ate, bathed, and got acquainted. The food was awful, according to my companions, but I thought it was delicious.

With the exception of a couple of rural boys from South Alabama, most of the other recruits were from Birmingham and more northerly cities. As far as I know, I was the only one from North Alabama. The next day the sergeants begin trying to shape us into a military unit. We learned to throw hand grenades, disassemble and reassemble M-1 rifles, and march and maneuver in some sort of military order. On the rifle range, I discovered I was in my element. I was always a passably good marksman, but in the company of boys who had never held a gun, I was the star of my company. One of the less distinguished moments of my military experience occurred when a three-star general, commander of the 31st or Dixie Division, strolled by with his aides to inspect the scene. I had just knocked out the center of my target. "Where'd you learn to shoot like that, son?" asked the kindly old general. "Back on the farm, I suppose, sir. We always had guns around and I'm used to shooting." I felt like an Alabama version of movie star Audie Murphy (and a genuine hero of World War II). The general smiled, told me to carry on, and walked away with his aides. Whereupon, a young lieutenant rushed up and began to scream and curse. "Don't you know who that was?" he raged, summoning me to attention. And without waiting for a response, he explained, "that, private Raley, was a three-star general, the Commander of our division. And so what the hell did you do, private Raley? You lay there on the damn ground without a salute, without even standing at attention when addressed by an officer, and by the Commanding General no less. I can't believe it. My God, Raley, what in hell were you thinking?" "Guess I wasn't thinking, and I'm sorry, sir." "Sorry won't cut it in this army," he snapped as he walked away. I soon surmised, however, that the higher the officers the less they stood on rigid protocol. It was the lesser ranks that made life miserable.

The major part of our training was our time on bivouac. They took us out into the deep woods miles from the base and ordered us to set up our tents—two men to a tent—and prepare for our first march. First, they fed us a smelly fish broth around which gnats were swarming. The city boys, some of whom had slipped off base and gotten drunk the evening before, were ready to vomit, but since the woods and bugs of South Carolina looked and felt exactly like those of Alabama, I thought nothing of it. I simply dipped out the gnats and ate my food as I always had. They gave us salt tablets to take, but I tossed mine in the bushes. I had never needed extra salt and saw no reason now to take the army's. The march with a sixty-pound backpack was an ordeal for many in the company. Not only were they unused to walking but also the heat was stifling, more than several of the Northern boys could endure. A few of them got dizzy from the heat—and their hangover—and had to fall out of line and sit for a time. The cadre taunted them for their softness but saw to their welfare as they did so.

The most impressive of our experiences was the firepower display the army staged for us. Pointing to targets miles away on the side of a hill, the gunners then aimed the big guns and commenced to demolish them with incredible accuracy. Standing guard in the early morning hours was no fun. The main enemy was drowsiness.

Early one morning back on base I awoke to find men filing out of the barracks. "Where're you going?" I inquired. "To get our masturbation orders," one of the South Alabama boys told me, "like we was ordered to do. We're supposed to line up down at the Colonel's quarters." "Who told you about the orders?" I asked. "Gus told us. and he got the order from the Lieutenant." I smiled and turned to go back to sleep. "Aint you goin', Raley?" my buddy wanted to know. "Naw, y'all go ahead. I'll take my chances," I replied, smugly grateful for my education.

Ole Gus, Gus Vlahos, was the jokester and star of the camp. The tall, handsome son of the Greek owner of the Mary Ball Candy Company in Birmingham, Gus seemed to have all the privileges and none of the privations of life. To him a little time in the Reserves seemed a good way to avoid long term duty in messy places like Korea. As different as daylight and dark, he and I hit it off from the first. He assisted me on the firing range and was mightily impressed by my accuracy. He was even more impressed when it turned out that I was the only other man in our company who knew the kind of orders he was talking about. The Colonel pretended to be furious over having his sleep disturbed, but we heard that privately he appreciated the joke and had a good laugh about it with his officers. When our summer training was over, Gus invited me to visit him in Birmingham. "Raley," he told me, "you come on down to Birmingham and I'll introduce to the prettiest girls you've ever seen, and we'll have parties like you never dreamed of." I did not doubt his word, but Gus's world was light years from mine and too rich for my country blood. At that point in my life I would have been a buffoon in such company. For all his bluster and bravado, I sensed that Gus was a man's man and a person you could depend on. I wonder what happened to him and hope life dealt him a good hand.

Having finished summer basic training and returned to Alabama, I spent a week at home before heading north again. The fenders were falling off the old Buick after a few days on our dirt roads and it was missing on one cylinder. I suspected a burned valve. The day before leaving I drove the old wreck into a Cullman junkyard and sold it for $25.00. Not a bad deal considering it had brought me from Michigan.

Then it was time to leave. Daddy (to whom I had made my proper apologies) and Tootsie Russell took me across the Tennessee River in the '40 Ford, now limping along with burned valves and other problems. Not long after that I caught a ride and eventually made it to Louisville, Kentucky. There I decided to take the bus on to Michigan. My friends were glad to see me. I settled in again at Ma Britt's and soon got a new job on the motor line at the Buick Division. (I had replaced my lost documents.) For the next few months I prospered, and life ran fairly smoothly for me. I sent money weekly to my parents and made the payment on the farm that year. My work on the motor line was monotonous but less fatiguing than spot welding over at Fisher Body. The man next to me whom we called "Missouri" was skilled at his job and before long he and I were able to do both jobs at once, freeing either of us to take off and wander up to the lunchroom or elsewhere. My job consisted of putting on fuel pumps with an air wrench and screwing a small tube to the carburetor. My partner had a similar trivial job that required some manual dexterity but no special skill.

Our arrangement lasted only a few days before one of the UAW union stewards saw what we were doing and cautioned us against it. "If management sees you doing that, one of you will be fired and the other will have all the work to do." We took his caution seriously and got back to our place.

On weekends I roamed around with Waymon and Marlon. We soon discovered that Flint was full of people from Cullman County and surrounding areas. Among them were the Burch brothers Norman and Gene, high school buddies of mine who were especially good friends to Marlon and his family. The whole Burch family had resettled in Flint, and visits to their home were like a return to Alabama. I have never forgotten their wonderful hospitality. One day we pulled into a service station in Waymon's Oldsmobile and who should come out to help us but Donald Cheatham from the Panama community. We had a happy reunion and Donald asked us where we were headed. We told him, and he asked us to wait a minute and he would go with us. "But Donald," I objected in astonishment, "you mean you're just going to walk off and leave the service station unattended?" "Yeah, I'm tired of workin' fer this old fart and ready to do somethin' else." With that he filled the tank, took an extra quart of oil, placed the keys above the door, and rode away with us. And without charging Waymon for the gasoline, I should add. Donald was now married but unchanged in his fun-loving, few-wheeling way of life.

We made several trips, one to Sarnia, Canada, and another up to Saginaw Bay. Even though Waymon was supposedly engaged to the girl he eventually married, he had gotten involved with a local girl and was terrified she was pregnant. He tried to talk us all into going to Buffalo, New York, but nobody was interested, least of all not to get him out of a fix he had willingly brought on himself. Waymon was scared and one night got drunk to alleviate his miseries, but instead his escapade brought on a new one. That day he had bought a pair of shoes that were too tight for him. But drunk out of his mind he felt nothing and proceeded to run through the streets of Flint daring us to catch him and shouting drunken insults to any and all within hearing. Finally, we overtook him and got him back home. The next morning his feet were a swollen, bloody mess. He pleaded for sympathy and got very little from us. For several days he could barely walk and had to limp to work.

In November GM's Buick division phased out the last of its straight-8 engines and with a promise to rehire us eventually, laid off almost all the workers. The hiring boom was over for the time being, and I decided to go back to Alabama.

Before leaving Flint, however, I heard about an old lady who for years had kept a fabulous 1940 Buick coupe locked away in her garage. I was intrigued and found her house. Sure enough, the Buick was a beauty, cream and light green with white sidewall tires. The inside was immaculate and even the clock still worked. "No one has driven it since my husband passed away," she explained. Afraid I couldn't afford it, I timidly inquired about her asking price. Apparently, the lady had not been out in recent years and was unaware how much prices had inflated. "Well, I was thinking about $250.00," she answered almost apologetically. My heart was pounding as I counted out the money. Car transfers were a simple cash transaction in those years, and I am not sure I even got a bill of sale. In any case, getting tags and title for any car was ridiculously easy in Alabama, a mecca for stolen automobiles in that era.

The layoff increased my disillusionment with factory work. True, the money was good, but prices were high, and paychecks seemed to melt away. I got back to Alabama happy with my 1940 Buick, but unhappy and aimless. During that time Aunt Phoebe got sick and passed away in the Cullman hospital. I drove over into Winston County to inform Uncle Bud Waid's family. We buried her in the Friendship cemetery next to Grandma and Grandpa Hooper.

The following weeks in Alabama were some of the dreariest of my life. I was resentful at the world in general and disgusted with myself. I expressed my frustration in alcoholic escapades that led to several brushes with the law. Finally, not having any better options, I reluctantly headed back to Michigan in December. My fancy old Buick had sprung an oil leak that damaged the engine. It still looked great, but I decided to sell it to Tootsie Russell, now living in the Johnson house.

I arrived on the Greyhound bus around three in the morning. According to a bank marquee the temperature had dropped to 8 below zero, as I recall, and I was dressed only in levi pants and a jacket. Luckily, I did have fur lined gloves but no cap. Rather than risk walking out to the west side of Flint in the sub-zero cold, I ducked into a seedy, all-night movie theater frequented by winos and bums. But it was deliciously warm, and I stayed there the rest of the night. When morning came, I had eggs and bacon in a diner next door to the movie. Then warm and fortified, I set out for Ma Britt's about fifteen blocks away. My ears were freezing by the time I got there but luckily my friends were home and once again I settled in with them. A day or so later I hired in at the same Fisher Body plant where I had worked under Waymon's name.

A few weeks after I arrived, we had a surprise visit from our old classmate Willard Butler. Willard may have been the most intelligent student in our class but so diffident and withdrawn that his brilliance remained a secret to all but a few of us who got to know him. A tall blond boy, he had played center for our basketball team. We all expressed our surprise at seeing him because we had heard that he had joined the Marines. "I am in the service but on furlough and just wanted to come up and see you boys," he explained. I have no idea how he found us in Michigan, and neither did anybody else in the house. But we were glad to see him and offered him a place to sleep.

Waymon's mother had come to spend some time with us. Under her kindly but firm direction we cleaned up the place, which had been as chaotic as three undisciplined boys could make it. A widowed lady, Mrs. Rutherford kept a .38 revolver for protection. The next morning when we got up Willard was gone and so was the .38 and several other items of value, including my billfold, a dollar or two, and newly restored birth certificate and social security card. A few days later the national news services reported that a Marine deserter named Willard Butler hijacked a car in Kentucky and forced a couple to drive him to another state where he went on a crime spree. Eventually he was caught, tried for several crimes, and sentenced to prison. He died there many years later, one of the earliest victims of AIDS. Looking back, it is reasonable to suppose from the signs he showed that Willard was gay, or better said, wretched and in deep conflict over his condition. At the time, however, we had no way of knowing and probably would have been horrified had we known. In those days there was no tolerance, legal or social, of homosexuality.

As I said, at Fisher Body I was assigned a job just a few yards from where I had worked as Waymon Rutherford. My old partner saw me and came over to greet me.

"Hey, Waymon, it's good to see you back."

"I'm not Waymon," I corrected him with a straight face. "You must have me confused with somebody else."

"But you look just like a boy I used to work with a few months ago," he protested. "His name was Waymon. You've got to be him. Don't you remember? You bought my old Buick," he insisted, peering at my face from different angles.

I continued the farce for a few days before confessing to him that I really was the same guy he knew, only I had a different name from the one I used during my first stint at Fisher Body.

A few days later Marlon, Waymon, and Mrs. Rutherford left for Christmas in Alabama and I remained alone in our apartment. The next few days, especially Christmas and the New Year, were the loneliest I have ever experienced. Everybody I knew had gone south. I was alone in a dark, frozen, snowed-in city. I spent time walking the streets, going to movies, and reading, but the sense of isolation was overwhelming. I promised myself that I would never spend another Christmas alone. So far, I haven't.

Marlon and Waymon returned—Mrs. Rutherford stayed in Alabama—and the next weeks passed in unchanging sameness: snow, cold, and semi-perpetual darkness. From December to March I do not remember seeing the sun. Then one day in middle March—I have forgotten the exact date—the clouds finally broke, the sun came out, the temperature rose, and I felt a boundless euphoria. Only someone who has experienced the gloom of a Northern winter can really appreciate the glory of spring. It was so marvelous that instead of taking the bus I walked five or six miles to my work. And promptly came down with my first cold of the winter.

A few days later, two unpleasant things happened. First, Cousin Owen James showed up looking for a job and, second, I received word that I would have to answer legal charges in Cullman. It involved some allegedly stolen property that Bode

Woods had loaded in a car with Nathan's and my help. I considered ignoring the summons and thumbing my nose at Alabama. But I thought better of it and asked to be away from work for a few days. My foreman refused to give me the time off, but the GM plant manager overruled him. Meanwhile, Owen almost convinced me of his sincerity, and I helped him find a good job. The automobile industry was in a downturn and jobs were becoming scarce. I told Owen he was lucky to find such an opening and a place with us at Ma Britt's. He reported to work and then quit after one shift. "Them ole Yankee sonsabitches aint gonna tell me what to do," he explained defiantly. "What did they tell you to do?" I asked. "They wuz tryin' to get me to work that conveyor belt with them transmissions on it." "But wasn't that your job?" "Yeah," he admitted but I was restin' for a little bit and they started in rarin' at me."

Instead of choking Owen, as I was at first inclined to do, I ignored him and packed my things.

"I reckon I'll go back home with you," he said after a while.

"Do as you please, Owen."

"Onliest thing is I reckon I'll need to borrow some money to get back on. I'll pay you back soon's I can. You know me, Harold, you can always count on me to keep my word."

It was all I could do not to laugh in his face, but I decided it was better to get him back to Alabama than to have to support him in Michigan.

We rode the bus back to Cullman and took a taxi out to the house. The next day he went on down to Jones Chapel. He never repaid me, thus living up my expectations of him.

At the hearing I received a strong lecture about bad choices and unsavory associations, but after the complexities of the case were examined—the official worth of the items in question amounted to about $25)—the court let me walk free of charges because I was gainfully employed. I explained that I was determined to stay clear of problems and troublemakers. There was an ironical twist to the case that I learned about many years later. I ran into Nathan shortly before he died of cancer and learned that Bode had told the truth—for once—and that the things we helped him load really were his property. There was no theft to begin with. Nathan explained that the owner of the house where the things were stored had framed Bode for supposedly having wronged his daughter. That part may have been true; the alleged theft was not.)

With that load lifted from my shoulders, I returned to Michigan only to discover that the humiliated foreman had managed to get me laid off. I was not surprised, in fact not even disappointed. GM had a practice of laying workers off just before they became eligible for UAW membership (90 days), and I had reached that point. Three times I had tried to make it in Flint, and three times I had failed. Enough was enough, I thought. I barely had time to unpack my things before I packed my suitcase again, said goodbye to my friends and left Flint, first for Wyandotte and then for Alabama.

Tolbert and Armon had also decided to return to Alabama. Tolbert planned to work a few months longer but meanwhile wanted us to take his car back home. It was a long 1941 Buick and we cruised south without any problem to speak of. The only difficulty I had was Aunt Viola's remark in a letter to Tolbert and Sarah that I was "driving the Buick around in Alabama." Such was not the case at all; I think I made one short trip in the Buick before parking it at Tolbert's house. Unfortunately, it was to Viola's house to deliver some things Armon had left in the car, which led her to the erroneous conclusion.

Chapter 32:
One Bale for College

But despite the sense of relief I felt as I left Flint for the last time, I was still in a quandary. Tired of factory labor in the North and the farm work in the South and convinced from my army experience that the military was not for me either, I did not know which way to turn. Stymied by indecision, I would stay home for the time being and help the family with the crop.

Darrell, Janice, and Joyce were growing up and it pained me to see them caught in a deeper version of the same poverty that had squeezed the joy out of our family and driven me to the brink of disaster. Daddy seemed to have lost interest in the farm, although looking back, I suspect his health had deteriorated more than any of us realized. The world had passed us by, and it broke my heart to see my younger siblings suffering the consequences. I wanted to help them, but my own dilemma absorbed all my thoughts. The old house, barn, and other buildings were dilapidated and falling apart. We moved to the Walker place with high hopes and enthusiasm, but the dream had failed.

I did my last farming in 1954 and also had my first and last experience as a tenant farmer. The Evans place south of us, where the Blackwoods, Browns, Bradfords, McReaths, Dentons, and others had lived, was now vacant. I went down to Falkville and rented a few acres from old Mrs. Evans for a corn crop which, following in Bufus's footsteps, I planned to peddle in Hartselle and Decatur. If I recall correctly, instead of paying her in kind, that is, in corn, I paid her $20 for the use of as many acres as I wanted. I planted about four.

That spring John Thomas Johnson, my Cousin Gene's grandfather, asked Daddy and me to come over and help him plant his corn. Mr. Johnson was in his late sixties and unable to do the heavier farm work, yet still spy enough to finish a crop with a little help. He was a meticulous man who liked Daddy but not his lax farming skills. "Sigh, son," he said to me. "Go see if you can lay off my corn rows." I obliged him and in his own words proceeded to lay off the most perfect corn rows John Thomas had ever seen in all his farming days in Cordele, Georgia and Alabama. "Sigh, Barthel," he said to Daddy, using his odd preface to everything he thought important, "that boy of yours is something else. I aint never seen better plowin'." To this day I treasure the praise of that old perfectionist.

For a part of the summer Daddy worked away. It may have been in the Bessmer iron mines, or perhaps Chicago. In any case, once again I was primarily responsible for the crop. But nothing was the same as it had been. I knew I was there only temporarily but had no idea about what was next in my life. As the summer wore on, a word began to obsess me: "expansion." I must expand my life. but my frustrations mounted as I failed to find my direction. I went to the Dough Ball revival, but it did not resonate with me at all. I do recall with gratitude that my Uncle Athel, who later became the Pastor of Roundtop Church, came to me, put his arm around my shoulder and prayed for me to come back to the right pathway. I loved my Uncle Athel but was indifferent to Dough Ball religion. Now much of it seemed off-track and poorly interpreted. I thought of the time volatile Henry Milligan got the shouting urge and leaping to his feet with a piercing scream, kicked out a section of the heater pipe in his exuberance. Smoke and soot filled the church. Surely, I reasoned, Christianity is more than this; surely life is more than this. I was now traveling in another direction, or so I thought. I made my move;

in time God would make His.

Daddy had traded the 40 Ford for a 1946 or 47 Chevrolet pickup with an unusable second gear. I drove it to Cullman a few times, but it was too rough and run down to ask a girl to ride in it. One night on the Corn Road a black cat darted in front of me and I ran over it unintentionally. Had I killed my bad luck?

Meanwhile, I traded vehicles several times, starting with a Harley Davidson 45 motorcycle I bought from Junior Heck (Willie Heck Blackman's son and husband to Christine Woods Heck). Riding it was an exhilarating but dangerous experience. Our sandy, rutted road was not made for motorcycles and I took several spills trying to make it over to the bumpy but hard packed Corn Road.

That summer I played a few games of baseball with a team Tal Woods, friend Billy's father, organized and coached as best he could. We had a lackluster record against better teams, and I think I lost the only complete game I pitched. Because of my years of rock throwing, naturally my control was excellent, too good in fact because I centered every pitch squarely over the plate instead of nipping the corners. But no one coached me. My best pitch was a lively knuckleball, but it was hard to catch and nearly as hard to hit when it was dipping and weaving. Enough runs scored on passed or dropped balls and poor defense to defeat our light hitting team. Usually I played shortstop or third base and did a passable job. I was the top hitter on our team, which was no great accomplishment, but I can boast that I always made contact with the ball and never struck out. One day I was hit on the right thigh by a real fastball. I stayed in the game and scored a run but for a week or two my leg was painfully sore. Then it seemed to heal but apparently adhesions or scar tissue developed that bothered me until I was in my late thirties. Whenever I ran hard it would tear loose again and the pain would return. Luckily, it finally cleared up on its own.

Lonzo was temporarily back in Alabama and wanted to go up past Lawrenceburg, Tennessee to see a girl we had known in Hartselle. We set out riding double on the Harley and made the trip without incident. The visit was pleasant but Lonzo's girlfriend and her free-wheeling mother liked their liquor. Before the day was done, we consumed more than our share of malt liquors. Late in the afternoon we started back to Alabama, recklessly weaving and singing along the Tennessee roads. By the time we reached the south alternate of Highway 72 in Alabama it was starting to get dark and the Harley had no lights. Lonzo had to stop for a restroom break and in my haste to get started again before dark, I accelerated too quickly and Lonzo slid off the back, badly scraping his legs and bruising himself. He moaned the rest of the way, but with luck—or perhaps a guardian angel or two—we made it home sober and in one piece.

In midsummer I had to report for another round of Army Reserve training, this time in Fort McClellan, Alabama. Brother-in-law Bunk and I drove down together in his 1940 Chevrolet. The two weeks were much less eventful than the previous summer. I had a day or two of maneuvers, and about the only field training we did was a couple of sessions on the rifle range. There was one moment, however, that resembled wartime conditions. While the sergeants were giving our team instructions about target pulling on the mound behind the targets, an obnoxious young lieutenant by the name of Spidel gave orders to his men to begin firing. Bullets began to thud around us, and we made a mad dash for cover behind the bunker. It was never clear, at least not to me, but one of the men may have been hit in the ankle. Spidel was reprimanded, perhaps demoted, to the delight of us all.

The rest of the training was better than anything I could have dreamed of. I was assigned to the base theater and spent the time learning to run the projectors and watching the latest movies. And in air-conditioned comfort no less, a true rarity in those days. After my second round of basic, I asked my Cullman commanding officer, Lt. Abt, if I could go on the inactive roster. He obliged after first offering to send me to Officers Training School. But I was finished with the military, though I always said, and said sincerely, that I would serve if my unit was called up. The Reserves scheduled me for a physical in 1957 or 58 in Huntsville, and in 1961 I received an Honorable Discharge in the mail. So it was that without really spending much time in the military I was honorably discharged from the Army.

The Harley developed several mechanical problems, and lacking money to repair it I looked around for a trade. Before I did, however, while I still had a few dollars in my pocket, Donald Cheatham showed up and announced that he had a dynamite business deal. A man he knew was going into the whiskey business and for $40.00 Donald could get us in on the ground floor with a chance to make some real money. I forgot my resolution to walk the strait and narrow and lent him the money even though I was skeptical of the deal. We rode the Harley to the Valley. Donald left me by the side of road and rode off to deliver the money. He explained that since the man didn't know me, it would be better if he went alone to deliver the money. He returned an hour later, and we raced back to the Mountain with Donald at the controls. It was now completely dark, and I was afraid we were going to run off the lonely mountain road, but Donald had excellent vision and we made it to his house. Not unexpectedly, the whiskey deal went as sour as the corn mash. The odd way I recovered my money from Donald belongs to a later chapter.

As summer wore on, I traded the Harley for a 1941 Chevrolet with a good chassis but a smoking engine and clattering lifters.

A couple of days later in Hartselle I ran across the desperate boy I had traded with. "You've got to give me back my Chevrolet!" he pleaded. "The car's got a note on it and the man holdin' it's gonna have the law after me." I didn't think that much of the Chevrolet anyway, so we traded again. I convinced him, nevertheless, that I was doing it out of the goodness of my heart. He thanked me profusely in gratitude.

Not long afterwards I traded the Harley, for good this time, for a 1940 Plymouth that lasted me the rest of the summer. I do not remember who I made the trade with. It was almost as rickety as the old mule that died on us, but with care and frequent repairs I kept it running and used it to haul my Evans farm corn to Hartselle and Decatur. The passenger side front door had a tendency to swing open on left turns. One day, Momma was riding with me and the door popped open. Momma grabbed for support but finding none, was about to roll out into the road when I caught her by the arm. I forgot about the incident until she reminded me many years later that I probably saved her life. I doubted it, but it was gratifying to me that she thought so.

One of the last times I ventured out in the rapidly deteriorating Plymouth I ran out of gasoline and left it on the side of the Corn Road near the Knopp farm. That night some hooligans from west of Battleground pushed it into a deep ditch, and I had to pay five dollars to have it pulled out. I knew the boys and my first impulse was to take revenge myself. But then I decided not to take matters into my own hands in classic Corn Road style, but instead to call the sheriff's office and report the boys. It was a novel, and for some, censurable action, for a cardinal rule was to leave the law out of our local business. But my thinking was changing. Duly fined for their vandalism, which neighbors had witnessed, the boys spread the word they would get even with me. I was gone before they had the chance, but if I remember correctly, they tried to take it out on my brother Darrell in a later run-in. Instead of revenge, however, all they got from tough Darrell was a beating with a tire iron and a trip to the hospital for one of them. Toward the end of summer, I sold the Plymouth for $30 to Howard Turney. He paid me $15 and never the rest. A typical Corn Road deal.

Meanwhile, a growing fascination with science fiction displaced—but did not entirely replace—my interest in history and adventure stories. Robert Heinlein's stories and books, especially a short novel called <u>Universe</u>, jarred me out of mental complacency and for a time induced a kind of intellectual vertigo. At the same time, I became interested in the craft of writing and worked on outlines of books that never got beyond the opening paragraphs. Many years later Momma told me she found and saved my first literary attempts. She confessed to me that she, too, had always wanted to write poetry but felt that her education was too limited. I scolded her and urged her to write.

Even as I yearned for a better life and a higher understanding of things, the seductive, downward pull of the Corn Road world was a powerful counter incentive. How easy, how natural and reasonable it would be to live where I had always lived, to marry and dwell among my own people, comfortable amongst familiar faces and hereditary virtues and vices, to be an acceptable version of what my family and people had always been.

As if to prove my counter thesis and despite my earlier resolutions to do things right, there were two or three more drinking escapades that summer, one near Birmingham with Tootsie Russell and his brother-in-law. Another time Armon and I bought a case of beer in Huntsville and drove his 1948 white Ford into a deep ditch on a dirt road near Hartselle. Addled by alcohol, we set off in different directions to get help. I walked to Morris Sammons' house in Hartselle, but Morris was gone. And so were Armon and the car when I got back out in the country where I had left him. Thinking that he would come back for me and still groggy from the beer, I lay down in a pile of leaves or hay and slept soundly till daylight. Armon failed to show and I walked out to Highway 31 and hitchhiked my way home. When next time I saw Armon he explained that he managed to extract the car from ditch and after waiting for a long time, decided I must have caught a ride home.

Such pointless, dangerous escapades made me realize I was using up my chances and getting ever closer to a moral and legal precipice. But the question remained, where was I to go from here? Weeks passed, the crops were laid by, and still no answer. Then one day as I was walking and mulling over the bad choices and alternatives, I discovered Brownie's dry little bones at the back side of a deserted field. Looking down at them, I was seized by the futility of my life. All the hopes for my life here were dead too, just like little Brownie. My life was elsewhere. But where? I was nearly twenty years old and every way I had taken had turned out to be a disappointment.

Then, suddenly, a daring idea flashed through my mind. Why not college? It came to me as something inevitable, something I was destined to do. Now it seemed so obvious, as though the option had been there all along, waiting for me to discover it—or for it to discover me. I saw it as deliverance from farm drudgery and factory dreariness. It was the "expansion" of life that I had been seeking all summer.

The idea thrilled me, even though I had not the slightest idea how I would go about actually doing it. In that era college was far outside the norm for people like us. It was remarkable enough, people told me, that I was the first in my family to finish high school. College was nearly unthinkable, an option reserved for the affluent elite, an order of life totally alien to us. But the idea became an obsession and I knew I had to act on it.

I inquired first at St. Bernard College in Cullman, but the young priest who interviewed me was not very encouraging and the campus did not seem right for me. Not long afterwards I drove the wobbly old Plymouth to West Point High School to get advice from Principal York, a man for whom I had great respect. "Harold," Mr. York told me, "you have one of the finest academic records at West Point High School, and I think you would do extremely well in college. Why don't you get in touch with Dr. James, President of Athens College? Tell him I recommend you. He's a friend of mine."

The Plymouth was in no shape to drive up to Athens, so the first chance I got I hitchhiked the fifty miles to Methodist-run Athens College, remembering as I walked onto the campus the time years earlier I had ridden by on a bus with John Chaney and wondered what strange things went on there. After some inquiries, I was directed to the President's office inside stately Founders Hall. "How may I help you, young man?" asked the imposing Mrs. Porter, secretary to President James. "I'd like to see the President," I answered. "Do you have an appointment?" she wanted to know, perfectly aware I am sure that I was not on his agenda. "No ma'am, but I need to see him if possible." At that moment Dr. James himself walked in.

"You need to see me, Mr. ____?"

"Raley, Harold Raley," I answered, shaking his hand. "And yes sir, I would like to see you, if you can spare me the time."

"Come into my office," he said cheerfully as Mrs. Porter glowered behind us.

I explained my business and mentioned Mr. York.

"Why, yes, Earl York, a fine man and a friend of mine," he commented approvingly. We talked a bit more then suddenly as if on impulse, he asked me,

"How would you like to be our mailman and perform other chores for the College, for room, board, and tuition?" I accepted at once, hardly daring to believe my good fortune.

"You walked in just at the right moment," he told me.

I hitchhiked home with a new spring in my step. But there was still farm work to do. Bemis and Armon helped me pick the cotton and gather the corn. After we had ginned a few bales, I told Momma that I intended to hold out one bale for myself, "to go to college on." "You better wait till your Daddy gets home," she admonished me. "Momma," I informed her firmly, "I made this crop and I'm keeping one bale for college. You can tell Daddy that when he gets back."

And so it was. Howard Turney bought the Plymouth, or at least took it off my hands, the bale of cotton sold for close to $150.00, and as far as I know, Daddy never objected at all. He had his faults, but stinginess was not among them. In September I asked Armon if he would drive me to Athens. He agreed and said he would pick me up on the appointed day.

There was a final quirky episode before I left. Powell's Chapel Holiness Church just over on Highway 31 in Morgan County was running a revival and days before I was to leave for college Armon and I attended the service. We sat behind the Turney girls who flirted outrageously with us, especially Yvonne, a brunette beauty who had been provocatively eyeing me off and on for a couple of years. So loud were their giggles and disruptive our responses in the steamy church that preacher Walter Powell stopped in mid sermon, looked over at us, and announced in his stentorian voice to the congregation,

"Brothers and sisters, the Devil's in church tonight!"

I thought his disturbing remark was directed at me, and it caused me some distress. But later I decided it was directed at the whole group.

Two days later, it was time to go. Armon showed up, I said goodbye to Momma and the family, and we drove off in swirl of dust headed for Athens College. On the way, we talked and laughed about many things we had experienced together over the years. It seemed to be a time for summaries and finalities. He let me out in front of Naylor Hall, in those days the dormitory for resident male students. We shook hands, wished each other well, and then he waved and drove away. I stood watching him go until the white ford turned a corner and vanished from view. I felt a sudden rush of emotions, for I sensed at some unspoken level that we were parting ways forever.

And as it turned out, we were. Armon returned home and married Yvonne a few months later. Soon afterward he would leave Corn Road country, father several children, and live and die in inner-city Chicago. I saw him only three times after that: first, a few weeks after I started college; second, soon after his oldest son David was born; and last, in Chicago in December of 1968. Of course, I went back home, too, but only for short visits, never to live there again. My life on the Corn Road was also over. College and a very different world lay head.

Afterthoughts

These are the memories of the boy I was long ago, not the confessions of the man I am today. As I said at the start, they are limited the first twenty years of my life that I think of as the Corn Road years. After I went off to begin my college and university work my life changed drastically. Whether I shall ever get around to telling the second and much longer portion remains to be seen. What I can say is that the two parts are so different as to be almost two different worlds.

I look back in sorrow at the mistakes I made, particularly those acts that hurt and disappointed people close and dear to me. But I remain thankful for the way I lived and the lessons I learned the hard way. For later I came to realize that the hard way is really the best way, a way that has no substitute, least of all, a classroom or university lecture. For this reason, I would not exchange those early years for any other way of life, even if it were possible. I consider it one of the advantages I had during my fifty plus years in the University. Let me explain that belief with one or two points and then I shall be finished.

There was never any doubt that a university career was my destiny. From the day Cousin Armon dropped me off at the Athens College campus, I knew I that I had found my place and sensed that I was zeroing in on my purpose. But here is the point: I took much of my rural way of life with me. I have never willingly surrendered or cast aside as useless any part of my past. Who I once was, I am still, and in an odd way maybe even more so. The hard and sometimes harsh experiences of farm life—animals, crops, breakdowns, illnesses, failures—have acted as an anchor that have kept my feet on the ground even when sophisticated theories and subtle philosophies threatened to send my head into the clouds. When you work with real things—hands on, as they say these days—you become—and remain--a realist. It is a vaccine against bogus reasoning. I like to think that as a result I have retained the ability to separate the wheat from the chaff, the true from the apparent, the real from the clever. If your mind is clear of phony things, it is ready for truth, like a spring field plowed and primed for planting instead of cluttered with ideological weeds. For these and many other reasons I treasure my formative past on the Old Corn Road. If in one sense I am no longer a part of it in body, it remains very much a part of me in spirit.

To sum it up, country life steadied me so that I could get on with the task of becoming the person I was born to be without crashing and burning along the way. A few things I learned quickly; deeper matters have taken me much longer and at great cost. And I am not there yet. I am still trying to become myself, my real self, my eternal self. But aren't we all?

Well, that's about all I had on my mind at the moment. And that said, I have said enough.

Friendswood, Texas

Family Photographs

Aug. 1966
My parents Vernie Lou and William Barthel Raley

TOM AND MARY RALEY AROUND 1943
(OUR PATERNAL GRANDPARENTS)

WILLIAM A. HOOPER AND ZONA WAID HOOPER AROUND 1896 (OUR MATERNAL GRANDPARENTS)

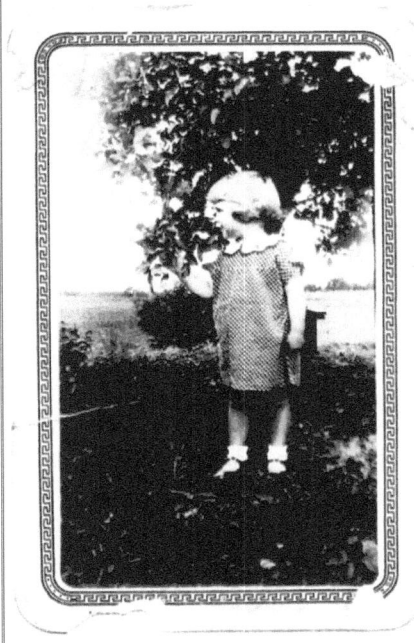
GERALDINE IN 1934

HAROLD 1941 WITH OLE TED AND PUPPY.

DARRELL IN 1955-56

SCHOOL DAYS 1955-'56
West Point High

MOMMA (VERNIE HOOPER) AROUND 1928-29)

JOYCE, JANICE, DARRELL, HAROLD, GERALDINE (ROBIN HOLDING JOYCE'S HAND (AROUND 1963)

JANICE, MOMMA (HOLDING JOYCE), HAROLD, DARRELL (1949)

SIBLINGS WITH MOMMA AT DADDY'S BURIAL (1968): JOYCE, JANICE, DARRELL, MOMMA, HAROLD, GERALDINE

THE OLD CORN ROAD LOOKING EAST

HAROLD AND GERALDINE IN 1941 (THE RED HILL YEAR)

Children of Barthel and Vernie Raley:
Geraldine, Harold, Darrell, Janice, Joyce

Joyced, Geraldine, Momma, Janice, Harold

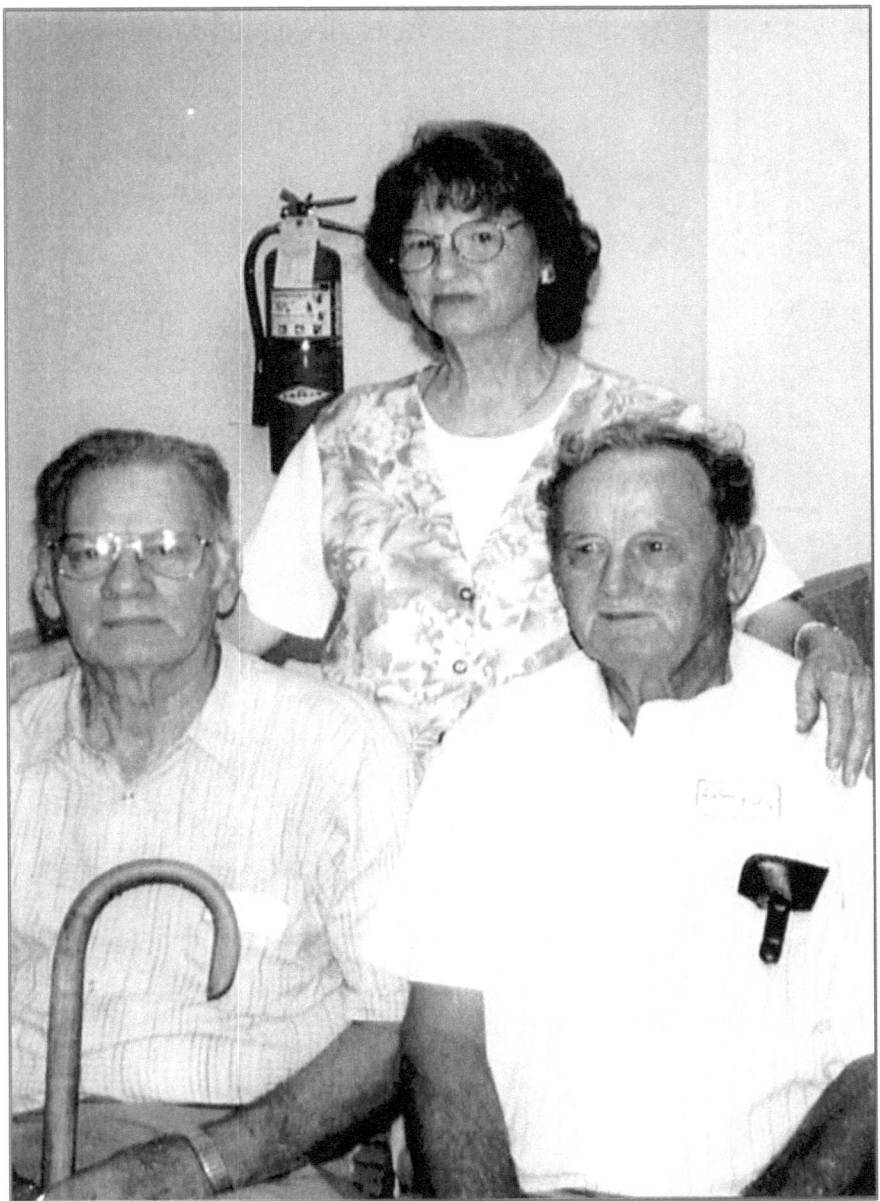

Aunt Azalee Raley Frick with her
brothers Felton and Elton Raley in 2002

Kinfolks and neighbors from Roundtop community
Tom ana Mary Raley in back right

Momma's Drawing of our old house on the Walker place

Memories of Appalachia 277

Ancestral Baptist Church
on the Raley Road in South Carolina

Raley Brothers: Athel, Felton, Bertis, Barthel, Bemis, Tolbert
(Missing: Felton)

REBECCA RODEN RALEY

WILLIAM "BILL" RALEY HUSBAND OF REBECCA OUR GREAT-PARENTS (WATER DAMAGED PHOTO),

THE FLINT MICHIGAN GANG IN 1953: MARLON ALVIS, DONALD CHEATHAM, HAROLD RALEY, WAYMON RUTHERFORD

The Raley Coat of Arms:

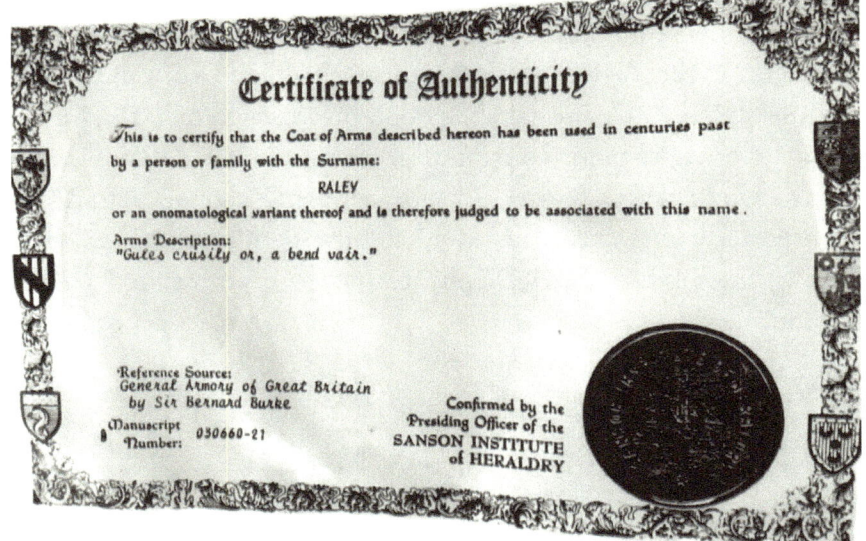

OFFICIAL DESCRIPTION
"Gules Crusily, or, a Bend Vair"
Translation: Crosses in a red field, or, A Fur band
Symbolic Meanings:
1. Crosses symbolize family's Christian heritage
2. Bells symbolize family's noble heritage
3. Helmet symbolizes family's noble heritage
4. Red field: from the family name: RA (red) and LEY (lea or field)

Title: Louisiana Rogue
- Author: Harold Raley
- Publisher: Lamar University Press
- Paper Back: ISBN: 9780985255275
- eBook: Kindle
- Pages 306
- Publication Date: April 2013

This wonderfully entertaining picaresque novel by Harold Raley falls in the tradition of rogue literature established by Tom Jones and other early novels. Set in the nineteenth century, Louisiana Rogue will take you on a wild, fast-paced romp through all levels of Cajun society in the 1830s. The title page says the book promises to tell "The Life and Times of Pierre Prospère-Tourmoulin, Picket-pocket, Thief, Gambler, Fugitive, Undertaker, Barber, Doctor, Priest, Prisoner, Bandit, and Count; Latterly penned in his hand for the gentle reader of leisure, Spanning the years 1831-1839" and claims to be translated by Peter Tourmoulin.

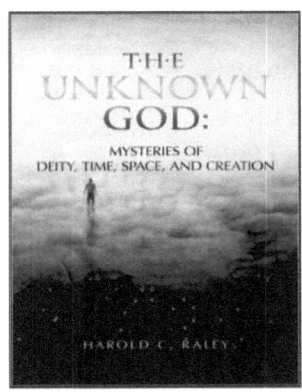

Title: The Unknown God: Mysteries of Deity, Time, Space, and Creation
- Author: Harold Raley
- Publisher: CreateSpace
- Paper Back: ISBN: 9781466273184
- Pages 142
- Publication Date: October, 2011

In his powerful Introduction to The Unknown God, religious thinker and writer Harold Raley makes this unusual request of the reader: "Suspend, if you will, everything you know about God. Put aside for the duration of this reading your traditional theologies and hear a new and more reverent way of thinking about God. When you return to your old understandings, they will have deeper meanings, unless those you once professed were meaningless to start with. If you are unwilling or unable to do as I ask, read no further. This message is not for you. The truth it contains will find you later when it is ready for you and you have been made ready for it." To approach Deity from this radically new perspective--arguably the greatest advance in theological thought of modern times--is to expose and shed light on the baffling paradoxes, improbable notions, and misleading errors not only about God but also about time, space, creation, and immortality. In each of these categories this book offers stunning new insights that incorporate not only the efforts of classical theologians but also the latest discoveries in science. Outline in these advanced insights is a new understanding of human life. By the law of corresponding identities, Raley explains, a more elevated theory of God necessarily means a more elevated theory of mankind. Each of the many themes and aperçus packed into this slender volume could have been a hefty tome. With pristine eloquence Raley reduces them to the essentials, believing as he does that clarity of style is courtesy to the reader.

Title: The Light of Eden:
A Christian Worldview
- Author: Harold Raley
- Publisher: John M. Hardy Publishing
- Paper Back: ISBN: 9780979839122
- Pages 196
- Publication Date: May 2008

An inspiring vision of richer Christian life and thought. In the tradition of C. S. Lewis and G. K. Chesterton, this extraordinary book is both a spiritual adventure and an intellectual feast. Packed with illuminating insights and written in beautiful language, The Light of Eden introduces its readers to a vast treasury of creative ideas, innovative concepts, and possibilities contained in Christianity.

Title: The Spirit of Spain
- Author: Harold Raley
- Publisher: Halcyon Pr Ltd
- Paper Back: ISBN: 9780970605498
- Pages 212
- Publication Date: October, 2011

    The Spirit of Spain brims with aperçus and revelations, many of them controversial, others startling, all engrossing. From Roman Hispania to the most recent Spanish trends, Professor Raley narrates the unique story of Spanish civilization. Examples of his original thinking include a "phenomenology of Spanish history," a new theory of the Spanish Renaissance, new concepts of Spanish patriotism and nationalism, and a reinterpretation of Spanish "Stoicism." As the book unfolds he also takes many sidelong looks into Hispanic America and offers a new explanation of Spain's relationship to Moslem Al-Andalus and modern Europe. The book culminates in a radical analysis of "Quixotic life" and its unsuspected significance for the post-modern age.

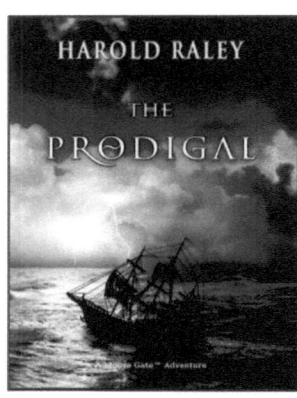

Title: The Prodigal
- Author: Harold Raley
- Publisher: Mouse Gate Press
- Paper Back: ISBN: 9781590953402
- eBook ISBN: 9781590953419
- Pages 96
- Publication Date: October, 2016

In the tradition of Crusoe and Sabatini, The Prodigal is a story of the shipwreck and struggle for survival of a young ship's carpenter who escapes one captivity only to fall into more dangerous circumstances. The story unfolds from Boston to Mexico, Cuba, Africa, and back again. At critical points a mysterious stranger intervenes to lend a hand and guide him to his destiny.

Title: Barefoot On A Frosty Morn
- Author: Harold Raley
- Publisher: Mouse Gate Press
- Paper Back: ISBN: 9781590953426
- eBook ISBN: 9781590953433
- Pages 352
- Publication Date: October, 2016

Barefoot on a Frosty Morn is a literary and genealogical tapestry of several families over three centuries. The genealogical threads stretch back to England and France and unfold in step with America's continental expansion. The families crisscross north, south, and west as the tapestry grows in richness and complexity. A final episode sheds light on the earliest roots of the story. The reader has a perspective only partially available to the personalities immersed in the stories. Episodes are woven around some American milestones: the Revolution, the Civil War and WWII. These resonate and enrich but do not hinder the genealogical flow of the novel. In its conception and execution *Barefoot on a Frosty Morn* is unlike any writing before it. It surpasses the limits of history and narrates the essence of the American vision of life.

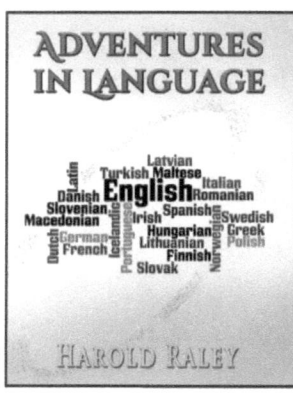

Title: **Adventures in Language**
- Author: Harold Raley
- Publisher: TotalRecall Publications
- Paper Back: ISBN: 9781590955321
- eBook ISBN: 9781590955352
- Pages 216
- Publication Date: October, 2017

In these *Adventures in Language* linguist Harold Raley explores fascinating features of English and many other languages in different cultures and historical eras.

Even though at times I point out obvious errors in the languages as they are currently structured, I realize that the rules of grammar and usage in English or any other living language are, or can be, subject to change. This may not be true of, say, ancient Sanskrit, but then we note that despite its perfection—or perhaps because of it—ancient Sanskrit ceased to be a spoken tongue many centuries ago.

Over the ages thinkers have pondered the qualities that define humanity and set mankind apart from other species. In my view, no stronger case than language can be made for human uniqueness. Animals can communicate and mimic but they cannot speak. Language, sung, recited, or spoken, is archly human, and for that reason also deeply mysterious, beautiful, and fascinating.

Title: Points Of Light
- Author: Harold Raley
- Publisher: TotalRecall Publications
- Paper Back: ISBN: 9781590955369
- eBook ISBN: 9781590955376
- Pages 238
- Publication Date: October, 2017

These *Points of Light* centered on the beauty, humor, and mystery of human life present many perspectives flowing out of the unifying philosophical premise that life, not physical reality, is the foundational reality in which all others are rooted.

A noted thinker once said that clarity is the courtesy an author extends to the reader. Insofar as my abilities permit, I have tried to add another kindness: word economy, which I understand to mean saying as much as possible in the fewest words. In those cases in which there is neither clarity nor economy, I alone take the blame.

www.ingramcontent.com/pod-product-compliance
Lightning Source LLC
Chambersburg PA
CBHW030512080526
44586CB00011B/157